T0309314

# REPOSITIONING BUSINESS:
## A STRATEGIC RESPONSE
## TO COVID-19

Proceedings of the 3rd International
Conference on "Impact of Current Events
on the Future of Business" (3rd ICEFB, 2021),
23 & 24 April, 2021, Hyderabad, India

# REPOSITIONING BUSINESS:
## A STRATEGIC RESPONSE
## TO COVID-19

Proceedings of the 3rd International
Conference on "Impact of Current Events
on the Future of Business" (3rd ICEFB, 2021),
23 & 24 April, 2021, Hyderabad, India

**Dr. Yamini Meduri**
*Assistant Professor, Vignana Jyothi Institute of Management*

**Dr. Vishal Kutchu**
*Sr. Assistant Professor, Vignana Jyothi Institute of Management*

First published 2022
by Routledge
605 Third Avenue, New York, NY 10158

and by Routledge
2 Park Square, Milton Park, Abingdon, Oxon, OX14 4RN

*Routledge is an imprint of the Taylor & Francis Group, an informa business*

*Library of Congress Cataloging-in-Publication Data*
A catalog record for this title has been requested


ISBN: 978-1-032-11465-1(pbk)

# Contents

# About the Authors

**Dr. Yamini Meduri**

*Assistant Professor, Vignana Jyothi Institute of Management*

A Design Thinking professional, Dr. Yamini Meduri is an HR by passion and a teacher by Profession. A recipient of 'Young Scientist' research grant from Dept. of Science & Technology, Govt. of India for her research in Disaster Recovery study, her research interest facilitated her to publish 8 indexed publications to her credit along with talking her research in international conferences. A member of Humanitarian Logistics Association and part of Technical Advisory Group of Universal Logistics Standards representing Asia Pacific region, she closely follows the disaster managements. Dr. Yamini also involves herself in consulting assignments with corporate organizations and conducting training sessions to mid and senior level managers.

**Dr. Vishal Kutchu**

*Sr. Assistant Professor, Vignana Jyothi Institute of Management*

Dr. Vishal Kutchu teaches Financial Accounting, Corporate Finance, Financial Statements Analysis, Enterprise Valuation and Working Capital Management and is a visiting faculty at MANAGE and NIAM, Jaipur. His research interests include market efficiency studies and case studies especially in accounting and valuation. He has published papers on testing weak form efficiency and semi strong efficiency of Indian Stock Market in national journals and presented papers in national and international conferences. He has completed online courses in Python viz., Investment Management with Python & Machine Learning and Python for Financial Analysis and his current research interest is in identifying and testing profitable trading strategies which can be translated into an algorithm.

# List of Figures

# List of Tables

# List of Contributors

**Dr. Yamini Meduri**
*Assistant Professor, Vignana Jyothi Institute of Management*

**Dr. Vishal Kutchu**
*Sr. Assistant Professor, Vignana Jyothi Institute of Management*

**Prof. Abhijit Vasmatkar**
*Assistant Professor, Symbiosis Law School, Pune*

**Ms. Suma Dadke**
*Student Researcher, Symbiosis Law School, Pune*

**Ms. P Sriya**
*Student Researcher, Symbiosis Law School, Pune*

**Mohammad Ali (Corresponding Author)**
*Department of Business Administration in Management Studies*
*Bangladesh University of Professionals, Dhaka, Bangladesh*

**Sabrina Sharmin Nishat**
*Department of Business Administration in Management Studies*
*Bangladesh University of Professionals, Dhaka, Bangladesh*

**Farzana Tazin**
*Department of Business Administration in Management Studies*
*Bangladesh University of Professionals, Dhaka, Bangladesh*

**Mohammad Rabiul Basher Rubel, PhD**
*Department of Business Administration in Management Studies*
*Bangladesh University of Professionals, Dhaka, Bangladesh*

**CS Divyesh Patel**
*PhD Scholar at Dharmsinh Desai University, Nadiad, Gujarat*

**Prof. (Dr.) Naresh K. Patel**
*Professor & Dean, Faculty of Management and Information Sciences*
*Dharmsinh Desai University, Nadiad*

**B. Prathyusha**
*Assistant Professor in Management Science, Department of Humanities and Sciences*
*VNR Vignana Jyothi Institute of Engineering & Technology, Hyderabad, Telangana, India*

**Ch. S. Durga Prasad**
*Director, Vignana Jyothi Institute of Management, Hyderabad, Telangana, India*

**Prof. K.V. Bhanu Murthy**
*Professor, Delhi Technological University, East Delhi Campus, Vivek Vihar II, Delhi*

**Dr. Manisha Choudhary**
*Assistant Professor, Govt. College Rithoj, Gurugram, Higher Education Department, Haryana*

**A. Ramesh**
*Sr Assistant Professor, Vignana Jyothi Institute of Management, Hyderabad, Telangana, India*

**Dr. Sheeja R**
*Associate Professor, CMS Institute of Management Studies, Coimbatore, Tamil Nadu, India*

**Mrs Namitha Krishnan**
*MPhil Scholar, Nehru College of Management, Coimbatore, Tamil Nadu, India*

**Raghupriya. A**
*Full-time PhD scholar, Department of Management Studies, CEG, Anna University, Chennai*

**Dr. Thiruchelvi. A**
*Associate Professor, Department of Management Studies, CEG, Anna University, Chennai*

**Sameer Kulkarni**
*Department of Technology Management, Defense Institute of Advanced Technology [DU], Girinagar, Pune*

**Dr. Sumati Sidharth**
*Department of Technology Management, Defense Institute of Advanced Technology [DU], Girinagar, Pune*

**Dr. Poonam Jindal**
*Assistant Professor, Vignana Jyothi institute of Management*

**Jaya Lakshmi Vakiti**
*Assistant Professor, Department of Management Studies*
*Nalla Malla Reddy Engineering College, Hyderabad, Telangana, India*

**Gutti R K Prasad**
*Research Scholar, Faculty of Management, Kalinga University, Naya Raipur, Chhattisgarh, India*

**Prof. Byju John**
*PhD, Research Supervisor and Director General, Department of Management*
*Kalinga University, Naya Raipur, Chhattisgarh, India*

**Manmath Deshpande**
*Research Scholar, Dr. Ambedkar Institute of Management Studies and Research*
*Rashtrasant Tukdoji Maharaj, Nagpur University, (India)*

# Foreword

The multi-faceted Covid-19 pandemic hit every individual, every business, and every nation. The impact might be different for different stakeholders, but none is missed. The unparalleled pandemic of Covid-19 pushed the boundaries of the environments that the employees, employers, businesses, and economies are operating in. A sudden drift in the work environment has brought in unexpected challenges to a lot of organizations and hence, the economies around the world. The impact is felt in cultural, social, business, political and technological spheres. As people, businesses and nations are impacted, the imperative to understand, temper and manage these forces is taking center stage. Identifying the path forward has become the primary focus for all businesses and nations, both big and small.

The current pandemic has presented unprecedented complexities to businesses around the world and organizations are attempting to survive and sustain through the complexities. The workplace and business transformation has been backed by the every growing technological advancements that rapidly rearranging the concept of work. We are now witnessing a call for smart capabilities powered by Machine Learning (ML) and Artificial Intelligence (AI). As AI is entering new markets or adding new products to existing markets, marketers are testing which of these technologies enable faster and less expensive time-to-market strategies. Furthermore, we are witnessing a resounding applause to remote workplaces which was a distant dream earlier. Also, a need for developing sustainable economic and financial capabilities is exponentially increasing as the time progresses. More than ever, the value of sustainable supply chains driven by quality, quantity and reach is understood now. The prominence of building performance driven organic infrastructure using renewable solutions has earned enough attention.

Against this backdrop, a two-day virtual International Conference was held to provide a forum to showcase relevant research. The conference was held by Vignana Jyothi Institute of Management (VJIM), Hyderabad, India, on 23rd & 24th April 2021. The book is an attempt to bring together some selected research content that was presented during the conference which provide research recommendations about how organizations can respond to the pandemic.

**Dr. Ch. S Durga Prasad**
*Director, VJIM & Convener, III International Conference*

# Preface

The Covid-19 pandemic has impacted businesses globally. The year 2020, was an eyeopener as well as a myth buster to one and all. Establishments, however large and professionally managed, had to learn new lessons from and for the situation. Companies, big and small, had to innovate and adapt to match the mercurial events taking shape. It is by now apparent to all stakeholders that anticipation, innovation, and adaptation are the 'mantras' for sustainability. As the adage reads, 'when the going gets tough, the tough get going', only those who have seasoned from man-made and natural calamities can perdure.

Businesses across the world are struggling to survive as the pandemic forges ahead. However, it is not impossible to find examples of innovative businesses that have learnt how to thrive during this crisis. One such striking example is telemedicine. Patients and health service providers have been forced into live-video visits, which are surprisingly effective. To quote Michael Okun, National Medical Director for the Parkinson's Foundation, 'We accomplished in 10 days what we have been doing for 10 years - fighting and advocating and trying to get telemedicine up and going'. Virtual classes, workshops and online training have emerged a blessing not only for academic purposes but also for corporate communication as well as gym and yoga classes. As consulting firm McKinsey writes in their recent article, Ready, set, go: Reinventing the organization for speed in the post-COVID-19 era, companies must "increase the speed of decision making, while improving productivity, using technology and data in new ways, and accelerating the scope and scale of innovation."

The life lesson that the pandemic roller coaster teaches us is in fact contradictory to the Darwinian theory of 'the survival of the fittest.' What we need to realize now is 'the survival of those who can sustain, innovate and adapt'.

In our efforts to understand and build sustainable solutions, we have tried to put together the required resources to discuss and deliberate through our 3rd international Conference on "Impact of current events on the future of business".

**Dr. Yamini Meduri & Dr. Vishal Kutchu**

# Acknowledgements

It brings us immense pleasure to acknowledge the team organizing the 3<sup>rd</sup> International Conference on "Impact of current events on the future of business". We are happy that the academic conference is focussed on understanding how businesses responded strategically to the complex and volatile Covid-19 Pandemic.

We would like to place on record the support of our Governing Council whose encouragement and support made this conference possible. We thank our President, Dr. D N Rao and our General Secretary, Mr. K Harishchandra Prasad for their inspiring leadership and support throughout the conference.

We thank our conference partners AMDISA (Association of Management Development Institutions in South Asia) for being a supporting partner for our conference and helped us through the process of the promotion and conduct of the conference. It was because of AMDISA that we were able to provide a platform for discussing inter-country research initiatives through an interaction among academics and business leaders.

We also acknowledge the team from Journal Press India who helped us managing the conference through a hassle-free conference management system and being the single point for all the participants.

It becomes vital for the researchers, academicians, business professionals, corporate houses to come together to learn from each other to understand the challenges and learn about the opportunities that the global pandemic has thrown to the world around. We thank our participants from across borders who participated and presented their research in our conference. It is their participation and research which has made this book possible.

The life lesson that the pandemic roller coaster teaches us is in fact contradictory to the Darwinian theory of 'the survival of the fittest'. Thanks to our conference team without whose support this conference wouldn't have been possible even in thought. We place on record our sincere thanks to Dr. Sagyan Sagarika Mohanty, Mr. N Srinivas Chakravarthi & Mr. Raghu Mantha for their support throughout the conduct of the conference.

**Dr. Yamini Meduri & Dr. Vishal Kutchu**

# CHAPTER ONE

## An Expensive Price to Pay: How Article XXI(b) Protects International Hegemony at the Cost of Good Governance

**Prof. Abhijit Vasmatkar**
*Assistant Professor*
*Symbiosis Law School, Pune*
*abhivasmatkar@gmail.com*

**Ms. Suma Dadke**
*Student Researcher*
*Symbiosis Law School, Pune*
*17010125232@symlaw.ac.in*

**Ms. P Sriya**
*Student Researcher*
*Symbiosis Law School, Pune*
*17010125121@symlaw.ac.in*

**Abstract**—*In 2020, the Trump Administration's decision to impose 25 per cent tariffs on aluminium derivatives and 10 per cent tariffs on steel derivatives took effect. Despite widespread outrage from the international community, which is evidenced by the multitude of retaliatory measures and complaints against the United States of America before the World Trade Organization, it is certainly not the first time that this International Hegemon has subverted international trading regulations. Presently, the US has invoked the security exception under Article XXI(b) of the General Agreement on Tariffs and Trade, 1994. These tariffs were defended by the Trump Administration as a measure to protect the viability of the domestic industry to meet national defence requirements. The security exception, which as the name suggests, is an exception carved out for states that allows them to take any action they consider necessary for the protection of their essential security interests. It has, thus, largely been a self-judged provision used by states to justify trade decisions that protect their national interest. Two questions arise in this context: whether the existence of this exception serves to perpetuate international hegemony due to the sensitive aspect of state sovereignty it covers in* *its self-judging character, and whether this then transforms it into a tool to challenge good governance. The WTO as a governing body is founded on the ideals of good governance, however, it has been ineffective in regulating the exploitation of its provisions by powerful and developed states due to the non-recognition of such principles explicitly. If status quo remains, where states misuse the provisions of GATT increasingly and repeatedly, and the WTO remains unable to discharge good governance and hold such states accountable, it may result in monumental changes in the world order including the eventual collapse of the multilateral international trade regime. This paper explores the relationship between good governance and the WTO and how the security exception functions within this context. It examines the nature and usage of said exception by the US and how this has created a pressing issue for the multilateral trade regime. It proposes carving out an exception to the exception as a reinforcement to ensure that there is a check and balance of measures imposed under Article XXI(b). The proposed exception is of a qualifying nature that lays down international standards which must be met to retain the self-judging character of the national security exception, failing which, such measures would be open to judicial scrutiny.*

**Keywords**—international trade, good governance, international hegemony, national security exception, state sovereignty, tariffs, WTO

## A. INTRODUCTION

By the end of the Cold War era, consensus was that international organizations lacked institutional depth and existed to serve the interests of the rich and powerful instead (Kentikelenis & Voeten, 2020; Mearsheimer, 1995). In this background of global dissatisfaction and the failure of the International Trade Organization, the World Trade Organization was institutionalised as a product of one of the most successful trade negotiations of the time, the Uruguay Round, on the ideals of liberal trade and economy, international cooperation and global good governance.

The term 'good governance' was first used while discussing the need for institutional reform and efficiency in the public sector within Sub-Saharan African countries (Kaufmann et al., 1999). It can be traced back to the development of the normative concept of 'governance' by the World Bank, which was defined as *"the manner in which power is exercised in the management of a country's economic and social resources for development"* (World Bank, 1992). This concept has evolved over the years, and today when viewed from the perspective of international economic relations, good governance is understood as having three dimensions (Christie et al., 2013):
  i)   The usage of rules, resources and power in the functioning of institutions,
  ii)  participation in terms of equal representation and equal access to decision making and inclusion, and
  iii) factors ensuring transparency, accountability and fair administration.

Time and time again, the WTO has reiterated its commitment to the twin ideals of good governance and sustainable development . However, notably, when it comes to acting on such commitments the WTO seems to favour one twin over the other (Weiss & Steiner, 2007) – while sustainable development is explicitly provided for as an objective in the preambulatory paragraphs of the Marrakesh Agreement, 1994, and regularly invoked by the Appellate Body (US – Import Prohibition of Certain Shrimp and Shrimp Products), the principles of good governance are merely alluded to and decidedly more obscure.

It may be argued that while the concept of good governance is hardly visible in the WTO's broader framework, the organization itself is a rules-based system (Mayer, 1981; Keohane, 1984; Jackson, 1989) rooted in the elements of participation, transparency and accountability. The origin of the consensus rule that the WTO negotiations are based on, lies within the principle of participation and the effort to reduce the economic hierarchy between the developed and developing statesalike, and is aimed at ensuring accountability and effectiveness in the regime (Woods, 1999, p. 52). The establishment of the Dispute Settlement Body with the objective of delivering unbiased decisions on trade issues, as well as its model of functioning, is based on the principle of accountability, framed on the idea that the world economic order is accountable not to powerful states, but to the international trading regime instead (Woods, 1999, p. 44). The requirement that tariff measures be reasonable, internally consistent, transparent, and non-discretionary points to the procedural element of the principle of fairness seen within the regulations of the WTO, while the demand for equal distribution of power to ensure equitable outcomes of WTO measures points to the substantive element of the principle (Woods, 1999, p. 46). Essentially, the broad idea of good governance, intrinsic within the WTO, entails equal representation and power divisions amongst the world with no one state being able to act as an unaccountable hegemon (Botchway, 2001, p. 177). It stands to reason, then, that the WTO is against the notion of international hegemony.

Unfortunately, it would seem that the lack of explicit recognition of good governance principles in the WTO's legal framework, and particularly within the General Agreement on Tariffs and Trade, 1994, has fostered a consequent lack of any semblance of good governance in the multilateral trade system. In fact, it may very well be true that there exist certain provisions in GATT itself that have been used in an attempt to subvert the principles of participation, transparency, accountability and fair administration.

The multilateral trading regime has experienced several devastating setbacks in 2020, however thesystem was already in shambles due to the paradigm shift from multilateralism to multipolarity.This shift can be attributed to the growing flavour of 'economic nationalism' over the past decade and the United States of America, particularly under the Trump Administration, has been the most recent state to embrace the phenomenon. This is evident in the state's short-sighted foreign policy, pronounced trade wars and abuse of power to suit national interest that all served to spell severe ramifications for the rest of the world. This policy orientation is not a consequence of Trump's presidency and can be seen within the moderate democrat administrations of Obama and Biden as well. In fact, the Appellate Body crisis started to build up in 2011 when the reappointment of Jennifer Hillman was blocked, followed by the unilateral decision to block the appointment of Seung Wha Chang in 2016 (United States Blocks Reappointment of WTO Appellate Body Member, 2016). Economic nationalism is on the rise with protectionist measures increasing rapidly, threatening liberalised trade. This is also a direct consequence of two issues: the rise in regional trade, or Mega-Regionalism, and the abuse and misuse of the WTO regulations and provisions, such as Article XXI(b), by powerful states and trade giants.

Article XXI(b), or popularly referred to as the national security exception (hereinafter referred to as NSE), is an example of this. Not only has it been used with increasing frequency in recent years, resulting in an arguable absence of transparency and accountability by virtue of the nature of this provision, but its invocation has also been accompanied by a host of unsavoury suspicions and hostile retaliation. While this is worrisome, what is even more unsettling is how the NSE itself is being used with impunity by powerful member states to serve their own hegemonic ends, thereby actively undermining the WTO's claim of good governance. It is, perhaps, obvious at this juncture that the discussion around NSE cannot be continued without the study of the one state which has invoked it multiple times in the past decade. In other words, the United States of America has once again assumed centre stage.

In 2017, the Trump Administration directed the initiation of an investigation into steel imports and their effect on US national security (US Department of Commerce, 2017).

In 2018, the Trump Administration imposed 25 per cent tariffs on steel products and 10 per cent tariffs on aluminium products ("Adjusting Imports of Steel into the United States," 2018).

In 2020, the Trump Administration imposed 25 per cent tariffs on steel derivatives and 10 per cent tariffs on aluminium derivatives ("Adjusting Imports of Derivative Aluminum Articles and Derivative Steel Articles into the United States," 2020).

Section 232 of the Trade Expansion Act, 1962, empowers the President to regulate imports on the grounds of national security, beginning with an investigation by the Department of Commerce and ending with a recommendation, based upon which the President may issue proclamations adjusting imports. So far, only imports of steel and aluminium products and derivatives have been adjusted under this law, however, it is speculated that restrictions on automobiles and their parts ("Adjusting Imports of Automobiles and Automobile Parts into the United States", 2019) and as well as on uranium and titanium sponges follow closely ("Notice of Request for Public Comments on Section 232 National Security Investigation of Imports of Titanium Sponge," 2019). This move of the then Administration invited harsh criticism, both domestically and internationally.

On the domestic front, the very constitutionality of Section 232 (American Institution for International Steel, Inc. v United States, 2019) is being challenged in federal court along with the tariffs themselves (Severstal Export GMBH v. United States, 2018), and Congress is deliberating measures to limit the President's powers in this respect, in the aftermath of Trump's affinity for tariffs (Fefer et al., 2018). More importantly, this situation draws attention to the complications arising on the international front: although the US imposed such tariffs under Section 232, it also invoked Article XXI(b) to justify the imposition.

These tariffs were defended by the Trump Administration as a measure to protect the viability of domestic industries to meet national defence requirements which is linked to protecting US national security interest. Nevertheless, this move has been the cause of outrage and retaliatory measures including from the European Union, China and India (Fefer et al., 2018, p. 28). It has also resulted in numerous complaints against the US before the WTO (Fefer et al., 2018, pp. 39-41), as it is seen not only as yet another violative act by the US but also as a threat to the multilateral trading regime – a threat that still holds under the Biden Administration.

This article, while briefly touching upon these tariffs and their legitimacy under NSE, aims to answer this question: whether the very existence of the NSE serves to perpetuate international hegemony due to the sensitive aspect of state sovereignty it covers in its self-judging character, thus, not simply becoming the perfect clause to exploit, but also a tool to challenge good governance. It further discusses what this ultimately means for the WTO as well as the continued existence of liberalised multilateral trade.

For the purpose of this article, the authors will be restricting their study of the exploitation of this exception to this particular instance of steel and aluminium tariffs levied by the US.

## B. AN ANALYSIS OF ARTICLE XXI(B) OF GATT

The NSE can be invoked to justify violations of member obligations assumed under GATT, creating a caveat in the system. Article XXI(b) allows for states to take any trade-related measures that they consider necessary for the protection of their essential security interests relating to *fissionable materials, traffic of arms or ammunition, any material directly or indirectly involved in supply for the military establishment, measures taken during any emergency in international relations or during the time of war.* The keywords that warrant deliberation are "it considers necessary" and "essential security interests", "supply for the military establishment" and "emergency in international relations".

By and large dormant for decades, this clause, predominantly an affirmation of the recognition of the sovereignty of members (Federer, 2018; Alexandroff & Sharma, 2005), has become the centre to many disputes and virtually the ideal provision to exploit the WTO multilateral trade system. The NSE was created to ensure the sovereignty of states over their national security, as is reflected by the text. It has a clear discretionary nature, conferring upon states absolute power in matters of determining essential security interests, and it is this nature that lends the provision a self-judging character. This can further be substantiated by drawing a comparison with the exception clause under Article XX, where the subjective term "considers necessary" is absent, and whose invocation has been examined objectively by the DSB, creating a general rule that the absence of unjustified discrimination is to be established by the invoking member state (EC – Measures Affecting Asbestos and Products Containing Asbestos, 2001).

Due to lack of WTO judicial precedent on the NSE clause until 2019, the primary tool of interpretation has been state practice, a *lex specialis* of GATT treaty interpretation (Alford, 2011, p. 708). Individual interpretation of member states can be broadly classified into two competing interpretations, the *ultra vires* and the *intra vires* perspective (Federer, 2018). The *ultra vires* perspective argues that the sole judge of the NSE invocation is the invoking member and that the DSB has no right to adjudicate on the security interests of a sovereign WTO member which, it is contended, is substantiated by the intention behind the clause: to ensure sovereign liberty over their essential security interests (Federer, 2018; U.N. Conference on Trade and Employment, 1947). The *intra vires* interpretation, further divided into two sub-classes, argues that the NSE falls within the jurisdiction of WTO Dispute Settlement Body. Where the first sub-class argues that the review power of the DSB is limited to whether the good faith requirement attached to invocation has been met with, the second sub-class argues that the invocation in its entirety is open to judicial scrutiny (Alford, 2011). This view is supported by the language used by the drafters of the text and the accepted rule that no member state can unilaterally justify violation of longstanding GATT principles (Federer, 2018, p. 230). Viewed from the lens of good governance, this *intra vires* interpretation is reflective of the principles of transparency, accountability and fairness. Unfortunately, the majority view and reigning state practice is that NSE is a self-judging clause, however, a strong minority argues that the invocation can be objectively reviewed based on whether the measure was taken in good faith and has any objective nexus to essential security interests (Akande & Williams, 2003).

This also happens to be the view taken by the DSB in the very recent, and first of its kind, ruling on the NSE in 2019 (Russia – Measures Concerning Traffic in Transit, 2019). Ascertaining the DSB's jurisdiction over disputes on the invocation of the NSE, the body defined certain key terms of the Article and chalked out the limits of the provision. Despite upholding the historic, and currently protested, self-judging character of the NSE, the DSB stated that such discretion is limited to what the state deems are its security interests and the WTO cannot scrutinise what interests pertain to the quintessential functions of the state. However, in rejecting Russia's claim that the NSE is non-justiciable altogether, the DSB held that the invocation can be reviewed where there is evidence of the absence of good faith and where the nexus between the measure and the security interest is implausible. The same stance was mirrored in the Saudi Arabia dispute regarding the invocation of the security exception (Saudi Arabia – Measures Concerning the Protection of Intellectual Property Rights, 2020) under the Agreement on Trade-Related Aspects of Intellectual Property Rights.

The authors submit that the majoritarian *ultra vires* interpretation is exactly what is creating a fissure in the framework of GATT, as it has allowed the NSE to morph into an anti-transparency, anti-accountability and anti-fairness weapon that can be wielded at will. This is evidenced by the way the US has been employing the NSE to further its agenda at the expense of others, and thus requires urgent attention. The multilateral trading system appears to be crumbling from within, a gradual destruction brought on by the very international hegemony it sought to counter and yet seemingly perpetuates.

## C. THE US AND THE NATIONAL SECURITY EXCEPTION – A CLOSE FRIENDSHIP

Much of Trump's electoral campaign consisted of assuring people he would "make America great again" (Simoes, 2017). It was apparent since then that should he assume office, his America First policy would bring about dramatic changes in the way America dealt with the rest of the world. His attempts to "put American steel and aluminum back into the backbone of the country" (Whitehouse, 2017) were what we began to see shortly after his inauguration, in the form of extreme tariffs. It was the promise of a politician being honoured. It is for this reason, among others, that it appears that the reason behind these measures was political, and not exactly pertaining to national economic security interests. In fact, economists are contending that these tariffs hurt American economic interest, particularly those of the manufacturing sector quite severely (Fajgelbaum et al., 2020).

What may have begun as a promise to voters, and arguably retained that character as does any promise made by a politician hoping to be re-elected, quickly turned into an irrational display of power by someone who thinks trade wars are "good and easy" (Griswold, 2019). Although the Administration defended the imposition of tariffs saying its domestic industries need to be self-sufficient in the interest of its national security, i.e., in case a war breaks out the US must be able to manufacture enough weaponry on its own and currently it is dependent on imports to do so – these tariffs have been applied selectively. The application against the US allies including the EU, does not bode well for international relations, but the fact that Argentina, Australia, Brazil, Canada, Mexico and South Korea are exempt from the tariffs on derivative steel products, and Argentina, Australia, Canada and Mexico are exempt from the tariffs on derivative aluminium products (Fefer et al., 2018, p. 9), has led to many states regarding this act as *malafide*. Indeed, the EU and other members have filed complaints against the US in the WTO (Fefer et al., 2018, p. 43). However, the one that is suffering the brunt of these restrictions is growing superpower China – a state Trump often accused of employing "unfair trade practices" (Whitehouse, 2018). Trump's acts were presumably in an attempt to pressure China into revising its policies on intellectual property protection, technology transfers, industrial subsidies and market access (Guohua, 2019a) – something he consistently criticised.

China has not taken these restrictions lying down – the US is now staring at retaliatory tariffs in return (Guohua, 2019a), as well as Chinese complaints before the WTO (Fefer et al., 2018, p. 39). This has the potential to turn into a full-blown trade war quickly, if not already presenting as one. There appears to exist a political vendetta against China, originating well before Trump, which has resulted in several US-China clashes before having reached this point where the US is formulating policies that have a strong undercurrent of 'beggar thy neighbour.' Often credited to Adam Smith, the beggar thy neighbour policy refers to a policy that is enacted by one state in an attempt to resolve its economic issues but also worsens another state's economic issues (Smith, 2007). Protectionist policies such as trade barriers including tariffs, quotas and sanctions are examples of this. 25 per cent tariffs on aluminium and steel are *certainly* examples of this. Such policies were sought to be prevented by the institution of GATT, an agreement that embodies principles of free trade.

The crux of the problem, however, is not that one does not recognise what the US did under the Trump Administration specifically, although that in itself is extremely concerning. Retaliatory beggar thy neighbour policies that result in a trade war will affect developing countries the most, destroying multilateral trade and world economies. The problem is that International Hegemon United States of America has always been doing this – flouting norms of international trade with impunity to further its interests, economic or otherwise, regardless of the detriment to others (Jordan, 2019). Over and over it has bent rules to suit its purpose, always hidden behind the farce of "the greater good," parading as environmental concerns (US – Measures Concerning the Importation, Marketing and Sale of Tuna and Tuna Products, 2018; US – Import Prohibition of Certain Shrimp and Shrimp Products, 2001) or moral duties and no amount of world pressure or WTO rulings have resulted in changed behaviour. Thus, in a sense, Trump merely furthered the legacy of a superpower interested in preserving power, and President Biden seems in no hurry to undo said legacy.

## D.  A SYSTEM IN NEED OF CHANGING

It is apparent that a global trade war rooted in preserving power and establishing supremacy is beneficial to none – especially developing states. The implications for the multilateral trading regime should the US continue indulging in such behaviour, made not only possible but also convenient by the NSE, are dire.

Today, once again, the legitimacy of the multilateral trade system is being contested by developing states who feel inadequately consulted within international organizations that are catering to the interests of the powerful (Woods, 1999, p. 41). A classic example of this is how China is still eligible for the Special and Differential Treatment despite being the world's third largest economy (Cimino-Isaacs et al., 2021). One of the consequences of this dissatisfaction is, harkening back to the 90s, the rise in the number of Regional and Free Trade Agreements over the years, that has led to a sense of multipolarity within the sphere of global trade, weakening the WTO (Garzon, 2017, p. 102). It is becoming increasingly common for states to develop bilateral and plurilateral RTAs such as the EU-Singapore Free Trade Agreements, or the Comprehensive and Progressive Agreement for Trans-Pacific Partnership. There are currently 342 RTAs in force, 7 of which were entered into in 2021 (WTO Database, 2021). This positive trend in the creation of RTAs suggests that there may come a time where the WTO becomes defunct, indeed it is already viewed as obsolete by some (Creamer, 2019), what with the flagrant abuse of its provisions and its inherent inability to counter wilful misuse. This may exacerbate brewing discontent further and lead to the ultimate collapse of the system.

The WTO is already plagued by a plethora of issues including the debacle of the Doha Development Agenda (Araujo, 2018, p. 245) and the crippling of the Appellate Body by the US resulting in its stagnation since December 2019 (Cimino-Isaacs et al., 2021). The US' continued blocking of the appointment of judges to the Appellate Body has created a situation where there is, effectively, no grievance redressal mechanism left to members. This is not to say that the US would abide by unfavourable rulings of the Appellate Body, in all likelihood – as evidenced by history – it will not. While a change in the US Administration may seem like a ray of hope for numerous issues like immigration, on the trade front, Biden's approach and goals appear to be much the same as his predecessor. Granted, Biden provides a more diplomatic and civilized approach to negotiations, but the economic nationalistic perspective still colours his core policy (Sloan, 2020). Even if Biden decides to extend cooperation to the WTO in an effort to salvage the situation, he has no plans to do so until the current global pandemic has been tackled by the state whose timeline, based on current statistics, cannot be predicted at this point. Further, with more and more states beginning to prioritise their interests and protect and promote regional trading regimes – it means the end of an era that was built on the principles of free trade. This has been aggravated by the COVID-19 pandemic, which has shifted focus to domestic interests and slowed down the ministerial negotiations (Cimino-Isaacs et al., 2021), ultimately pointing towards the question of the continued relevance of the body itself. The NSE, compounding these issues, is a polarising provision that is sabotaging the WTO's very existence.

However, as much as a systemic change seems warranted, any radical change must be approached with caution. Propounded by Sir Charles Kindleberger, the Hegemonic Stability Theory contends that for the world to remain stabilized, there is a need for one stabiliser – a hegemon, if you will – committed to the ideals of a liberal trade regime including free trade and peace (Brawley, 2004). Arguing in favour, Robert Gilpin cites hegemony, liberal ideology and common interests as the key factors essential for the formation and expansion of a liberal trade regime and market. The theory predicts the decline of the hegemony eventually, where the hegemon gets weary of 'free-rider nations' and begrudges its economic partners who enjoy similar benefits with lesser input from their side, so to speak (Schubert, 2003 as citing Gilpin, 1987).

This precisely resembles the current scenario with the US. Although the framing of the 1994 GATT is mostly credited to the US, it no longer holds the same values of the liberal economy as it did back then and its policies now are overwhelmingly nationalistic. The Trump Administration made its discontent with the regime clear, threatening to withdraw from the WTO if "they don't shape up" and going as far as to call the treaty "the worst trade deal ever made." (Jordan, 2019, p. 177). The WTO system, the US claims, has enabled the rise of countries like China at the cost of millions of manufacturing jobs in the US (Johnson, 2020). Therefore, any radical change to reform the system and the NSE clause particularly, might have very well been the straw that broke the camel's back. While the Biden Administration has now replaced Trump in office, it is clear that his position on the WTO is not dissimilar, although perhaps not as extreme (Sloan, 2020). It has been categorically stated that the US would be less willing to cooperate if its interests are not prioritised (Guohua, 2019b). Thus, it may lead to the withdrawal of the US from the WTO regime and although such withdrawal may not lead to the abolishment of the WTO directly, it will significantly weaken the already crumbling system, maybe fatally.

Given the current state of affairs, there is no one clear successor to the seat of International Hegemon. The baton may pass to China, which has slowly begun its hegemonic journey, with increased contribution to the global economy and quantitative lead on the US since 2013 (Lisewski, 2020) or to the EU, the current trade giants of the world alongside the US. However, it is also true that international trade and economy is not a relay race – such major transitions, more accurately the vicious battle for hegemonic dominance, disrupt the world order and create a flux. If the WTO were to collapse, and with-it GATT, there would exist a vacuum in the sphere of international trade where there would be no global trade facilitating and regulating body. In the long term, this implies that smaller developing states would be left to defend themselves, with no institution to champion their cause and protect them from exploitation from developed states in unbalanced negotiations. The descent into multipolarity would become more rapid and intensive, attributed to numerous conflicting trade blocs with zero cooperation amongst them. A glimpse of this future is already visible, with an increasing number of states opting for Mega-Regionals, such as the Trans Pacific Partnership (TPP), and the Regional Comprehensive Economic Partnership (RCEP). RCEP alone accounts for 30 per cent of global GDP (McDonald, 2020) and TPP over 40 per cent (McBride et al., 2021). The numbers are so high and so many trade partners have entered into RTAs that even if the WTO shattered, their trade lines would remain intact, albeit presenting as a cut-throat warring wolf-pack model of global trade with incredibly high stakes. Moreover, should trade wars break out, which is neither a foreign nor a far-fetched notion, there would be no impartial body to help end the trade crisis before it disrupts the world economy drastically. This also means that states would have to resort to measures of dispute settlement that are fraught with diplomatic tension, politically motivated agendas and selfish interests. Ultimately, the cumulative effect of all these contributing factors would then trigger economic crises and threaten the ideals of sovereignty.

However, it is not merely in the interest of the world for world order to remain as is with a functional WTO backed by the US. The US' withdrawal might hurt the US more than the WTO. The US has only 20 FTAs in force with relatively smaller states, and the recent withdrawal from the TPP (Office of the US Trade Representative, 2017) and the abandonment of Transatlantic Trade and Investment Partnership (TTIP) negotiations, coupled with unregulated trade relations without GATT principles might be counter-productive for the US as 60 per cent of the US trade is outside the purview of its FTAs (Costa & Cimino-Isaacs, 2016). It would also lose its Most Favoured Nation status with 163 member states and the state would become a less attractive base for manufacturing, thus increasing the cost of US production and diminishing its competitiveness which essentially comes down to an increased price burden on the consumers (Brown & Irwin, 2018).

The US has lost too many lives, jobs and opportunities to the COVID-19 pandemic, and like several other states, now faces a disrupted supply chain and high unemployment rate (Weinstock, 2020). Although backing out of the WTO may seem beneficial to its economic nationalism and in dealing with its economic crisis, it would further cripple the US economy and expose it to the danger of tariff hikes and more stringent restrictions from member states, who are no longer bound by MFN obligations and other protections that the WTO offers. This would also then contribute to a faster hegemonic decline which may spell unimaginable and unmitigable disaster for the rest of the world.

## E. THE ROAD AHEAD

As established, the need for a systemic change is imminent and extremely necessary, beginning with the self-judged national security exception that has turned into a dangerous tool foretelling ruin. However, a delicate balance must be struck between creating real change while also not disturbing the current system too severely lest we run the risk of unleashing trade instability and the breakdown of the multilateral trade system.

The authors believe that what is required is a regulatory character to the framework of the NSE that will ensure transparency in application and clarity in interpretation. Such character would fall in line with the *intra vires* interpretation of the NSE, thereby strengthening the WTO's supposed commitment to good governance as well, without interfering with state sovereignty enforced through the provision. This can be done by way of modification of the clause itself that involves laying down a set of qualifications testing the veracity of the invocation that must be satisfied for member states to be eligible to claim the NSE for their proposed trade measures.

The authors propose carving out an exception within the exception as a means of reinforcement within Article XXI(b) to ensure equilibrium between sovereign security concerns and independence, and prevention of the possible misuse of GATT.

## Article XXI(b)

*"Nothing in this Agreement shall be construed*

*(b) to prevent any contracting party from taking any action which it considers necessary for the protection of its essential security interests*

   (i)   *relating to fissionable materials or the materials from which they are derived;*

   (ii)   *relating to the traffic in arms, ammunition and implements of war and to such traffic in other goods and materials as is carried on directly or indirectly for the purpose of supplying a military establishment;*

   (iii)   *taken in time of war or other emergency in international relations; or..."*

***Provided that, the self-judging character shall be extinguished where one or all of the qualifications for the invocation have not been met in the interest of transparency, accountability and fairness.***

*Explanation 1.* – In Clause b, "**qualifications**" include:

(a)   (a) The measure imposed under this exception

   (i)   must be uniformly applied to all contracting parties in consonance with Article I. Where certain member states are exempted, a statement of reason for such exclusion must be provided by the invoking member to all contracting parties, subject to judicial scrutiny upon institution of complaint by the aggrieved member;

      (i)   Should the statement of reason provided by the invoking member relate to exceptions available under Articles XXIV and XX, then such measure imposed must satisfy the requirements of such articles.

   (ii)   must aim to impart a higher degree of benefit upon the invoking member than the degree of disadvantage created to another member;

   (iii)   must be in consonance with the standard and principles of good faith;

   (iv)   must be proportionate to the threat to national security of the invoking member. Where tariff measures are being sanctioned, they must be in quantitative proportion to the security interest aimed to secure;

   (v)   must have a prima facie plausible nexus with the security interest aimed to be secured.

The authors are aware of the difficulty that accompanies modifying a treaty, especially one as complex as GATT. However, it is necessary that GATT, being an extremely important instrument in international trade falling under the ambit of the WTO, explicitly recognises the principles of good governance. It is desirable that this loophole in the current system is addressed appropriately, particularly to combat international hegemony. Considering the recent trend of judicial pronouncements by the WTO in regards to the NSE, it is hoped that member state acceptance and willingness to formulate a remedy – this specific remedy, would be strengthened through precedent.

Article XXI(b) is enabling powerful states to violate free trade norms and introduce policies best suited to their interests and in the process, exploit developing states that are bound by GATT norms. The cumulative effect of this is the ever-widening gap between the developed and developing member states. If remaining unchecked, the consequence will be the inevitable decline of the WTO as well as its standing as a paragon of good governance, with members repudiating obligations. They may resort to protectionist policies, or devise an alternate trade regime rather than remain part of a pseudo system that panders to superpower interests and where the authority of members to twist existing provisions to their advantage is not curtailed – such a development might trigger recession eventually and liberal economic principles may be at stake. Global cooperation is not enough, the need of the hour is good governance – what meets the eye today is an appalling lack of governance from the WTO, made possible by the simultaneous lack and presence of certain provisions in GATT used by member states to their advantage and the WTO's ultimate disadvantage. If such practice of twisting provisions to undermine good governance continues to go unaddressed and remains non-remedied, the future for multilateral international trade and world economies looks inarguably bleak.

The WTO must take concrete steps to save the world from a polarised trade regime and must push for more decisive negotiations and consequential reforms. This, it is submitted, begins with introducing a well-balanced reform to the NSE framework to combat the impunity with which superpowers navigate international trade and its hegemonic set-up, while still respecting state sovereignty.

## REFERENCES

Adjusting imports of automobiles and automobile parts into the United States. (2019). 84 FR 23433. A Presidential Document by the Executive Office of the President. Retrieved March 14, 2021 from https://www.federalregister.gov/documents/2019/05/21/2019-10774/adjusting-imports-of-automobiles-and-automobile-parts-into-the-united-states

Adjusting imports of derivative aluminum articles and derivative steel articles into the United States. (2020). 83 FR 5281. A Presidential Document by the Executive Office of the President. Retrieved March 14, 2021 from https://www.federalregister.gov/documents/2020/01/29/2020-01806/adjusting-imports-of-derivative-aluminum-articles-and-derivative-steel-articles-into-the-united

Adjusting imports of steel into the United States. (2018). 83 FR 11625. A Presidential Document by the Executive Office of the President. Retrieved March 14, 2021 from https://www.federalregister.gov/documents/2018/03/15/2018-05478/adjusting-imports-of-steel-into-the-united-states

Akande, D. & Williams, S. (2003) International adjudications on national security issues: What role for the WTO? *Virginia Journal of International Law*, 43(1), 365–404.

Alexandroff, A. & Sharma, R. (2005) The national security provision – GATT article XXI. In P. Marcrory, A. Appleton & M. Plummer (Eds.), *The World Trade Organization: legal, economic and political analysis* (pp. 1572). Springer.

Alford, R. P. (2011). The self-judging WTO security exception. *Utah Law Review*, 2011(3), 697–760.

American Institute for International Steel, Inc. v. Unites States, 376 F. Supp. 3d 1335 (Ct. Int'l Trade 2019).

Appellate Body Report, *European Communities - Measures Affecting Asbestos and Products Containing Asbestos,* WTO Doc. WT/DS 135/AB/R (Adopted Mar. 12, 2001).

Appellate Body Report, *United States - Measures Concerning the Importation, Marketing and Sale of Tuna and Tuna Products,* WTO Doc. WT/DS381/AB/RW/ (Adopted on Dec. 14, 2018).

Appellate Body Report, *United States – Import Prohibition of Certain Shrimp and Shrimp Products: Recourse to Article 21.5 of the DSU by Malaysia,* WTO Doc. WT/DS58/AB/RW/ (Oct. 22, 2001).

Araujo, B. (2018). Labour provisions in EU and US mega-regional trade agreements: Rhetoric and reality. *International and Comparative Law Quarterly*, 67(1), 233–254.

Botchway, F.N. (2001). Good governance: The old, the new, the principle, and the elements. *Florida Journal of International Law*, 13(2), 159–210.

Brawley, M. R. (2004). Hegemonic leadership: Is the concept still useful. *Connecticut Journal of International Law*, 19(2), 345–358.

Brown C.P. & Irwin D.A. (2018). *What might a Trump withdrawal from the World Trade Organization mean for US tariffs?.* Peterson Institute International Economics, no. 18–23. Retrieved March 14, 2021 from https://www.piie.com/publications/policy-briefs/what-might-trump-withdrawal-world-trade-organization-mean-us-tariffs

Christie, A., Smith, D., & Conroy, K. (2013). Transport governance indicators in Sub-Saharan Africa. *SSATP Africa transport policy program working paper, no. 95.* World Bank.

Cimino-Isaacs, C., Fefer, R., Fergusson, I. (2021) WTO: ministerial delay, covid-19, and ongoing issues. Congressional Research Service.

Costa, P.N.D & Cimino-Isaacs, C. (2016). *US exit from WTO would unravel global trade.* Peterson Institute International Economics. Retrieved March 14, 2021 from https://www.piie.com/publications/policy-briefs/what-might-trump-withdrawal-world-trade-organization-mean-us-tariffs

Creamer, C. D. (2019). From the WTO's crown jewel to its crown of thorns. *AJIL Unbound*, 113, 51–55.

Fagjelbaum, P., Goldberg, P., Kennedy, P. & Khandelwal, A. (2020) The return to protectionism. *NBER working paper, no. 25638.* National Bureau of Economic Research.

Federer, H. (2018). GATT article XXI: trade sanctions and the need to clarify the security exceptions. *Cambridge Law Review,* 3, 212–233.

Fefer, R., Hammond, K., Jones, V., Murrill, B., Platzer, M., Williams, B. (2018), Section 232 investigations: Overview and issues for Congress. *Report, no. 45249.* Congressional Research Service.

Griswold, D. (2019). Assessing president Trump's trade priorities. *CATO Journal*, 39(1), 199–212.

Guohua, Y. (2019a). International law in the 2018 China-US trade war. *Journal of WTO and China*, 9(1), 28–55.

Guohua, Y. (2019b). The causes of the crisis confronting the WTO appellate body. *Journal of WTO and China*, 9(4), 102–126.

Jackson, J. H. (1989). *The world trading system: law and policy of international economic relations.* Cambridge, MA: MIT Press.

Johnson, K. (May 27, 2020). *US effort to depart WTO gathers momentum,* Foreign Policy, Retrieved March 14, 2021 from https://foreignpolicy.com/2020/05/27/world-trade-organization-united-states-departure-china/.

Jordan, B. (2019). The WTO versus the Donald: Why the WTO must adopt review standard for article XXI(b) of the GATT. *Wisconsin International Law Journal*, 37(1), 173–206.

Kaufmann, D., Kraay A. & Zoido-Lobatón P. (1999). Governance. Policy Research Working Paper 2196.

Kentikelenis, A. & Voeten, E. (2020). Legitimacy challenges to the liberal world order: evidence from United Nations speeches, 1970–2018. *The Review of International Organizations*, 1–34. https://doi.org/10.1007/s11558-020-09404-y

Keohane, R. (1984). *After hegemony*. Princeton, NJ: Princeton University Press

Lisewski, M. (2020). The weakening of the hegemon and the future of the liberal international order. *Journal of Politics and Law*, 13(3), 166–179.

Mayer, W. (1981). Theoretical considerations on negotiated tariff adjustments. *Oxford Economic Papers New Series*, 33(1), 135–153.

McBride, J., Chatzky, A. & Siripurapu. (February 1, 2021). *What's next for the Trans-Pacific Partnership.* Council for Foreign Relations. Retrieved March 14, 2021, from https://www.cfr.org/backgrounder/what-trans-pacific-partnership-tpp

Mearsheimer, J. (1994). The false promise of international institutions. *International Security, 19*(3), 5–49. doi:10.2307/2539078

McDonald, T. (November 16, 2020). *What is the Regional Comprehensive Economic Partnership (RCEP)?*. BBC News. Retrieved March 14, 2021, from https://www.bbc.com/news/business-54899254

Notice of request for public comments on section 232: National security investigation of imports on titanium sponge. (2019). 84 FR 8503. Notice by Industry and Security Bureau. Retrieved March 14, 2021 from https://www.federalregister.gov/documents/2019/03/08/2019-04209/notice-of-request-for-public-comments-on-section-232-national-security-investigation-of-imports-of

Office of the US Trade Representative. (2017). *The United States officially withdraws from the trans-pacific partnership*, Press Release. Retrieved March 14, 2021, from https://ustr.gov/about-us/policy-offices/press-office/press releases/2017/january/US-Withdraws-From-TPP

Panel Report, *Russia-Measures Concerning Traffic in Transit,* WTO Doc. WT/DS512/R (Adopted Apr. 26, 2019).

Panel Report, *Saudi Arabia- Measures Concerning the Protection of Intellectual Property Rights,* WTO Doc. WT/DS567/R (Appeal on July 28, 2020).

Schubert, J. (2003*). Hegemonic stability theory: The rise and fall of the US – leadership in world economic relations*. GRIN Verlag.

Severstal Export GMBH v. United States, No. 18-00057, 2018 Ct. Intl. Trade LEXIS 38.

Simoes, F. (2017). Making trade policy great again: What policymakers should learn from Trump's election. *Asian Journal of WTO and International Health Law and Policy, 12*(2), 265–288.

Sloan, S.R. (2020). US foreign policy in 2021. *Atlantisch Perspectief*, 44(5), 38–43.

Smith, A. (2007). *Wealth of nations* (S. M. Soares Ed., Dig. Ed.)

Trade Expansion Act 19 USC. § 1862 (2012).

U.N. Conference on Trade and Employment, Havana, Cuba, Nov. 21, 1947-Mar. 24, 1948, An Informal Summary of the ITO Charter, U.N. Doc. E/CONF.2/INF.8 at 35 (Nov. 21, 1947).

US Department of Commerce. (2017). The effect of imports of steel on the national security: An investigation conducted under section 232 of the trade expansion act. Bureau of Industry and Security. 482–4883.

United states blocks reappointment of WTO appellate body member. (2016). *American Journal of International Law*, 110(3), 573–579.

United states blocks reappointment of WTO appellate body member. (2016). *American Journal of International Law*, 110(3), 573–579.

Weinstock, L. (2020). Covid-19 and the US economy. Congressional Research Service.

Weiss, F., & Steiner, S. (2007). Transparency as an element of good governance in the practice of the EU and the WTO: Overview and comparison. *Fordham International Law Journal*, 30(5), 1545–1586.

Whitehouse. (2017). *President Donald J. Trump stands American made Aluminum.* White House Briefings. Retrieved March 14, 2021, from https://www.whitehouse.gov/briefings-statements/president-donald-j-trump stands-american-made-aluminum/

Whitehouse. (2018). *President Donald J. Trump is Confronting China's Unfair Trade.* White House Briefings. Retrieved March 14, 2021, from https://www.whitehouse.gov/briefings-statements/president-donald-j-trump-confronting-chinas-unfair-trade-policies/

Woods, N. (1999). Good governance in international organizations. *Global Governance*, 5(1), 39–62.

World Bank. (1992). *Governance and development (English).* Retrieved March 14, 2021 from http://documents.worldbank.org/curated/en/604951468739447676/Governance-and development

WTO Agreement: Marrakesh Agreement Establishing the World Trade Organization, Apr. 15, 1994, 1867 U.N.T.S. 154, 33 I.L.M. 1144 (1994).

WTO. (2021). *RTAs in force.* Regional Trade Agreements Database. Retrieved Mar. 15, 2021, from https://rtais.wto.org/UI/PublicAllRTAList.aspx

## CHAPTER TWO

# COVID 19: Effect of Job Insecurity on Employee Performance: Mediating Role of Depression

**Mohammad Ali (Corresponding Author)**
*Department of Business Administration in Management Studies*
*Bangladesh University of Professionals, Dhaka, Bangladesh*
*E-mail: rana.ali0191@gmail.com*

**Sabrina Sharmin Nishat**
*Department of Business Administration in Management Studies*
*Bangladesh University of Professionals, Dhaka, Bangladesh*
*E-mail: sabrina.nishat@bup.edu.bd*

**Farzana Tazin**
*Department of Business Administration in Management Studies*
*Bangladesh University of Professionals, Dhaka, Bangladesh*
*E-mail: farzana.tazin@bup.edu.bd*

**Mohammad Rabiul Basher Rubel, PhD**
*Department of Business Administration in Management Studies*
*Bangladesh University of Professionals, Dhaka, Bangladesh*
*E-mail: rabiul.basher@bup.edu.bd; asstprof_sub@yahoo.com*

**Abstract**—*The focus of the current study is to see the influence of job insecurity (JI) on employee performance in the form of in-role (IR) and extra-role (ER) performance with the mediating effect of depression. Data were collected from front-line employees of 4-star and 5-star hotels of Bangladesh. Findings of the study showed significant effect of employee JI on both IR and ER performance. Again, JI exhibited positive relationship with employee depression in the workplace. For depression, both employee IR and ER performance also showed significant relationship. Finally, both the mediating relations were also found significant. Thus, it can be revealed that management of the organization needs to be more concerned on employee performance which may help them to attain sustainable competitive advantage in the industry. Therefore, it is essential for the organization to ensure employee continuity in the workplace which may minimize their depression to contribute more.*

**Keywords**—Job insecurity, employee performance, depression, hotel industry, Bangladesh

## INTRODUCTION

The Coronavirus disease 2019 (COVID-19) epidemic revealed a global bump with approximately 25.1 million verified incidents and over 8,44,000 deaths in 216 countries up to 31ˢᵗ August 2020 (World Health Organization, 2020). This condition generated an adverse impact on the economies (Gössling et al., 2020; Nicola et al., 2020), societal connection, association, bonding (Balanzá–Martínez et al., 2020) and health. COVID-19 has brought about a dire catastrophe to all industries across the globe. Business sectors like tourism, accommodation, and travel agencies are facing a steep plunge in demand because of being vulnerable to severe tremors like the occurrence of pandemics (Nicola et al., 2020). In specific, the hotel industry has faced massive sales decreases as service availing rates have massively fallen owing to the social distancing rule imposed by the world health organization as well as the local government. Thus, worldwide, the hotel organizations faced a radical drop in the number of visitors (Sobieralski, 2020). In consequence, the hotel business across the world is facing an employment shockwave in comparison to other industries, with a sharp drop in the employment ratios and a theatrical increase in the frequency of short-term leaves.

In response to the upsurge of the pandemic in Bangladesh, the appearance of visitors into the country was controlled, and the percentage of travelling inside the country also declined remarkably, initiating an undeniable managerial crisis in hotels. Employment uncertainty is generated by the spread of the virus in these industries, thus, causes an unavoidable threat to organizational operations and viability-an unusual situation that demands the hospitality industry to search for a variety of alternative approaches (Carnevale & Hatak, 2020). In this situation, examining job insecurity (JI), as seen by hotel employees, and its negative implications might prove to be noteworthy in defining how industries can replenish and how fast-changing industries can experience a persistent future.

Undoubtedly, contemporary working conditions have been incapable to ascertain employment security for all employees owing to unpredictability arising from technological upgradations, economic shifts, political instability, even from time-period before the upsurge of the pandemic (Etehadi & Karatepe, 2019). Employee conceptions about JI - the prejudiced and insensate conception of losing jobs have boomed on account of organizational re-engineering and cut-downs, and now the current pandemic has also severed the condition. Employees might fall prey to JI for two particular causes (Mauno et al., 2014); mostly, changes in an organization brought by JI, like employee cut-offs, dismissals, and mergers that affect specific workgroups of an organization, incorporating their conceptions of JI, and furthermore, separate work groups might perceive commonly or jointly about notions like particular threats or stressors. Henceforth, it cannot be avoided that employees face tremendous stress in the form of JI

(Gaunt & Benjamin, 2007) signifying a negative correlation between factors of job attitude and employee mental health conditions (De Witte et al., 2015). A study by Chirumbolo (2015) explored the consequences of JI throughout the pandemic referring to the fact that JI triggers workers to get involved in damaging actions due to damaging psychosomatic behaviors.

A contemporary study identified that psychological condition moderates the potential correspond of work performance (Ford et al., 2011). The current research also considered depression as a mediator between JI and employee performance (in-role and extra-role). The discrete expenses of depression are fairly recognized (Lacko & Knapp, 2018), and recent calculations propose that approximately $925 billion annual cost is being incurred by the global economy in consequence of the productivity lost due to depression and anxiety conditions. Depression is a prevalent mental health condition, declared by the Diagnostic and Statistical Manual of Mental Disorders (DSM–5), as the existence of continual dejected spirit infused with cognitive and somatic changes that considerably intervene with typical routine activities. The segregated costs of depression are well recorded, and updated statistics signify that reduced output arousing from depression and anxiety disorders cause an annual charge of approximately $925 billion to the global economy (Chisholm et al., 2016).

The contributions of this study are two-tiered. Primarily, we addressed the impact of JI on employee performance in the shape of IR and ER in the hotel industry in Bangladesh with mediating effect of depression in COVID 19 situation. There has been little research on assessing the effect of JI on employee work outcome in hotel organizations as service industry (Jung et al., 2021). Another, here is a lack of research considering depression as a mediator between JI and both employee IR and ER performance. Therefore, this contextual study adds to this track of study as well. Henceforth, figure-1 presents the research framework of the current study that portrays the relationship between JI and employee IR and ER performance with the mediating role of depression.

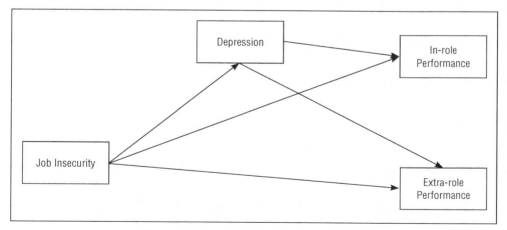

**Figure 1.** Proposed Research Framework

# LITERATURE REVIEW

## Employee Performance

Performance is expressed as the acquired result of competent workers in some situations (Prasetya & Kato, 2011). As stated by Hawthorne studies, and scores of other research work on productivity of worker showed up the reality that employees who are pleased with their job will have maximum job performance, in consequence, foremost job retention, than those who are not satisfied with their jobs (Landy, 1985).

Employee performance can be stipulated based on IR and ER performance. IR performance alludes to the behavior directed toward formal tasks, duties and responsibilities designated to the sole employee previously referred in their job description (Williams & Anderson, 1991). Contrarily, ER performance indicates those activities that are vitally important for organizational success but are discretionary in nature, for example, acting respectfully, assist others, quality relationship with fellow workers and superiors (Niehoff & Moorman, 1993). Scholars also termed ER performance as organizational citizenship behavior (Colquitt et al., 2009).

## Job Insecurity

JI was initially defined in the eighties as the powerlessness to maintain the steadiness of work of an individual in an endangered working condition (Greenhalgh, 1984). There is huge uncertainty facing the employees around the world due to globalization, technological innovation, economic and political changes. Thus, resulting in the replacement of stability and predictability with JI (Dewitte, 2015). Employees expecting a possible layoff results in stress which are traumatic and life-disrupting (Alaina & Keim, 2014). JI appears from workers' perception about events, signal link with work, people and social atmosphere. Employees have a negative perception of JI when new managers arrive. It can threaten an individual's personal resources and identity (Shoss, 2017).

JI as a significant work stressor resulting in drastic consequences does not only impact both employees and their employers. Alongside the advent of continuous changes in the working environment inducing feelings of JI, employers are now forced to deal with new demands or master skills not relating to their jobs (Jiang & Lavaysse, 2018). Employees feel threatened by the prevalence of JI owing to the concept that they may lose their jobs. JI means to behold idiosyncratic conceptions about employment settings, overtly, about losing job constancy and continuance of employment relationship with the organization (Laura Bernardi, 2008). So far, JI has been linked with adverse job-related outcomes. For example, upon confrontation with perceived JI, employees may reveal lower level of motivation and they become depressed.

## Depression

Depression is not just a form of acute unhappiness. It is a jumble that influences both brain and body as well as behavior, immune system and nervous system. Depression is observed as a disorder because it is imbalanced in a person's work activities or relationships (PDM Task Force, 2006). Depression also varies from ordinary sorrowing in that the person feels the world as empty or cruel, in contrast to, clinically depressed persons who hold their sense of emptiness or badness in themselves. In most cases depression ranges from light to extremely severe (PDM Task Force, 2006).

Depression has also been viewed as a veto subject in the organization. A lot of employees face organizational depression. Maximum employees conceal their sadness due to the fear of job loss or discrimination among their colleagues (Lacko & Knapp, 2018). Due to depression and anxiety, employees face negative reactions from employers and colleagues. Organizational depression is a mental sickness related to drawbacks due to a poisonous workplace atmosphere (Rasool et al., 2016). According to the grouping of DSM-5, depression is a familiar mental health condition that confirms continuous dejected temper collective with perceptive and sensual deviations which pointedly intervenes with everyday routine working. Beyond all health conditions, depression has far-reaching consequences on individual work performance (Kessler et al., 2008). Depression is a psychological discomfort that encompasses a tireless feeling of sorrow and loss of attraction (American Psychological Association, 2020; Sandoiu, 2020). Owing to the upsurge of COVID-19, tension arises among the employees regarding their careers. This COVID-19 triggers job loss of employees and unstable future job market which grows depression among the employees (Sandoiu, 2020; Morath & Guilford, 2020; UN News, 2020). Normally, employees with depression shows low concentration, lethargy and decreasing decision-making capacity (Kessler et al., 2008). Several areas of job performance are deteriorated by depression such as interpersonal relationships, innovation, time management, workplace safety, etc.

# HYPOTHESES DEVELOPMENT

## Job Insecurity and employee performance

JI is adversely related with employee job related outcomes (Darvishmotevali et al., 2017) as it is perceived as a job stressor. Employees who are mostly worried about JI cannot perform with full spirit (Darvishmotevali et al., 2017). Shin and Hur (2020) found that JI negatively controls employee job performance and acts as a mediator between the association of supervisor rudeness and employee job performance. JI acts as a negative determinant of role performance (Schreurs et al., 2012). Piccoli et al. (2019) believed that JI leads to negative behavioral consequences like poor performance, absenteeism, job switching intention, etc.

Rubel et al. (2018) suggested that employee feelings towards the insecurity of jobs can play as an important hindrance in IR service and ER service behavior. Based on the previous empirical evidence on the relationship between JI on employee performance, the following hypotheses may be developed.

**Hypothesis 1a:** Job insecurity is negatively related to IR performance.

**Hypothesis 1b:** Job insecurity is negatively related to ER performance.

## Job insecurity and depression

JI as a psychological stressor (Kim & Kim, 2018) leads to high stress on employees' mentality. It acts as a determinant of job anxiety that causes depression (Kim et al., 2017). Kim & Kim (2018) claimed that JI significantly contributes to increase employee depression which may even lead suicidal attempt. Amid Covid-19, employees feel insecurity about their job and as a result of which anxiety and depression exist among young adults (Ganson et al., 2021). JI creates mental burden for employees that becomes the reason of poor mental health (Ganson et al., 2021). Therefore, it could be hypothesized that JI may act to enhance depression.

**Hypothesis 2:** Job insecurity is positively related to depression.

## Depression and employee performance

Depressed employees are less productive employees because depression prevents dedication and engagement towards performance (Anwar et al., 2021). Depressed employees tend to be frequently absent and less involved in the assigned tasks which lead poor job performance (Parent-Lamarche et al., 2020). Lerner et al. (2015) concluded that job stressors like depression, anger and fear have a detrimental impact on employee performance. Alam (2020) concluded that work stress causes depression, which, in turn, is negatively correlated with employee performance. Lack of coworker and supervisor support may lead to high depression which may significantly deteriorate the IR and ER performance of employees (Talebzadeh & Karatepe, 2020). These arguments might be induced into the following hypotheses:

**Hypothesis 3a:** Depression is negatively related to IR performance.

**Hypothesis 3b:** Depression is negatively related to ER performance.

## Depression as a mediator

We encompass the present study by assessing depression as a mediator in the relationship between JI and employee performance. Literature has emphasized the significance of negative relationship between JI and employee performance which decreases IR and ER performance (Piccoli et al., 2019; Rubel et al., 2018; Shin & Hur, 2020). Similarly, researchers have claimed depression plays a prominent role to reduce the level of employee performance (Alam, 2020; Anwar et al., 2021; Parent-Lamarche et al., 2020; Talebzadeh & Karatepe, 2020). Common beliefs of the scholars support that JI is a psychological threat for employees which creates high depression (Ganson et al., 2021; Kim et al., 2017; Kim & Kim, 2018). However, researchers are still investigating the impact of JI on employee performance. It can be argued that JI is a determinant of depression which decreases employee performance.

Accordingly, depression has been experimented as a mediator by the researchers. Morasco et al. (2013) identified that depression influenced by JI is a potential mediator between JI and chronic pain. Furthermore, it was supported that depression mediates the relationship between workplace culture and employee productivity (Laing & Jones, 2016). Parent-Lamarche et al. (2020) found that depression mediates the influence of working condition on job performance. Recent research also provides the evidence of mediating role of depression (Bianchi et al., 2015; Fazeli et al., 2020). Therefore, the present study argues that depression plays a mediating role in the relationship between JI and employee performance and the hypotheses are as follows.

**Hypothesis 4a:** Depression mediates the relationship between job insecurity and IR performance.

**Hypothesis 4b:** Depression mediates the relationship between job insecurity and ER performance.

## METHODOLOGY

### Sample

The current research is cross-sectional in nature where data were collected in 2020 (October 2020-November 2020). A structured questionnaire is employed to collect data for the current research. Front-line employees were included of the 4-star and 5-star hotels in Bangladesh. Approximately there are 105 (4-star and 5-star) hotels in Bangladesh (Bangladesh Civil Aviation and Tourism Ministry Report, 2020). Among these 105 hotels, almost 76% (80) hotels are in Dhaka, the capital city, and Chottogram division, and the rest 24% (25) are situated in other locations of the country (Bangladesh Civil Aviation and Tourism Ministry Report, 2020). Thus, these two locations are considered as the sampling frame of the current research.

With the help of the human resource department the researchers distributed 800 questionnaires equally to all participated organizations. Of 800 questionnaires distributed, 478 were reverted. 60 questionnaires were discarded due to inconsistent information. In total 418 questionnaires were found suitable for further analysis. The current research employed purposive judgmental sampling a category of non-probability sampling design. Judgmental sampling is suitable when there is no complete list of the respondents and very difficult to identify the actual number of population (Sekaran & Bougie, 2016).

## Measures and Data Analysis Technique

The current study adapted all items from the previous validated literature. Such as JI and depression were measured by 8 and 5 items adapted from Jung et al. (2021) and Ganson et al. (2021). Finally, both IR and ER performance were measured by 3 items for each adapted from Rubel et al. (2018). In this study, independent and mediator variable were assessed by 5-point Likert scale whereas, 7-point Likert scale was employed to measure both dimensions of dependent variable. Statistical Package for Social Science (SPSS) was employed to insert data, analyze the descriptive statistics and measure the demographic profile of the respondents. Whereas, Partial Least Square (PLS 3.2.7) was used to assess both measurement and structural model of the research framework based on the hypotheses.

## RESULTS

The respondents of the current research were from front-line employees; therefore, their perceptions were examined. The average age of the respondents who participated in this survey is 34 years. Approximately half (50%) of the participants are between 25–34 years. Two-thirds portion of the respondents is male (67.80%). On average, the span of work experience of the respondents is around eight years.

## Measurement model

The measurement model has been evaluated using a confirmatory factor analysis (CFA) to confirm the reliability, convergent validity and discriminant validity of the model. The data presented in Table 1 reflects that the value of all item loadings is higher than 0.5 while both AVE's and CR outcomes are predominantly higher than 0.5 and 0.7 respectively as recommended by Hair et al. (2014). Among the values presented in this table, the lowest value of CR is 0.843, and AVE is 0.519. Henceforth, it can be concluded that the study confirms convergent validity by achieving the parameter for acceptability.

**Table 1.** Measurement Model

| Constructs | Items | Item Loading | AVE | CR |
|---|---|---|---|---|
| Depression | Depre 1 | 0.768 | 0.519 | 0.843 |
| | Depre 2 | 0.647 | | |
| | Depre 3 | 0.737 | | |
| | Depre 4 | 0.728 | | |
| | Depre 5 | 0.714 | | |
| Extra-role Performance | ERP 1 | 0.876 | 0.735 | 0.892 |
| | ERP 2 | 0.913 | | |
| | ERP 3 | 0.825 | | |
| In-role Performance | IRP 1 | 0.825 | 0.733 | 0.845 |
| | IRP 2 | 0.886 | | |

| Job Insecurity | Job Ins 1 | 0.763 | 0.692 | 0.931 |
| | Job Ins 2 | 0.893 | | |
| | Job Ins 3 | 0.799 | | |
| | Job Ins 4 | 0.866 | | |
| | Job Ins 5 | 0.848 | | |
| | Job Ins 6 | 0.813 | | |

Furthermore, this study tested discriminant validity by an empirical standard to show how each construct was different from others following Hair et al. (2014). This study used Heterotrait-monotrait (HTMT) method suggested by Henseler et al. (2016) for discriminant validity analysis. Henseler et al. (2016) proposed value ≥ 0.85 as the stricter criterion or value ≥ 0.90 as the lenient criterion. The present value was found supporting the limit of the stricter criterion of ≥ 0.85. Therefore, the discriminant validity standard was justified (see Table 2).

**Table 2.** Discriminant Validity

| | Depre | ERP | IRP | Job Ins |
|---|---|---|---|---|
| Depre | | | | |
| ERP | 0.265 | | | |
| IRP | 0.242 | 0.637 | | |
| Job Ins | 0.223 | 0.337 | 0.346 | |
| Mean | 3.61 | 4.67 | 4.81 | 3.72 |
| SD | 0.66 | 0.87 | 0.92 | 0.69 |

## Structural model

A structural model is developed by studying the hypothetical relationships among the variables. Following Table 3, the path from depression to employee ER performance ($\beta = -0.164$, $p < 0.01$) and IR performance ($\beta = -0.126$, $p < 0.01$) also illustrate significant relationships. Moreover, the path from JI to depression shows significant relation ($\beta = 0.196$, $p < 0.01$). Finally, the paths from JI to both outcome variables (extra-role and in-role performance) indicate their substantial relationships having values of ($\beta = -0.274$, $p < 0.01$) and ($\beta = -0.249$, $p < 0.01$), correspondingly. Table 3 shows the results of the hypothesized relationship.

**Table 3.** Result of Direct Effect

| Direct Path | Std. Beta | Std. Error | t-Value | P-value | Decision |
|---|---|---|---|---|---|
| Job Insecurity > In-role Performance | −0.249 | 0.045 | 5.58** | 0.000 | Supported |
| Job Insecurity > Ex.-role Performance | −0.274 | 0.042 | 6.51** | 0.000 | Supported |
| Depression > In-role Performance | −0.126 | 0.048 | 2.65** | 0.008 | Supported |
| Depression > Ex.-role Performance | −0.164 | 0.046 | 3.58** | 0.000 | Supported |
| Job Insecurity > Depression | 0.196 | 0.049 | 4.02** | 0.000 | Supported |

**p < 0.01, (based on one-tailed test with 1, 000 bootstrapped replications)

This research also measures the mediating effect of depression on both JI and employee IR and ER performance following Preacher and Hayes (2008). The current results indicate considerable mediating effect of depression on JI and employee IR performance ($\beta = -0.025$, $p < 0.01$) and ER performance ($\beta = -0.032$, $p < 0.01$).

Preacher and Hayes (2008) recommend that the upper and lower limit values of confidential interval should not include zero to get mediation effect. The present study supports this requirement to get the mediating effect of depression between JI and employee IR performance (LL 0.013, UL 0.123), and ER performance (LL 0.056, UL 0.142).

**Table 4.**   Result of Indirect Effect

| Indirect Path | Std. Bet. | Std. Erro | t-Value | 95% LL | 95% UL | P-value | Decision |
|---|---|---|---|---|---|---|---|
| Job Ins > Depre. > ERP | −0.032 | 0.011 | 2.87** | 0.013 | 0.123 | 0.004 | Supported |
| Job Ins > Depre. > IRP | −0.025 | 0.011 | 2.26** | 0.056 | 0.142 | 0.024 | Supported |
| **p < 0.01, (based on two-tailed test with 1, 000 bootstrapped replications) | | | | | | | |

## DISCUSSION

The aim of this research is to examine how JI influences employee performance through the mediating effects of depression in the setting of a developing country. Specifically, the influence of JI on employee performance through depression among the front-line employees of the organizations in the Bangladeshi hotel industry. The outcome of the study is congruent with the past studies. The results of the current study accepted the first hypothesis on the relationship between JI and employee IR and ER performance. Earlier Shin and Hur (2020) supported that JI directly and indirectly makes negative link with employee performance.

The second hypothesis was also supported; JI can reinforce the depression of employees as the two are positively related. Similar results were also supported by the empirical analysis of Ganson et al. (2021). The result shows that when employees are concerned about the security of their job during COVID-19, they tend to be depressed. The results of the study confirmed the third hypothesis. The current findings showed a significant relationship between employee depression and IR and ER performance as advocated by Talebzadeh & Karatepe (2020). In the present context of the hotel industry, due to COVID-19, depressed front-line employees cannot psychologically engage themselves in the job that ultimately deteriorate their performance.

In this study, hypothesis four presumed that depression mediates the association between JI and both IR and ER performance. The result confirmed the mediating role of depression between JI and employee IR and ER performance, which is reliable with the previous study directed by Morasco et al. (2013). Since JI increases employee depression (Ganson et al., 2021) and depression decreases employee performance (Alam, 2020), the results establishes the mediating effect of depression between JI and employee performance.

In the present study, JI was found as a negative determining factor of employee performance that eventually impedes the performance of the organizations in the hotel industry as well. Moreover, depression was found as an intervening variable between JI and employee IR and ER performance. Therefore, hotel organizations should ensure the job security of employees which will contribute to reduce depression and ultimately improve their current level of performance.

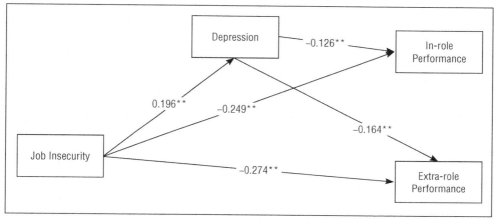

**Figure 2.**  Output of Structural Model

## THEORETICAL AND PRACTICAL IMPLICATIONS

The findings of this research prioritize the importance of pragmatic style when managing employees' conceptions of job security in controlling their depression and refining their performance. At the instance of ensuring the job security by an organization, employees believe that their well-being is considered. They respond by enhancing their enactment beyond the specific task-related errands for which they are cared for and recognized by their organization. The current study imparts empirical evidence to believe that organizations can reduce depression when job security is ensured and well communicated with employees. Such insight may enrich human resource management (HRM) theories imparting support of employee IR and ER outcomes as well as recognizing JI as a job stressor. Moreover, the findings accelerate the argument of mediating impact of employee attitude by presenting depression as a mediator between JI and employee IR and ER performance. On theoretical aspect, the present results differentiate the study from the existing literature of HRM. The findings of the study contribute to the literature on HRM and employee outcomes by providing insights into JI, depression and employee performance in a developing country context. The current study provides the evidence of negative impact of JI on employee performance and the positive linkage of depression with JI amidst COVID-19.

Specifically, in practice, the results of the study provide Bangladeshi hotel organizations with a comprehensive understanding of the dimensions of JI and their applicability in the service sector for an improved economy. Proper security of job may lead to better performance of the employees. The study assesses how JI has an impact on front-line employees' performance through depression. The study suggests that hotel managers must concentrate on job security to make employees more devoted towards their performance. Fear of COVID-19 creates psychological pressures which becomes acute due to depression that arises from insecurity of job. Hence, hotel managers should take care of the issues of employee depression.

The findings help in presuming that job security is an important factor of goodwill of an employer when employees are not depressed. As a result, employees become more enthusiastic to perform effectively for the organizations. Hence, the outcome of this research will help the managers of hotel organizations to gain better insights into the reduction of employee performance due to depression and the extent to which job security is crucial in this regard. Moreover, the findings will be beneficial to the organizations of other service industry and other developing countries.

## LIMITATIONS AND FUTURE RESEARCH DIRECTION

The study admits some limitations though it has been designed carefully. This study is cross sectional in nature; therefore, longitudinal approach can be used in the future study to examine the causal relations of the variables. Only three dimensions have been used in the present study whereas depression was incorporated as a mediator. Hence, researchers can analyze the impact of JI addressing the mediating effect of other altitudinal variables such as engagement, commitment, perceived support from leader, etc. The study focused on just hotel industry which is not enough to generalize the findings of service sector in a developing country context. Therefore, more service industry such as, insurance, banking, medical, etc. can be covered to achieve more generalizable results in the context of service sector of Bangladesh. Moreover, similar study can be performed in the developing and developed country context to extend the literature in JI and employee outcomes.

## CONCLUSION

This paper aims to examine how JI influences employee performance through depression during COVID-19. The study concludes that insecurity of job is significantly related with employee outcomes such as, IR and ER performance. Our findings prioritize the idea that when job security is not ensured, employee performance suffers. Hence, management of hotel industry can attain better performance when employees feel their jobs are secured. More specifically, hotel industry should pay more attention on job security and mental health such as, state of depression, to get maximum and sustainable employee performance.

# REFERENCE

Alaina C., & Keim, R. S. (2014). Why Do Employees Worry About Their Jobs? A Meta-Analytic Review of Predictors of Job Security. *Journal of Occupational Health Psychology, 19*(3), 269–290.

American Psychological Association. (2020). Retrieved from Depression: https://www.apa.org/topics/depression/

Anwar, A., Kee, D. M. H., Salman, A., & Jabeen, G. (2021). Impact of COVID-19 social media news on employee behavior: the mediating role of psychological well-being and depression. *Asian Education and Development Studies.*

Balanzá–Martínez, V., Atienza–Carbonell, B., Kapczinski, F., & De Boni, R. B. (2020). Lifestyle behaviours during the COVID-19–time to connect. *Acta Psychiatr Scand,141,* 399–400

Bangladesh Civil Aviation and Tourism Ministry Report (2020). *Ministry of Civil Aviation and Tourism.* Retrieved from https://mof.portal.gov.bd/sites/default/files/files/ mof. portal.gov.bd/page/5e31763f_f5b2_4ecb_bf9a_edc8609d2f3f/G3_22_53_Civil_English.pdf

Barlow, D. H. (2002). *Anxiety and Its Disorders.* The Guilford Press.

Barlow, D. H. (2010). Unraveling the mysteries of anxiety and its disorders from the perspective of emotion theory. *American Psychologist, 55*(11), 1247–1263.

Bianchi, R., Schonfeld, I. S., & Laurent, E. (2015). Burnout–depression overlap: A review. *Clinical psychology review, 36,* 28–41.

Bryner, J. (2020). *1st known case of coronavirus traced back to November in China.* Retrieved from Live Science: https://www.livescience.com/first-case-coronavirus-found.html

Carnevale, J. B., & Hatak, I. (2020). Employee adjustment and well-being in the era of COVID-19: Implications for human resource management. *Journal of Business Research, 116,* 183–187.

Cherry, K. (2020). *Overview of the 6 Major Theories of Emotion.* Retrieved from Verywell mind: https://www.verywellmind.com/theories-of-emotion-2795717

Chirumbolo, A. (2015). The impact of job insecurity on counterproductive work behaviors: The moderating role of honesty–humility personality trait. *The Journal of psychology, 149*(6), 554–569.

Chisholm, D., Sweeny, K., Sheehan, P., Rasmussen, B., Smit, F., Cuijpers, P., & Saxena, S. (2016). Scaling-up treatment of depression and anxiety: a global return on investment analysis. *The Lancet Psychiatry, 3*(5), 415–424.

Colquitt, J., LePine, J., & Wesson, M. (2009). *Organizational Behavior: Improving Performance and Commitment in the Workplace.* New York: Mc Grew Hill Irwin.

Darvishmotevali, M., Arasli, H., & Kilic, H. (2017). Effect of job insecurity on frontline employee's performance. *International Journal of Contemporary Hospitality Management, 29*(6), 1724–1744.

De Witte, H., Vander Elst, T., & De Cuyper, N. (2015). Job insecurity, health and well-being. In *Sustainable working lives* (pp. 109–128). Springer, Dordrecht.

Etehadi, B., & Karatepe, O. M. (2019). The impact of job insecurity on critical hotel employee outcomes: the mediating role of self-efficacy. *Journal of Hospitality Marketing & Management, 28*(6), 665–689.

Fazeli, S., Zeidi, I. M., Lin, C. Y., Namdar, P., Griffiths, M. D., Ahorsu, D. K., & Pakpour, A. H. (2020). Depression, anxiety, and stress mediate the associations between internet gaming disorder, insomnia, and quality of life during the COVID-19 outbreak. *Addictive Behaviors Reports, 12*, 100307.

Ford, M. T., Cerasoli, C. P., Higgins, J. A., & Decesare, A. L. (2011). Relationships between psychological, physical, and behavioural health and work performance: A review and meta-analysis. *Work & Stress, 25*(3), 185–204.

Ganson, K. T., Tsai, A. C., Weiser, S. D., Benabou, S. E., & Nagata, J. M. (2021). Job insecurity and symptoms of anxiety and depression among US young adults during COVID-19. *Journal of Adolescent Health, 68*(1), 53–56.

Gaunt, R., & Benjamin, O. (2007). Job insecurity, stress and gender: The moderating role of gender ideology. *Community, Work and Family, 10*(3), 341–355.

Giorgi, G., Lecca, L. I., Alessio, F., Finstad, G. L., Bondanini, G., Lulli, L. G., Mucci, N. (2020). COVID-19-Related Mental Health Effects in the Workplace: A Narrative Review. *International Journal of Environmental Research and Public Health, 17*(21), 7857.

Gössling, S., Scott, D., & Hall, C. M. (2020). Pandemics, tourism and global change: a rapid assessment of COVID-19. *Journal of Sustainable Tourism, 29*(1), 1–20.

Greenhalgh, L. Z. R. (1984). Job Insecurity: Toward Conceptual Clarity. *The Academy of Management Review, 9*(3), 438–448.

Hair Jr, J. F., Sarstedt, M., Hopkins, L., & Kuppelwieser, V. G. (2014). Partial least squares structural equation modeling (PLS-SEM): An emerging tool in business research. *European business review, 26*(2), 106–121.

Henseler, J., Hubona, G., & Ray, P. A. (2016). Using PLS path modeling in new technology research: updated guidelines. *Industrial management & data systems, 116*(1), 2–20.

Izard, C. E. (1971). *The face of emotion.* New York. Appleton-Century Crofts.

Izard, C. E. (1977). *Human emotions.* Springer.

Jung, H. S., Jung, Y. S., & Yoon, H. H. (2021). COVID-19: The effects of job insecurity on the job engagement and turnover intent of deluxe hotel employees and the moderating role of generational characteristics. *International Journal of Hospitality Management, 92*, 102703.

Kessler, R., White, L. A., Birnbaum, H., Ying, Q., Kidolezi, Y., Mallett, D., & Swindle, R. (2008). Comparative and interactive effects of depression relative to other health problems on work performance in the workforce of a large employer. *Journal of Occupational and Environmental Medicine, 50*, 809–816.

Kim, M. S., Hong, Y. C., Yook, J. H., & Kang, M. Y. (2017). Effects of perceived job insecurity on depression, suicide ideation, and decline in self-rated health in Korea: a population-based panel study. *International archives of occupational and environmental health, 90*(7), 663–671.

Kim, Y., & Kim, S. S. (2018). Job insecurity and depression among automobile sales workers: a longitudinal study in South Korea. *American journal of industrial medicine, 61*(2), 140–147.

Klerman, G. L., & Burrows, G. D. (1977). *Anxiety and depression.* Handbook of studies of depression.

Lacko, S.-L. E., & Knapp, M. (2018). Is manager support related to workplace productivity for people with depression: A secondary analysis of a cross-sectional survey from 15 countries. *BMJ Open, 8*.

Laing, S. S., & Jones, S. M. (2016). Anxiety and depression mediate the relationship between perceived workplace health support and presenteeism: A cross-sectional analysis. *Journal of occupational and environmental medicine, 58*(11), 1144–1149.

Landy, F. J. (1985). *Psychology of Work Behavior.* Homewood. I.L. Dorsey Press.

Laura Bernardi, A. K. (2008). Job Insecurity and the Timing of Parenthood: A Comparison between Eastern and Western Germany. *European Journal of Population, 24,* 287–313.

Lerner, D., Adler, D. A., Rogers, W. H., Chang, H., Greenhill, A., Cymerman, E., & Azocar, F. (2015). A randomized clinical trial of a telephone depression intervention to reduce employee presenteeism and absenteeism. *Psychiatric Services, 66*(6), 570–577.

Jiang, L., & Lavaysse, L. M. (2018). Cognitive and affective job insecurity: A meta-analysis and a primary study. *Journal of Management, 44*(6), 2307–2342.

Mauno, S., De Cuyper, N., Tolvanen, A., Kinnunen, U., & Mäkikangas, A. (2014). Occupational well-being as a mediator between job insecurity and turnover intention: Findings at the individual and work department levels. *European Journal of Work and Organizational Psychology, 23*(3), 381–393.

Morasco, B. J., Lovejoy, T. I., Lu, M., Turk, D. C., Lewis, L., & Dobscha, S. K. (2013). The relationship between PTSD and chronic pain: mediating role of coping strategies and depression. *Pain, 154*(4), 609–616.

Morath, E., & Guilford, G. (2020). Unemployment claims data point to record wave of job loss. *The Wall Street Journal.*

Nicola, M., Alsafi, Z., Sohrabi, C., Kerwan, A., Al-Jabir, A., Iosifidis, C., ... & Agha, R. (2020). The socio-economic implications of the coronavirus and COVID-19 pandemic: a review. *International journal of surgery, 78,* 185–193.

Niehoff, B. P., & Moorman, R. (1993). Treating employees fairly and organizational citizenship behavior: Sorting the effects of job satisfaction, organizational commitment, and procedural justice. *Employee Responsibilities and Rights Journal,* 209–225.

Parent-Lamarche, A., Marchand, A., & Saade, S. (2020). Does Depression Mediate the Effect of Work Organization Conditions on Job Performance? *Journal of occupational and environmental medicine, 62*(4), 296–302.

PDM Task Force. (2006). *Psychodynamic Diagnostic Manual (PDM).* Silver Spring: Alliance of Psychoanalytic Organizations.

Piccoli, B., Reisel, W. D., & De Witte, H. (2019). Understanding the relationship between job insecurity and performance: hindrance or challenge effect? *Journal of Career Development, XX*(X)1–16.

Plutchik, R. (1980). Measurement implications of a psychoevolutionary theory of emotions. *Assessment and modification of emotional behavior, 6,* 47–69.

Prasetya, A., & Kato, M. (2011). The Effect of Financial and Non-Financial Compensation to the Employee Performance. *The 2nd International Research Symposium in Service Management, 1.*

Preacher, K. J., & Hayes, A. F. (2008). Asymptotic and resampling strategies for assessing and comparing indirect effects in multiple mediator models. *Behavior research methods, 40*(3), 879–891.

Rasool, S. F., Koser, M., & Yan, Z. (2016). Two folded layers of organizational justice. *International Journal of Research, 3*(14), 368–381.

Rubel, M. R. B., Rimi, N. N., Yusliza, M. Y., & Kee, D. M. H. (2018). High commitment human resource management practices and employee service behaviour: Trust in management as mediator. *IIMB Management Review, 30*(4), 316–329.

Sandoiu, A. (2020, April 20). *COVID-19: How long is this likely to last?* Retrieved from Medical News Today: https://www.medicalnewstoday.com/articles/covid-19-how-long-is-this-likely-to-last.

Schreurs, B. H., Hetty van Emmerik, I. J., Guenter, H., & Germeys, F. (2012). A weekly diary study on the buffering role of social support in the relationship between job insecurity and employee performance. *Human Resource Management, 51*(2), 259–279.

Sekaran, U., & Bougie, R. (2016). *Research methods for business: A skill building approach.* John Wiley & Sons.

Shin, Y., & Hur, W. M. (2020). Supervisor incivility and employee job performance: the mediating roles of job insecurity and amotivation. *The Journal of psychology, 154*(1), 38–59.

Shoss, M. K. (2017). Job Insecurity: An Integrative Review and Agenda for Future Research. *Journal of Management, 43*(6), 1911–1939.

Sobieralski, J. B. (2020). COVID-19 and airline employment: Insights from historical uncertainty shocks to the industry. *Transportation Research Interdisciplinary Perspectives, 5*, 100123.

Talebzadeh, N., & Karatepe, O. M. (2020). Work social support, work engagement and their impacts on multiple performance outcomes. *International Journal of Productivity and Performance Management, 69*(6), 1227–1245.

UN News. (2020). *Looking back at 2020, In Case You Missed It.* Retrieved from UN News: https://news.un.org/en/story/2020/12/1081092

Williams, L. J., & Anderson, S. E. (1991). Job Satisfaction and Organizational Commitment as Predictors of Organizational Citizenship and In-Role Behaviors. *Journal of Management, 17*(3), 601–17.

Zhu, N., Zhang, D., Wang, W., Li, X., Yang, B., Song, J., China Novel Coronavirus Investigating and Research. (2019). A Novel Coronavirus from Patients with Pneumonia in China. *The New England Journal of Medicine, 382*(8), 727–733.

# CHAPTER THREE

# Covid 19 And Corporate Governance (India): Practical Issues, Implications and New Relief Measures

**CS Divyesh Patel**
*PhD Scholar at Dharmsinh Desai University, Nadiad, Gujarat*

**Prof. (Dr.) Naresh K. Patel**
*Professor & Dean*
*Faculty of Management and Information Sciences*
*Dharmsinh Desai University, Nadiad*

## Abstract

**Purpose/Objective:** *This research aims to study number of practical issues and risk faced by corporates and its implications and new relief measures introduced in relation to Corporate Governance (India) during COVID-19 outbreak. However, their extent and impact will naturally vary with the nature and size of a business.*

**Design/Methodology/Approach:** *Exploratory research is used to study and investigate practical issues and implications faced by Corporates regarding Corporate Governance practices in India during COVID19 outbreak.*

**Findings:** *COVID-19 Pandemic has impacted not only human but significant commercial impact being felt globally. It has come with inherent commercial risks impacting on business operations due to disruptions to Meetings, Dividend, Liquidity, Disclosure, Capital Allocation, Risk Management and Internal Control. Regulators should allow companies to conduct a hybrid AGM. It has compelled Companies to step up on building their technology infrastructure. Management should review of their share buyback programmes during such financial crisis. Remuneration committee should emphasize on Executive Pay matters. Government has initiated relief measures under Companies Act, 2013 and LLP Act, 2008 and relaxations from compliance with provisions of the SEBI (LODR) Regulations, 2015 due. Major initiative is contribution for COVID-19 is eligible CSR activity and introduction of schemes of Companies Fresh Start and revised the LLP Settlement to provide a opportunity to make good any filing related defaults and make a fresh start on clean slate.*

**Originality/value:** *Drawing on such analytical framework, this research provides further directions to amend and inculcate various corporate Governance practices for Government, Regulators, Companies and other stakeholders during such crisis. It also addresses the current policy issues that may have a significant effect on Corporates strategies.*

**Keywords**—Corporate Governance (CG), Virtual /Hybrid Meetings, COVID19

# 1. INTRODUCTION

World's economy is a corona patient. Corona virus disease (COVID-19) epidemic has affected many countries and the World Health Organization (WHO) has declared it 'Pandemic'. The WHO more specifically defines a pandemic as "a worldwide spread of a new disease." On March 11, 2020, the WHO officially declared the COVID-19 outbreak a pandemic due to the global spread and severity of the disease. It's possible that the corona virus threat will eventually fade, as the Ebola, Zika, and Severe Acute Respiratory Syndrome (SARS) viruses have in recent years. But even if it does, the next devastating, yet-unnamed outbreak is not so much a matter of "if" but "when." The profound impact of the measures being taken across the globe to contain the spread of the Coronavirus COVID-19 is creating a number of issues for companies. The Indian Government declared lockdown for a period of 21 days with effect from 25.03.2020 in compliance of Order of The National Disaster Management Authority (NDMA) chaired by Hon'ble Prime Minister Shri Narendra Modi, Ministry of Home Affairs (MHA) has issued an Order dated 24.03.2020 under Section 10(2)(l) of the Disaster Management Act, directing the Ministries/Departments of Government of India, State/Union Territory Governments and State/ Union Territory Authorities to take effective measures for ensuring social distancing so as to prevent the spread of COVID-19 in the country. While we are now focusing in India on securing the population from health hazards and on providing relief, especially to the poor, we also need to think long-term - to secure the health of the economy, the viability of businesses, and the livelihoods of people. The Indian Governments and Regulators have passed legislation introducing a series of measures including those relevant to maintaining the good corporate governance of companies. These measures have applied with immediate effect. Corporate governance involves a set of relationships between a company's management, its board, its shareholders and other stakeholders. Corporate governance also provides the structure through which the objectives of the company are set, and the means of attaining those objectives and monitoring performance are determined[1]. In his pioneering research, **Gottfried and Donahue (2020)** stated that as the global COVID-19 health emergency continues, the economic fallout is escalating as well and it would lead to logistical impediments and shifts in timing and strategy but, importantly, also creates opportunities for savvy investors. Global economic growth has gone into reverse, businesses have started cancelling service to customers, and millions of workers are technically unemployed or fired. It raises the question: what happened to "stakeholder capitalism", the enlightened

---

[1] Defined as per G20/OECD Principles of Corporate Governance.

economic model many companies embraced just months ago? How can it be squared with what we're seeing today? Corporate governance also comprises risk management; therefore, a key professional mandate of management is to ensure that risk is not diversified or spread to the detriment of the institution. Boards of directors are responsible for the governance of their establishments. The governing board is to ensure that management renders services that are appreciable to the stakeholders. **Jensen, M.C. (2001)** proposed that there should be a system of executing services that strengthen the connection between institutions and their stakeholders through effective communication. It is supported by **Davies, M. A. (2012)** in his research where he stated that it is the duty of the board to ensure a higher standard of performance and accountability by engaging in practices that foster good governance. Therefore, political and administrative reforms in many countries could directly shape what is to be referred to as good governance, especially in developing countries. Adherence to governance standards brings simplicity and reduction of risk in such institutions through the support of standard protocols, stakeholders, and government. Corporate governance is the system by which organizations are bound for and controlled. It is a configuration of checks and balances (both internal and external to organizations), to make sure that they discharge their duties well and accountable to all stakeholders **(Dignam, A. and Galanis, M., 2016)**. They are also to ensure that establishments deliver their duties in a socially responsible way, in all areas of their business activity **(Grayson, D. and Hodges, A., 2017)**. As we know that the heart of corporate governance is transparency, disclosure, accountability and integrity. Good corporate governance practice is an important element in attracting investors, and investors are willing to pay a premium of up to 25% for a well governed firm **(Barton, D. and Wong, S.C., 2004)**. **Todorovic (2013)** has inferred that implementation of CG practices such as disclosure, protection of shareholders rights and equal treatment of shareholders can ensure safeguard investments. **Drobetz, W. (2004)** researched that Good CG led to increase valuation, increase higher profit, higher sales growth and reduce capital expenditure.

The remainder of the paper is organized as follows. The next section reviews extant of the Research Methodology and the Course of the Research Process. Section three presents Practical Issues and Implications with reference to Corporate Governance (India). In Section four, New relief measures and Initiatives during COVID-19 relating to Corporate Governance have been discussed including Spending of CSR funds for COVID 2019. Summary and major conclusions are in section five.

## 2. THE RESEARCH METHODOLOGY AND THE COURSE OF THE RESEARCH PROCESS

The study is purely based on exploratory research or grounded theory approach aims to study number of practical issues and risk faced by corporate and its implications and new relief measures in relation to Corporate Governance during COVID-19 outbreak. This study used Secondary research methods namely Online research, Literature research and Case study research are carried out during stages of research process to narrow the scope of research objectives and to transform ambiguous problems into well-defined one. Running business in the midst of a pandemic is an unprecedented challenge for business leaders worldwide. The restrictions imposed by many governments all over the  world in handling the COVID-19 outbreak raise significant challenges as regards corporate governance. However, their extent and impact will naturally vary with the nature and size of a business, but the approach taken in respect of these issues could be crucial for the particular business to thrive or at least survive this new reality.

## 3.  COVID-19 AND CORPORATE GOVERNANCE (INDIA)

### 3.1  Practical Issues and Implications

The rapid outbreak of the corona virus presents an alarming health crisis that the world is grappling with. In addition to the human impact, there is also a significant commercial impact being felt globally. As viruses know no borders, the impacts will continue to spread. In fact, 94 percent of the Fortune 1000 is already seeing COVID-19 disruptions. With the rapidly-developing situation; we are still in the premature stages of understanding the impact that COVID-19 will have. However, some important issues and implications regarding corporate governance practices and standards has been depicted in Figure-1.

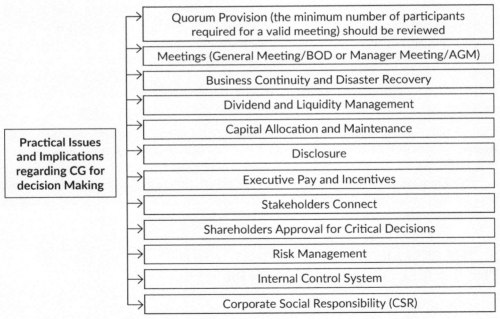

**Figure-1.**  Practical Issues and Implications regarding Corporate Governance for decision Making

*Source:* Compiled by Researcher

## 3.2 Meetings

Indian Government's directives of a 21-day lockdown and social distancing to avoid mass gatherings are likely to have an impact on Quorum Provision referred under section 103 of Companies Act, 2013 (i.e. the minimum number of participants required for a valid meeting). And in turn it would impact on format of Meetings namely General Meeting, B.O.D or Manager Meetings, AGM and NCLT Convened meetings. As in-person company meetings will largely no longer be possible. Hence, Small and Retail shareholders are likely to be the most exaggerated as compared to Institutional investors as they have several platforms to engage with company managements. The failure of not holding shareholder meetings will likely lead to a delay in urgent business transactions and to the adjournment or postponing of AGMs. That means it would lead to material impact on business. Although the board of directors can take all the crucial decisions relating to the working of a company, a set of critical decisions require shareholders' approval including appointment/re-appointment of directors, undertaking related party and inter-corporate transactions exceeding regulatory thresholds, issue of securities, schemes of arrangement, etc. Not obtaining shareholder approval in time might lead to non-compliance with the provisions of law or possibly even failed transactions. The only option for shareholder approval is via the postal ballot (i.e. Voting by post or through any Electronic mode) but subject to certain items of business under section 110 of Companies Act, 2013 read with Rule 22 of Companies (Management and Administration) Rules. 2014.

The major issue related to Closing of Financial Year. The statue state that AGMs are required to be held within six months of the close of the financial year subject to time between two consecutive AGMs cannot exceed 15 months. Financial year for most companies in India closes on March 31, unless the companies have got a separate relaxation of the rules from the Ministry of Corporate Affairs to have another year end keeping in the mind that MNCs typically close their financial year on December 31 to align with global practices. As many of companies have already sent out notices for shareholder meetings where the meetings were earlier scheduled to be held during the lockdown phase, are being postponed. Although most Indian companies do not include such a provision in their Articles of Association (AoA), during such unforeseen times, it is generally possible for a board to decide to postpone a meeting. If postponement is not possible, a company's AOA will likely allow adjournment of a meeting, which will have the same practical effect. The AOAs usually allow meetings to be adjourned either by the chairperson with the consent of a quorate meeting or by the chairperson unilaterally if no quorum is present. Companies can also go with delaying in holding their AGMs. The COVID-19 pandemic may significantly reduce accessibility, communication and physical meetings to conduct statutory audits. It may cause delays to audit-related activities, including the impossibility to conduct on-site audits and inspections, and exercising the relevant access rights.

## Virtual or hybrid AGMs

Among the measures introduced by the Government, certain rules introduce the possibility for the meetings of companies to be held exclusively in digital form without requiring the physical presence of their members[8] and will therefore be able to conduct such meetings in a manner that protects the health and safety of their shareholders and board members. It is advocated that companies must allow shareholders to participate via a two-way teleconferencing or WebEx. Currently, the top 100 companies by market capitalization are required to have a webcast of their AGMs, but this is a one-way transmission. Although the Ministry of Corporate Affairs has allowed board meetings and board committee meetings to be held via video conferencing, it has not extended this to shareholder meetings. The Companies Act, 2013, requires physical quorum to constitute a valid meeting. UK-incorporated listed companies are permitted to hold hybrid (a combination of physical and electronic) or virtual AGMs. The US Securities and Exchange Commission (SEC) has also released a guidance, which permits US-based companies to opt for virtual or hybrid meetings. Allowing companies to hold a virtual meeting, especially for listed companies where the shareholder base is large, is now a necessary requirement for social distancing. The regulators (Mainly SEBI and Ministry of Corporate Affairs (MCA) need to allow companies to do so. The other option would be for companies to conduct a hybrid AGM. A Hybrid meeting allows the attendees to decide whether they'd prefer to attend the meeting in person or online, this could be from the comfort of their home, office or mobile device. Alternative options would be **"Postponement of AGM", "Call and adjourn AGM" and "Delay of AGM"** if your Articles of Association (AOA) do not permit a hybrid or virtual meeting.

## 3.3 Business Continuity and Recovery

During the COVID19 outbreak, most of companies are facing difficulties to maintain business continuity. Most of companies would be facing difficulties from suppliers' end. It means suppliers are incapable to supply components which are crucial to the company's manufacturing or provision of services. In turn it would lead to Business Distress/Financial Distress of Companies. **Mehran, H., Morrison, A.D. and Shapiro, J.D., (2011)** concluded that If a corporate fail, the fallout can be restricted to the stakeholders. If a bank fails, the impact can spread rapidly through to other banks with potentially serious consequences for the entire financial system and the macroeconomic. Moreover, in case a bank crashes then it does not crash alone, it also takes away the lifelong investment and savings of its entire account holders too. The failure of banks can create huge consequences to financial system of the country concerned as a whole. So, Business continuity is a biggest issue that corporate is facing. Hence corporates should be proactively addressed, especially in light of the duty that directors have to exercise reasonable care, diligence and skill, and this involves assessing and minimizing the risks in similar extreme situations. It will be important for boards to attack this problem by anticipating how the spread of the coronavirus will affect its stakeholders and then communicate how the company plans to deal with those issues (**Scott, M., 2020**).

## 3.4 Dividend and Liquidity Management

Now, another issue surfacing would be regarding dividend, liquidity and working capital requirements during COVID19 outbreaks and lockdown. There are few issues like company recently declared dividends which have still not been distributed or Corporates are currently deciding about dividend distributions. Directors need to consider not only the position of the company when a dividend is proposed but also when it is made. Where the company is no longer competent to pay a dividend, it is advocated that directors should halt any dividend and communicate as appropriate to the market. The assessment of whether a dividend is appropriate should include consideration of current and likely operational and capital needs, contingency planning and the directors' legal duties, both in statute and common law. Bearing the current uncertainty and adverse market conditions in mind, it might be prudent to take a step back and gauge market, public and stakeholder reaction. In this sense it is also important to act in a manner which is in sync with both internal (management, employees etc.) and external sentiment. Liquidity and working capital requirements may naturally come under strain at such time and consideration will need to be given to cash flow management, banking arrangements and refinancing as well as available assistance/ incentives including moratoria.

## 3.5 Capital Allocation and Maintenance

One of the central pillars of corporate governance is capital allocation, and where companies decide to focus their funding. Over recent years we have seen companies using increasing amounts of cash to re-purchase stock rather than investing in their businesses or bolstering up their balance sheets. In the S&P 500, 50% of all free cash flow is now used to re-purchase stock.

At a time when balance sheets are under immense pressure and companies face significant unexpected costs, including how they dedicate resources to ensuring the welfare of their staff, management should review the appropriateness of their share buyback programmes both at this time and in the longer term. Although there is an expectation that certain sectors will receive government assistance, the most likely outcome for distressed companies will be the use of emergency capital raising through deeply discounted rights issues or placing. In these circumstances, we would like companies to minimize the dilution of existing shareholders by honoring their pre-emptive rights and giving them the right to purchase further shares before others in the market. India has witnessed that few corporates are exploring share repurchase. Fairfax backed Quess Corp is exploring share buyback on 25th March, 2020. Delta Corp to consider share repurchase on 28th March, 2020. Sterlite Technologies approves buyback of shares up to Rs145 crores on dated 24th March, 2020. Motilal Oswal Financial Services okaus Rs150 crore share buyback plan dated 21st March, 2020. Sun pharma has announced Rs1700 crore buyback on 17th March, 2020. These are buybacks that may give solid assured returns during COVID 19 outbreaks and lock down. It can be seen that all the buyback decisions were announced during the lockdown period and proved that positive reduction in equity would lead to increase in shareholders return.

## 3.6  Disclosure

Disclosure which is an essential ingredient of CG is the foundation of any structure of CG **Bhasin, M. (2012)**. With respect to regulated entities and companies listed on a regulated market which are subject to various laws and regulations aimed at securing investor protection, adequate disclosure without delay of information which should be made known to the public should remain a top priority. Proactive boards of such companies should thus continue assessing the situation, communicating with regulators and providing public disclosure where it is needed or warranted as new information constantly emerges. Cautious assessments should be made to analyze the extent of the negative impact of COVID-19 related developments and to determine any corrective action that might be needed to mitigate such impact as far as possible, with constant disclosure of significant developments to the general public. In fact, Ministry of Corporate Affairs (MCA) deployed a new simple web-based form w.e.f. 23rd March; 2020 focusing a purely confidence disclosure and building measure to assess the readiness of the companies to deal with COVID-19 threat in India.

## 3.7  Executive Pay and Incentives

It is advocated that Companies need to consider as consequence of the COVID 19 outbreaks
*   Shareholders will not generally look favorably on executives receiving pays and incentives following a year where shareholders have lost out, even though the impacts of the virus are non-controllable from Corporate ends.
*   Remuneration committees (An essential practice of CG) may make adjustments to schemes to permit rewards to executives who exhibit outstanding skill in navigating their company through the hard period ahead.
*   Close attention should be on individual company circumstances, including whether companies are consistent in their treatment of staff and executives (like self-quarantine).
*   For companies seeing an exceptional increase in demand for their services like Pharma, as a consequence of the virus and of related government measures, Remuneration committees should treat this as a windfall effect and be prepared to adjust pay downwards if appropriate.

## 3.8  Risk Management and Internal Control

Corporate governance also comprises risk management; therefore, a key professional mandate of management is to ensure that risk is not diversified or spread to the detriment of the institution. Relocation of staff and the inaccessibility of some business locations may lead to risk management processes and internal controls becoming impracticable or otherwise relaxed. Boards should monitor such changes carefully, introducing alternative mitigating controls where necessary and practicable to support the operation of an effective control environment.

## 4. NEW RELIEF MEASURES AND INITIATIVES DURING COVID-19 RELATING TO CORPORATE GOVERNANCE

### 4.1 Special Measures under Companies Act, 2013 and Limited Liability Partnership Act, 2008 in view of COVID-19 outbreak, dated 24th March, 2020

- No additional fees shall be charged for late filing during a moratorium period.
- BOD meetings stand extended by a period of 60 days till next two quarters i.e. till 30th September as per section 173 of Companies Act, 2013
- The Companies (Auditor's Report) Order, 2020 shall be made applicable from financial year 2020-21, instead of being applicable from the financial year 2019-20
- An additional period of 180 more days is allowed to file declaration for Commencement of Business for newly incorporate companies.

### 4.2 Spending of CSR funds for COVID-19

It is clarified by the Ministry of Corporate Affairs (MCA) in general circular No. 10/2020 dated 23.3.2020, that spending of CSR funds for COVID-19 is eligible CSR activity. Funds may be spent for various activities related to COVID-19 under item nos. (i) and (xii) of Schedule VII relating to promotion of health care, including preventive health care and sanitation, and, disaster management. Further, as per General Circular No. 21/2014 dated 18th June, 2014, items in Schedule VII are broad based and may be interpreted liberally for this purpose. It is further clarified that any contribution made to the PM CARES Fund shall qualify as CSR expenditure under the Companies Act, 2013. However, in continuation of above circular, it further supplemented that spending of CSR funds for "Setting up makeshifts hospitals and temporary COVID Care facilities would also come under the purview of eligible CSR activities as per Schedule VII of Companies Act, 2013 under item (i) and (xii) relating to heath care, including preventive health care, and disaster management respectively (**MCA, 2021**).

### 4.3 Relaxations from compliance with certain provisions of the SEBI (Listing Obligations and Disclosure Requirements) Regulations, 2015 (LODR) due to the COVID-19 virus pandemic

- Compliance Certificate under Reg. 40(9) from Practicing Company Secretary on timely issue of share certificates gets extended till may 31st, 2020 (period of relaxation – 1 month).
- Relaxation of holding AGM and meeting of Board/Committee(s) as earlier discussed.
- Extension of timeline for filings under Regulation 7(3) with 1 month, Regulation 13(3) relating to Statement of Investors Complaint for 3 weeks, Regulation 24A relating to Secretarial Compliance report for 1 month, Regulation 27(2) relating to Corporate Governance report for 1 month, Regulation 31 relating to Shareholding Pattern for 3 weeks, Regulation 33 relating to Annual Financial Results for 1 month.

- Relaxation of publication of advertisements in the newspapers under Regulation 47 gets exempted till 15th May, 2020.

## 4.4 "Companies Fresh Start Scheme, 2020" and "revised LLP Settlement Scheme, 2020"

In pursuance of the Government of India's efforts to provide relief to law abiding companies and Limited Liability Partnerships (LLPs) in the wake of COVID 19, the Ministry of Corporate Affairs, has introduced the "Companies Fresh Start Scheme, 2020" and revised the "LLP Settlement Scheme, 2020" which is already in vogue to provide a first of its kind opportunity to both companies and LLPs to make good any filing related defaults, irrespective of duration of default, and make a fresh start as a fully compliant entity. It's a one-time waiver of additional filing fees for delayed filings by the companies or LLPs with the Registrar of Companies during the currency of the Schemes, i.e. during the period starting from 1st April, 2020 and ending on 30th September, 2020.

## 5. CONCLUSIONS

This research reveals that rapid outbreak of the corona virus first and foremost a human tragedy. It has impacted not only human, there is also a significant commercial impact being felt globally. As viruses know no borders, the impacts will continue to spread. In fact, 94 percent of the Fortune 1000 is already seeing COVID-19 disruptions. COVID-19 pandemic come with inherent commercial risks impacting on business operations due to disruptions to Meetings (AGM,EGM, BOD Meeting and NCLT convened meetings), Administration, Business Continuity , Dividend and Liquidity management, Disclosure, Capital Allocation and Maintenance and lastly Risk Management and Internal Control. Among the measures introduced by the Government, certain rules introduce the possibility for the meetings of companies to be held exclusively in digital form without requiring the physical presence of their members and will therefore be able to conduct such meetings in a manner that protects the health and safety of their shareholders and board members. Regulators should allow companies to conduct a hybrid AGM (i.e. Virtual Meeting). COVID-19 has compelled Companies to step up on building their technology infrastructure. It is imperative that directors and managers are proactive in ensuring the appropriate strategies are put in place to anticipate and to mitigate the potential commercial impacts of a pandemic, and to ensure compliance with their duties and legal obligation. Its duty of Board to make sure that Corporate Governance should not be simply sets of rules or "Check the box" framework. Management should review the appropriateness of their share buyback programmes and proved that positive reduction in equity (i.e. Free cash flow) would lead to increase in shareholders return. Company and its remuneration committee should emphasize on Executive Pay matters as it is very sensitive during COVID 19 outbreak which is stipulated in the introduction of this article. Corporate honchos are worried about well-being of their employees and business. Indian Government has initiated various relief measures under Companies Act, 2013 and Limited Liability Partnership Act, 2008 and announced relaxations from compliance with certain provisions of the SEBI (Listing Obligations and Disclosure Requirements) Regulations, 2015 (LODR) due to the COVID-19 virus pandemic towards Corporate Governance which has discussed earlier of this article.

Major two important announcement first spending of CSR funds for COVID-19 is eligible CSR activity covered under Schedule-VII of Companies Act, 2013 and Secondly introduced the "Companies Fresh Start Scheme, 2020" and revised the "LLP Settlement Scheme, 2020" to provide a first of its kind opportunity to both companies and LLPs to make good any filing related defaults, irrespective of duration of default, and make a fresh start on clean slate as a fully compliant entity. That added feather towards Ease of doing Business in India. **Hirt, M., Smit, S., Bradley, C., Uhlaner, R., Mysore, M., Atsmon, Y., & Northcot, N. (2020)** advocated that Corporate need to think and act across five horizons namely "Resolve, Resilience, Return, Reimagination and Reform" to battle against COVID-19. COVID pandemic is considered as a systemic risk which is not controllable from risk point of view. Given these ongoing uncertainties, a recent McKinsey briefing note frames this as a situation calling for a scenario planning approach, and suggests three fundamental planning scenarios, labelled as: "quick recovery", "global slowdown" and "global pandemic and recession". Scenario planning is important for both governments and companies, but it remains far from clear which of these scenarios, if any, will prevail. In nut shell, Investors, companies and other stakeholders will need to work together in a constructive way in order to navigate through the current crisis of COVID19. Drawing on such analytical framework, this research provides further directions to amend and inculcate various corporate Governance practices for Government, Regulators, Companies and other stakeholders during such crisis. It also addresses the current policy issues that may have a significant effect on Corporate's strategies.

# 6. REFERENCES

## 6.1 Journals

Barton, D. and Wong, S.C., 2004. Asia's governance challenge.

Bhasin, M., 2012. 'Voluntary 'Corporate Governance Disclosures Made in the Annual Reports: An Empirical Study. *International Journal of Management & Innovation, 4*(1).

Davies, M. A. (2012). *Best practice in corporate governance: Building reputation and sustainable success*. Gower Publishing, Ltd.

Dignam, A. and Galanis, M., 2016. *The globalization of corporate governance*. Routledge.

Drobetz, W., 2004. The impact of corporate governance on firm performance. *Department of Corporate Finance. University of Basel.*

Fortune (2020). https://fortune.com/2020/02/21/fortune-1000-coronavirus-china-supply-chain-impact/, accessed on March 10, 2020

Gottfried, K., and S. Donahue. 2020. The impact of COVID19 on shareholder activism.

Harvard Law School Forum on Corporate Governance. Accessed from https://corpgov.law.harvard. edu/2020/04/12/theimpact-of-covid19-on-shareholder-activism/

Grayson, D. and Hodges, A., 2017. *Corporate social opportunity! Seven steps to make corporate social responsibility work for your business*. Routledge.

Hirt, M., Smit, S., Bradley, C., Uhlaner, R., Mysore, M., Atsmon, Y., & Northcot, N. (2020). Getting ahead of the next stage of the coronavirus crisis. *McKinsey & Company, 4.*

Jensen, M.C., 2001. Value maximization, stakeholder theory, and the corporate objective function. *Journal of applied corporate finance, 14*(3), pp. 8–21.

MCA. (2021, April 22). Retrieved from http://www.mca.gov.in/Ministry/pdf/GeneralCircularNo5_ 22042021.pdf

Mehran, H., Morrison, A.D. and Shapiro, J.D., 2011. Corporate governance and banks: What have we learned from the financial crisis? *FRB of New York Staff Report*, (502).

Scott, M., 2020. *Corporate Board Member*. [Online] Available at: https://boardmember.com/has-your-board-assessed-the-impact-of-the-coronavirus-outbreak/

Todorovic, I., 2013. Impact of corporate governance on performance of companies. *Montenegrin Journal of Economics, 9*(2), p. 47.

## 6.2  Online Documents

Affairs, M. o. C., 2020. *www.mca.gov.in*. [Online] Available at: http://www.mca.gov.in/Ministry/pdf/ Circular12_30032020.pdf

Affairs, M. o. C., 2020. *www.mca.gov.in*. [Online] Available at: https://www.mca.gov.in/Ministry/pdf/ Circular13_30032020.pdf

Africa, F. A. S., 2020. *Franchise Association South Africa*. [Online] Available at: https://www.fasa.co.za/ coronavirus-implications-for-business-corporate-governance/

Directors, I. o., 2020. *Institute of Directors*. [Online] Available at: https://www.iod.com/news/ news/articles/The-corporate-governance-of-coronavirus—what-boards-should-consider [Accessed 20 3 2020].

Governance, H. L. S. F. o. C., 2020. *Harvard Law School Forum on Corporate Governance*. [Online] Available at: https://corpgov.law.harvard.edu/2020/03/14/the-impact-of-coronavirus-fears-on-annual-shareholder-meetings/ [Accessed 14 3 2020].

India, I. o. C. S. o., 2020. *www.icsi.edu.in*. [Online] Available at: https://www.icsi.edu/media/ webmodules/REGULATORY%20UPDATE%20MARCH.pdf

# CHAPTER FOUR

# Determinants of Occupational Stress in Information Systems Professionals Post COVID-19: A Factor analysis approach

**B. Prathyusha**
*Assistant Professor in Management Science*
*Department of Humanities and Sciences*
*VNR Vignana Jyothi Institute of Engineering & Technology, Hyderabad, Telangana, India*

**Ch. S. Durga Prasad**
*Director, Vignana Jyothi Institute of Management, Hyderabad, Telangana, India*

**Corresponding author: B. Prathyusha**
*prathyusha_b@vnrvjiet.in*

---

**Abstract**—*The life of every individual has changed overnight with the arrival of COVID-19. The various surveys conducted at State and National Level stated that COVID-19 is not only disrupting organisations and institutions but also disrupting the work and personal lives of the employees. The invisible enemy made everyone alter the mode of communication with one another and made them to get engaged with different methodologies which lead to a new normal have caused occupational stress among employees. Occupational Stress is taking a toll on the mental, physical and emotional health and productivity of employees. The current study was planned to examine the various occupational stressors and to identify those stressors that influence Information Systems Professionals working in Hyderabad city. The primary data was collected using Occupational Stress Index (OSI) by stratified random sampling method from 1064 information systems professionals belonging to the Large, Medium, Small, and Start-up IT companies in Hyderabad. The factor analysis affirmed a twelve-factor model of occupational stressors in the Information Systems Professionals which confirms that the instrument used for the current research for assessing occupational stress has the high insightful/analytical capacity/ability for identifying areas requiring key concentration in the IT sector.*

**Keywords**—Occupational Stress, COVID-19, Information Systems Professionals, Factor Analysis, Hyderabad, Categories of IT Companies

# INTRODUCTION

The majority of employees knew what they were expected to do while working from office/ workplace/factory suddenly didn't have clarity on how to quantify the productivity while working from home. They started introspecting about the contribution and value that they are creating/should create in new normal post-pandemic has added stress to their daily lives. Information Systems professionals are experiencing high levels of stress as many of them have lost their jobs or are working for reduced hours. Occupational stress is identified a serious medical problem, which has serious emotional, physical and psychological implications on employees wellbeing. Pre COVID-19 around 80% of working professionals in India have complained that they are experiencing stress, anxiety and depression and this percentage have increased to around 90% during and post COVID-19 as employees were unprepared for the pandemic, job separation, salary reductions, working from home etc., Irrespective of age, gender, income, experience and designation every information system professional is experiencing stress due to above stated factors. While some level of stress is acceptable but high/chronic stress has become a common ailment that leads to issues such as anxiety, depression, high blood pressure, blurred vision, insomnia, skin rashes, migraines, and heart problems start affecting employee productivity and wellbeing. Combating the stress appears to be a key focal point for individuals and organizations.

Automation of business processes using artificial intelligence, IoT (Internet of things), surge in IT (Information Technology) and its applications and growing demand for high quality digitised services and products  (P.S. Manjula, 2015) has created an unprecedented demand for Information Systems Professionals around the world as well as in Hyderabad. The Information Technology (IT) Sector is the fastest growing sector in Telangana. Telangana IT/ ITES exports reached to Rs. 1,28,807 crores in 2019-20 when compared to Rs. 1,09,219 crores from the previous year 2018-19 at the rate of 17.93% against 8.09% all India. The sector provided direct employment to 5,82,126 professionals in 2019-20 in comparison to 5,43,033 professionals in 2018-19, there is an increase of 7.2% against the national growth rate of 4.93%. The growth story is phenomenal in the last quarter of FY 2019-20 (Jayesh Ranjan, 2020). According to the white paper prepared by Hyderabad Software Enterprises Association (HYSEA), CBRE, KPMG and Telangana Government and released by Minister for IT and Industries, Telangana expects a growth of 10% for the FY 2021 in IT sector in Telangana. But this is subjected to second and third wave of COVID-19. The recent survey conducted by HYSEA stated that 38% of the IT companies which took part in the survey believe that their revenues will be negative or remain flat. The report also stated that the number of layoffs were less during and post COVID-19 and the Telangana State Government has set-up a "Layoff Redressal Committee" and gave counseling several professionals and organisations during COVID-19 times.

## LITERATURE REVIEW

(Devi. T, 2011) examined the impact of high levels of stress on organisational level outcomes, its impact on behavior, mind, body and emotions and recommended the coping strategies to be implemented at organisational level among 200 Information Technology professionals belonging to technical and middle level of management from six IT companies. The major stressors identified were organisational changes, fear of job loss, emphasis on competition, lack of employee control, increasing technology, Workload, organization culture and push of multi-tasking. The stress coping strategies suggested were like finding triggers and stressors, stress management programs supportive organizational culture, physical activities, life style modification programs, proper job design, stress counseling and to participate in spiritual programs.

(Rani, 2013) identified that relationship with peers and superiors, working hours, programmes related to women development and role ambiguity were the factors that contribute to occupational stress among women IT professionals. Adoption of more stress coping strategies by the individuals and organisations was given as a suggestion.

(B. Prathyusha C. M., 2014) studied about the health problems faced by the software professionals which was carried among 90 software professionals in Hyderabad city. The study revealed that prolonged working hours and sitting; and the continuous viewing of the computer screens/monitors are crucial factors affecting the health of the software professionals. The study also mentioned the practices followed by the professionals to cope up with the occupational stress and health problems.

(B. Prathyusha C. M., 2014) identified the coping strategies used by the software professionals to handle stress and investigated gender wise differences with regard to coping strategies by software professionals. The data was collected using a structured questionnaire from 100 software professionals belonging to different IT companies in Hyderabad and the sampling technique adopted was convenience sampling. The results showed that diet, sleeping for long hours, exercise, yoga, art of living, and mediation are some of the popular stress coping strategies adopted by the software professionals.

(Misra, 2015) studied about the different predictors of stress and stressful work conditions among 50 software employees of age between 30-40 years working in 4Soft, Oracle, Satyam and Accenture in Hyderabad during the last five years. The results were that the employees who worked in these companies from past five to eight years experienced stress due work pressure and working hours and have high levels of dissatisfaction.

(B. Prathyusha C. M., 2015) conducted a survey using PLSS (Professional Life Stress Score) developed by David Fontana to assess the professional life stress among 150 software professionals belonging to different IT companies in Hyderabad. The data was collected by using convenience sampling method. The results showed that there the software professionals were experiencing moderate to high level of Professional Life Stress.

(B. Prathyusha C. M., 2016) measured occupational stress using Occupational Stress Index (OSI) given by Srivastava A. K. and Singh A. P. among 500 IT Professionals working in different IT companies in Hyderabad. The data collected was analysed using descriptive statistics and the results proved that the IT Professionals were experiencing high levels of stress.

(K.D.V. Prasad, 2016) conducted study to identify the factors causing occupational stress and its effect on job performance among 90 women and 110 men on the causes of occupational stress and its effect on performance at the workplace of IT companies. NASSCOM listed companies and the employees working more than 12 hours and were only considered for the study. The results indicated that women were experiencing high levels of stress when compared to men, the factors causing stress among them were same and were suffering from severe back and neck pain due to long sitting hours.

(Vimala Thomas, 2019) conducted a cross sectional study on occupational stress among Information Technology professionals working in Hyderabad. The study revealed that around 46%, 33%, and 21% of the professionals are experiencing low, moderate and high stress levels.

There were very fewer studies and it is also noticed that no holistic and exclusive study was conducted to determine factors affecting occupational stress among IS professionals in Hyderabad pre or post COVID-19. It involves a special mention that the studies conducted by the researchers prior to this study have done survey mostly in National Association of Software and Service Companies (NASSCOM) listed top five companies or in Indian based IT companies but not delved into and across the categories (Large, Medium, small and Start-ups) of IT companies. Hence, the present research is a pioneer study that endeavored to bridge this research gap.

## OBJECTIVES

1.  To examine or evaluate the various occupational stressors and to identify those stressors that are effecting the Information Systems Professionals post COVID-19.

## RESEARCH METHODOLOGY

### Sources of Data

Structured questionnaire was used to collect primary data from Information Systems Professionals in Hyderabad. The researcher adopted a standardized questionnaire of Occupational Stress Index (OSI) developed by Professors S.K. Srivastava and A.P. Singh (Srivastava A.K., 1984) consisting of 46 statements.

For this standardized questionnaire, Cronbach's alpha-coefficient was found to be 0.90 and Reliability coefficient determined by Split-half (odd-even) method was 0.937. Secondary data was collected from journals, newspapers, internet and business magazines.

## Sample

The sample for the study consisted of 1064 information systems professionals from categories of IT companies using proportionate stratified random sampling. Four categories of IT companies (Large, Medium, Small and Start-up) were considered into four strata. Using Simple Random Sampling Technique, the sample is taken from each stratum. Stratification was done on the principles that the strata are homogenous within themselves and categories of IT companies are non-overlapping in order to gain a fastidiousness in estimation of characteristics of population.

**Table 1.**    Break up of categories of IT companies (Strata)

| Sl.no | Category | Turnover | Number of professionals |
|-------|----------|----------|-------------------------|
| 1 | Large | More than 200,00,00,000 | More than 1000 |
| 2 | Medium | 10,00,00,000 - 200,00,00,000 | 301-1000 |
| 3 | Small | 50,00,000 - 10,00,00,000 | 51-300 |
| 4 | Start-up | Upto 50,00,000 | 0-50 |

*Source:* ICT Policy 2016

## Tools

To analyse the data the tools adopted were Factor analysis and Principal Component Analysis.

# RESULTS AND DISCUSSIONS

To identify the stressors which are influencing the information systems professionals, factor analysis was carried on 46 variables. The following table 2 shows the descriptive statistics (mean and standard deviation) related to sources of stress.

**Table 2.**    Descriptive Statistics (Mean and Standard Deviation) related to sources of stress

| Itemcode | Statement | Mean | Standard Deviation |
|----------|-----------|------|--------------------|
| Var1 | I have to do a lot of work in this job | 3.98 | .829 |
| Var2 | The available information relating to my job-role and its outcomes are vague and insufficient. | 3.02 | 1.095 |
| Var3 | My different officers often give contradictory instructions regarding my works. | 2.84 | 1.055 |
| Var4 | Sometimes it becomes complex problem for me to make adjustment between political / group pressures and formal rules and instructions | 3.12 | 1.121 |

| Var5 | The responsibility for the efficiency and productivity of many employees is thrust upon me. | 3.54 | .983 |
|---|---|---|---|
| Var6 | Most of suggestions are heeded and implemented here. | 2.48 | .875 |
| Var7 | My decisions and instructions concerning distribution of assignments among employees are properly followed. | 2.47 | .854 |
| Var8 | I have to work with persons whom I dislike. | 3.09 | 1.108 |
| Var9 | My assignments are of monotonous nature. | 3.08 | .983 |
| Var10 | Higher authorities do care for my self-respect. | 2.58 | 1.036 |
| Var11 | I get less salary in comparison to the quantum of my labor/work. | 3.74 | 1.105 |
| Var12 | I do my work under tense circumstances. | 3.24 | 1.102 |
| Var13 | Owing to excessive workload I have to manage with insufficient number of employees and resources. | 3.04 | 1.059 |
| Var14 | The objectives of my work-role are quite clear and adequately planned. | 2.37 | .885 |
| Var15 | Officials do not interfere with my jurisdiction and working methods. | 2.90 | 1.218 |
| Var16 | I have to do some work unwillingly owing to certain group /political pressures. | 3.08 | 1.068 |
| Var17 | I am responsible for the future of a number of employees. | 3.16 | 1.003 |
| Var18 | My co-operation is frequently sought in solving the administrative or other work related problems at higher levels. | 2.71 | .957 |
| Var19 | My suggestions regarding the training programmes of the employees are given due significance. | 2.56 | .864 |
| Var20 | Some of my colleagues and subordinates try to defame and malign me as unsuccessful. | 2.77 | 1.028 |
| Var21 | I get ample opportunity to utilize my abilities and experience independently. | 2.55 | .979 |
| Var22 | This job has enhanced my social status. | 2.36 | .925 |
| Var23 | I am seldom rewarded for my hard labor and efficient performance. | 3.26 | 1.011 |
| Var24 | Some of my assignments are quite risky and complicated. | 3.56 | .969 |
| Var25 | I have to dispose off my work hurriedly owing to excessive workload. | 3.12 | 1.029 |
| Var26 | I am unable to perform my duties smoothly owing to uncertainty and ambiguity of the scope of my jurisdiction and authorities. | 2.94 | 1.015 |
| Var27 | I am not provided with clear instructions and sufficient facilities regarding the new assignments entrusted to me | 2.88 | 1.071 |
| Var28 | In order to maintain group conformity sometimes I have to do/ produce more than the usual. | 3.68 | .836 |
| Var29 | I bear the great responsibility for the progress and prosperity of this organisation/ department/ project. | 3.81 | .857 |
| Var30 | My opinions are sought in forming important policies of the organisation/ department/project. | 2.79 | 1.031 |
| Var31 | Our interests and opinion are duly considered in making appointments for important posts. | 2.76 | .948 |
| Var32 | My colleagues do co-operate with me voluntarily in solving administrative and other work related problems. | 2.21 | .853 |

| Var33 | I got ample opportunity to develop my aptitude and proficiency properly. | 2.42 | .975 |
|---|---|---|---|
| Var34 | My higher authorities do not give due significance to my post and work. | 2.88 | 1.008 |
| Var35 | I often feel that this job has made my life cumbersome. | 3.02 | .957 |
| Var36 | Being too busy with official work I am not able to devote sufficient time to my domestic and personal problems. | 3.21 | 1.142 |
| Var37 | It is not clear that what type of work and behaviour my higher authorities and colleagues expect from me. | 2.89 | .987 |
| Var38 | Employees attach due importance to the official instructions formal working procedure. | 2.48 | .792 |
| Var39 | I am compelled to violate the formal and administrative procedures and policies owing to group/ political pressures. | 2.56 | .924 |
| Var40 | My opinion is sought in changing or modifying the working system, implements and conditions. | 2.81 | .902 |
| Var41 | There exists sufficient mutual co-operation and team-spirit among the employees of this organisation. | 2.31 | .918 |
| Var42 | My suggestions and co-operation are not sought in solving even those problems for which I am quiet competent. | 2.91 | .999 |
| Var43 | Working conditions are satisfactory here from the point of view of our welfare and convenience. | 2.46 | .892 |
| Var44 | I have to do such work as ought to be done by others. | 3.31 | .938 |
| Var45 | It becomes difficult to implement all of a sudden the new dealing procedures and policies in place of those already in practice. | 3.51 | .983 |
| Var46 | I am unable to carry out my assignments to my satisfaction on account of excessive load of work and lack of time. | 3.24 | 1.128 |

*Source:* Primary data and A. K. Srivastava and A. P. Singh, 'The manual of Occupational Stress Index', Manovaigyanic Parikshan Sansthan, Varanasi, 1984.

Kaiser-Meyer-Olkin (KMO) and Bartlett's Test result is shown in the table 3.

**Table 3.**   KMO and Bartlett's Test

| Kaiser-Meyer-Olkin Measure of Sampling Adequacy. | | .882 |
|---|---|---|
| Bartlett's Test of Sphericity | Approx. Chi-Square | 14766.935 |
| | df | 1035 |
| | Sig. | .000 |

*Source:* Primary data

0.882 is the value of the KMO measure of sampling adequacy which indicates that the sample data for conduct of factor analysis for the 46 variables is appropriate. To find the presence of correlation among the variables the statistical tool used was the Bartlett's test of Sphericity. There is a significant relationship among the variables as the p-value (Sig.) is 0.00. The test statistic value of chi-square with 1035 degrees of freedom (df) is 14766.935.

Communality value ranges from 0 to 1. The value '0' means no variance and value '1' means total variance explained by common factor and if the variance is less than 0.5, it can be removed from the further study.

**Table 4.** Communalities

| Itemcode | Initial | Extraction |
|---|---|---|
| Var1 | 1.00 | .638 |
| Var2 | 1.00 | .580 |
| Var3 | 1.00 | .578 |
| Var4 | 1.00 | .636 |
| Var5 | 1.00 | .523 |
| Var6 | 1.00 | .624 |
| Var7 | 1.00 | .604 |
| Var8 | 1.00 | .462 |
| Var9 | 1.00 | .557 |
| Var10 | 1.00 | .387 |
| Var11 | 1.00 | .526 |
| Var12 | 1.00 | .546 |
| Var13 | 1.00 | .587 |
| Var14 | 1.00 | .523 |
| Var15 | 1.00 | .600 |
| Var16 | 1.00 | .484 |
| Var17 | 1.00 | .573 |
| Var18 | 1.00 | .553 |
| Var19 | 1.00 | .546 |
| Var20 | 1.00 | .589 |
| Var21 | 1.00 | .563 |
| Var22 | 1.00 | .485 |
| Var23 | 1.00 | .399 |
| Var24 | 1.00 | .487 |
| Var25 | 1.00 | .616 |
| Var26 | 1.00 | .596 |
| Var27 | 1.00 | .616 |
| Var28 | 1.00 | .466 |
| Var29 | 1.00 | .618 |
| Var30 | 1.00 | .627 |
| Var31 | 1.00 | .627 |
| Var32 | 1.00 | .689 |
| Var33 | 1.00 | .596 |
| Var34 | 1.00 | .580 |
| Var35 | 1.00 | .574 |

| Var36 | 1.00 | .592 |
|---|---|---|
| Var37 | 1.00 | .599 |
| Var38 | 1.00 | .609 |
| Var39 | 1.00 | .530 |
| Var40 | 1.00 | .529 |
| Var41 | 1.00 | .578 |
| Var42 | 1.00 | .546 |
| Var43 | 1.00 | .496 |
| Var44 | 1.00 | .615 |
| Var45 | 1.00 | .682 |
| Var46 | 1.00 | .664 |
| Extraction Method: PCA (Principal Component Analysis) | | |

Table 4 exhibits communalities table. Variables like Var8, Var10, Var16, Var22, Var23, Var24, Var28 and Var43 are removed for further analysis as all these variables have the value of variance to be below 0.5. Remaining all variables are considered for further analysis.

**Table 5.** Total Variance Explained

| Component | Initial Eigen values | | | Extraction Sums of Squared Loadings | | | Rotation Sums of Squared Loadings | | |
|---|---|---|---|---|---|---|---|---|---|
| | Total | % of Variance | Cumulative % | Total | % of Variance | Cumulative % | Total | % of Variance | Cumulative % |
| 1 | 7.909 | 17.194 | 17.194 | 7.909 | 17.194 | 17.194 | 3.577 | 7.776 | 7.776 |
| 2 | 4.809 | 10.455 | 27.648 | 4.809 | 10.455 | 27.648 | 3.009 | 6.541 | 14.317 |
| 3 | 1.932 | 4.2 | 31.849 | 1.932 | 4.2 | 31.849 | 2.801 | 6.089 | 20.407 |
| 4 | 1.651 | 3.589 | 35.438 | 1.651 | 3.589 | 35.438 | 2.522 | 5.482 | 25.889 |
| 5 | 1.487 | 3.233 | 38.67 | 1.487 | 3.233 | 38.67 | 2.327 | 5.059 | 30.948 |
| 6 | 1.435 | 3.12 | 41.791 | 1.435 | 3.12 | 41.791 | 2.12 | 4.608 | 35.556 |
| 7 | 1.33 | 2.892 | 44.683 | 1.33 | 2.892 | 44.683 | 2.04 | 4.434 | 39.991 |
| 8 | 1.225 | 2.663 | 47.346 | 1.225 | 2.663 | 47.346 | 2.03 | 4.413 | 44.404 |
| 9 | 1.177 | 2.559 | 49.905 | 1.177 | 2.559 | 49.905 | 1.686 | 3.666 | 48.07 |
| 10 | 1.088 | 2.365 | 52.27 | 1.088 | 2.365 | 52.27 | 1.482 | 3.222 | 51.292 |
| 11 | 1.029 | 2.237 | 54.507 | 1.029 | 2.237 | 54.507 | 1.312 | 2.853 | 54.144 |
| 12 | 1.019 | 2.215 | 56.722 | 1.019 | 2.215 | 56.722 | 1.186 | 2.577 | 56.722 |
| Extraction Method: PCA (Principal Component Analysis) | | | | | | | | | |

The above table 5 exhibits the items of Principal Component Analysis (PCA) using varimax rotation. Factor analysis is conducted on all the 46 variables, on the criteria that Eigen value is greater than one. All the 46 variables were reduced to 12 components as shown in the Fig. 1 (Scree Plot) which together explain 57% of total variance.

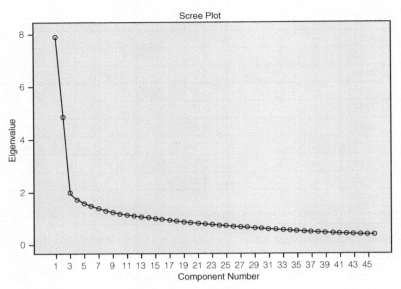

**Figure 1.** Scree Plot

More than 56.748% of the variance have been explained by the first twelve components, which proves that the variables chosen for the study are relevant. Rotated Component Matrix shown in table 6 indicate how each factor correlates with each item. For easy reading and understanding of the below table the values are suppressed to 0.4.

**Table 6.** a. Rotated Component Matrix

| | Components | | | | | | | | | | | |
|---|---|---|---|---|---|---|---|---|---|---|---|---|
| | **1** | **2** | **3** | **4** | **5** | **6** | **7** | **8** | **9** | **10** | **11** | **12** |
| Var1 | .672 | | | | | | | | | | | |
| Var2 | | .637 | | | | | | | | | | |
| Var3 | | | .681 | | | | | | | | | |
| Var4 | | | | .478 | | | | | | | | |
| Var5 | | | | | .520 | | | | | | | |
| Var6 | | | | | | .773 | | | | | | |
| Var7 | | | | | | | .583 | | | | | |
| Var9 | | | | | | | | | .773 | | | |
| Var11 | | | | | | | | | | | | .621 |
| Var12 | | | | | | | | | | .641 | | |
| Var13 | .454 | | | | | | | | | | | |
| Var14 | | .405 | | | | | | | | | | |

| | | | | | | | | | | | |
|---|---|---|---|---|---|---|---|---|---|---|---|
| Var15 | | | .672 | | | | | | | | |
| Var17 | | | | | -.548 | | | | | | |
| Var18 | | | | | | .490 | | | | | |
| Var19 | | | | | | | .705 | | | | |
| Var20 | | | | | | | | .819 | | | |
| Var21 | | | | | | | | | .460 | | |
| Var25 | .603 | | | | | | | | | | |
| Var26 | | .647 | | | | | | | | | |
| Var27 | | | .637 | | | | | | | | |
| Var29* | | | | | | | | | | | |
| Var30 | | | | | | .535 | | | | | |
| Var31 | | | | | | | .744 | | | | |
| Var32 | | | | | | | | .523 | | | |
| Var33 | | | | | | | | | .530 | | |
| Var34 | | | | | | | | | | .424 | |
| Var35 | | | | | | | | | | | .576 |
| Var36 | .661 | | | | | | | | | | |
| Var37 | | .409 | | | | | | | | | |
| Var38 | | | .777 | | | | | | | | |
| Var39* | | | | | | | | | | | |
| Var40 | | | | | | .524 | | | | | |
| Var41 | | | | | | | | .434 | | | |
| Var42 | | | | | | | | | .605 | | |
| Var44 | .618 | | | | | | | | | | |
| Var45 | | | .806 | | | | | | | | |
| Var46 | .751 | | | | | | | | | | |

a. Rotation converged in 16 iterations.
Var29* and Var39* are having values less than 0.4
Rotation Method: Varimax with Kaiser Normalization
Extraction Method: Principal Component Analysis.

The following are the measures and item loadings of the twelve factors in order of their importance.

## Component 1 - Role Overload

The first component accounted for 17.194% of the total variance. This component had significant loading of 6 statements. Table 7 shows the factor loadings of these variables.

**Table 7.**   Component 1 - Significant Loadings of Variables

| Itemcode | Statement | Loading |
|---|---|---|
| Var1 | I have to do a lot of work in this job | .672 |
| Var13 | Owing to excessive workload I have to manage with insufficient number of employees and resources. | .454 |
| Var25 | I have to dispose off my work hurriedly owing to excessive workload | .603 |
| Var36 | Being too busy with official work I am not able to devote sufficient time to my domestic and personal problems. | .661 |
| Var44 | I have to do such work as ought to be done by others | .618 |
| Var46 | I am unable to carry out my assignments to my satisfaction on account of excessive load of work and lack of time. | **.751** |

*Source:* Primary data and.A. K. Srivastava and A. P. Singh, 'The manual of Occupational Stress Index', Manovaigyanic Parikshan Sansthan, Varanasi, 1984

The component is named as "Role Overload" as all the statements are positively loaded as shown in table 7, it proves that the occupational stress is caused to Information Systems professionals due to excessive workload.

## Component 2 - Role Ambiguity

This component accounts for 10.456% of the total variance and has significant loading of four statements. Table 8 shows that the factor loadings of these variables.

**Table 8.**   Component 2 - Significant Loadings of Variables

| Itemcode | Statement | Loading |
|---|---|---|
| Var2 | The available information relating to my job-role and its outcomes are vague and insufficient. | .637 |
| Var14 | The objectives of my work-role are quite clear and adequately planned. | .405 |
| Var26 | I am unable to perform my duties smoothly owing to uncertainty and ambiguity of the scope of my jurisdiction and authorities. | **.647** |
| Var37 | It is not clear that what type of work and behaviour my higher authorities and colleagues expect from me. | .409 |

*Source:* Primary data and A. K. Srivastava and A. P. Singh, 'The manual of Occupational Stress Index', Manovaigyanic Parikshan Sansthan, Varanasi, 1984.

The component is named as "Role Ambiguity" as all the statements describe that the occupational stress is caused due to ambiguity and uncertainty of the job roles performed.

## Component 3 - Role Conflict

This component accounts for 4.21% of the total variance and has significant loading of five statements. Table 9 shows the factor loadings of these variables.

**Table 9.**    Component 3 - Significant Loadings of Variables

| Itemcode | Statement | Loading |
|----------|-----------|---------|
| Var3 | My different officers often give contradictory instructions regarding my works. | .681 |
| Var15 | Officials do not interfere with my jurisdiction and working methods. | .672 |
| Var27 | I am not provided with clear instructions and sufficient facilities regarding the new assignments entrusted to me. | .637 |
| Var38 | Employees attach due importance to the official instructions formal working procedure. | .777 |
| Var45 | It becomes difficult to implement all of a sudden the new dealing procedures and policies in place of those already in practice. | **.806** |

*Source:* Primary data and A. K. Srivastava and A. P. Singh, 'The manual of Occupational Stress Index', Manovaigyanic Parikshan Sansthan, Varanasi, 1984.

The component is named as "Role Conflict" as all the statements describe that the occupational stress is caused due to sudden changes in the procedures and policies, for not providing clear instructions regarding new assignments and job roles being ill-defined.

## Component 4 - Political Pressures

This component accounts for 3.590% of the total variance and has four statements, out of four, only one statement is taken into consideration. Remaining statements are removed from the study as Var39 has factor loading to be less than 0.4 and Var16 and Var28 have the value of variance to be below 0.5. Table 10 shows the factor loadings of these variables.

**Table 10.**    Component 4 - Significant Loadings of Variables

| Itemcode | Statement | Loading |
|----------|-----------|---------|
| Var4 | Sometimes it becomes complex problem for me to make adjustment between political/group pressures and formal rules and instructions | **.478** |
| Var39 | I am compelled to violate the formal and administrative procedures and policies owing to group/ political pressures. **(Loading is less than 0.4)** | **Not considered** |

*Source:* Primary data and A. K. Srivastava and A. P. Singh, 'The manual of Occupational Stress Index', Manovaigyanic Parikshan Sansthan, Varanasi, 1984.

The component is named as "Political Pressures" as all the statements describe that the occupational stress caused is due to make adjustment between formal rules and instructions and group/ political pressures.

## Component 5 - Persons Responsibility

This component accounts for 3.234% of the total variance and has significant loading of three statements, out of three, only two statements are considered. Var39 is removed from the study as it has the factor loading to be less than 0.4. Table 11 shows the factor loadings of these variables.

**Table 11.**   Component 5 - Significant Loadings of Variables

| Itemcode | Statement | Loading |
|---|---|---|
| Var5 | The responsibility for the efficiency and productivity of many employees is thrust upon me. | **.520** |
| Var17 | I am responsible for the future of a number of employees. | −.548 |
| Var29 | I bear the great responsibility for the progress and prosperity of this organisation/ department/project. **(Loading is less than 0.4)** | **Not considered** |

*Source:* Primary data and A. K. Srivastava and A. P. Singh, 'The manual of Occupational Stress Index', Manovaigyanic Parikshan Sansthan, Varanasi, 1984.

The component is labelled as "Persons responsibility" as the stress is caused due to the responsibility of productivity and efficiency of many employees is upon the Information System professional and the negative loading of var17 indicates that the extent of stress is reduced when the responsibility of the future of number of employees is in the hands of Information Systems professional.

## Component 6 - Under Participation

This component accounted for 3.13% of the total variance and has significant loading of four statements. Table 12 shows the factor loadings of these variables.

**Table 12.**   Component 6 - Significant Loadings of Variables

| Itemcode | Statement | Loading |
|---|---|---|
| Var6 | Most of suggestions are not heeded and implemented here. | **.773** |
| Var18 | My co-operation is frequently sought in solving the administrative or other work related problems at higher levels. | .490 |
| Var30 | My opinions are sought in forming important policies of the organisation/department/ project. | .535 |
| Var40 | My opinion is sought in changing or modifying the working system, implements and conditions. | .524 |

*Source:* Primary data and A. K. Srivastava and A. P. Singh, 'The manual of Occupational Stress Index', Manovaigyanic Parikshan Sansthan, Varanasi, 1984.

The component is named as "Under Participation" as all the statements describe that the occupational stress is due to the suggestions and opinions are not sought out from Information systems professionals for solving the problems or in changing the policies.

## Component 7 - Powerlessness

This component accounts for 2.894% of the total variance and has significant loading of three statements. Table 13 shows the factor loadings of these variables.

**Table 13.**    Component 7 - Significant Loadings of Variables

| Itemcode | Statement | Loading |
|---|---|---|
| Var7 | My decisions and instructions concerning distribution of assignments among employees are properly followed. | .583 |
| Var19 | My suggestions regarding the training programmes of the employees are given due significance. | .705 |
| Var31 | Our interests and opinion are duly considered in making appointments for important posts. | **.744** |

*Source:* Primary data. and A. K. Srivastava and A. P. Singh, 'The manual of Occupational Stress Index', Manovaigyanic Parikshan Sansthan, Varanasi, 1984

The component is named as "Powerlessness", as all the statements elucidate that the occupational stress in Information Systems professionals is caused due to not being involved in suggestions related to training programmes, opinions related to appointments for important positions and decisions relating to distribution of assignments.

## Component 8 - Poor Peer Relations

This component accounts for 2.664% of the total variance and has four statements, out of which three statements are considered. The statement Var8 is not considered for further study as the value of variance below 0.5. Table 14 shows the factor loadings of these variables.

**Table 14.**    Component 8 - Significant Loadings of Variables

| Itemcode | Statement | Loading |
|---|---|---|
| Var20 | Some of my colleagues and subordinates try to defame and malign me as unsuccessful. | **.819** |
| Var32 | My colleagues do co-operate with me voluntarily in solving administrative and other work related problems. | .523 |
| Var41 | There exists sufficient mutual co-operation and team-spirit among the employees of this organisation. | .434 |

*Source:* Primary data and A. K. Srivastava and A. P. Singh, 'The manual of Occupational Stress Index', Manovaigyanic Parikshan Sansthan, Varanasi, 1984.

This component is named as "Poor Peer Relations" as all the statements describe that the relationship with colleagues and subordinates lead to occupational stress.

## Component 9 - Intrinsic Impoverishment

This component accounts for 2.558% of the total variance and has four statements. Table 15 shows the factor loadings of these variables.

**Table 15.**   Component 9 - Significant Loadings of Variables

| Itemcode | Statement | Loading |
|---|---|---|
| Var9 | My assignments are of monotonous nature. | **.773** |
| Var21 | I get ample opportunity to utilize my abilities and experience independently. | .460 |
| Var33 | I got ample opportunity to develop my aptitude and proficiency properly. | .530 |
| Var42 | My suggestions and co-operation are not sought in solving even those problems for which I am quiet competent. | .605 |

*Source:* Primary data and A. K. Srivastava and A. P. Singh, 'The manual of Occupational Stress Index', Manovaigyanic Parikshan Sansthan, Varanasi, 1984

This component is named as "Intrinsic Impoverishment" as all the four statements describe that the occupational stress is caused due to monotonous assignments, cooperation and suggestions of the employee are not sought in in solving problems.

## Component 10 - Low Status

This component accounts for 2.364% of the total variance and has three statements, out of which only one variable is considered. The statements Var10 and Var22 are not considered for further study as the value of variance is less than 0.5. Table 16 shows the factor loading of the variable.

**Table 16.**   Component 10 - Significant Loadings of Variables

| Itemcode | Statement | Loading |
|---|---|---|
| Var34 | My higher authorities do not give due significance to my post and work. | **.424** |

*Source:* Primary data and A. K. Srivastava and A. P. Singh, 'The manual of Occupational Stress Index', Manovaigyanic Parikshan Sansthan, Varanasi, 1984

This component is labelled as "Low Status", as the statement describes that the occupational stress is caused due to higher officials not giving due respect and significance to the professional work and the designation.

## Component 11 - Strenuous working conditions

This component accounts for 2.238% of the total variance and has four statements, out of which two variables are considered. The statements Var24 and Var43 are not considered for further study as the value of variance is less than 0.5. Table 17 shows the factor loadings of the variables.

**Table 17.**   Component 11 - Significant Loadings of Variables

| Itemcode | Statement | Loading |
|---|---|---|
| Var12 | I do my work under tense circumstances. | **.641** |
| Var35 | I often feel that this job has made my life cumbersome. | .576 |

*Source:* Primary data. and A. K. Srivastava and A. P. Singh, 'The manual of Occupational Stress Index', Manovaigyanic Parikshan Sansthan, Varanasi, 1984

This component is named as "Strenuous Working Conditions" as the above statements describe that the stress is caused due to the working conditions.

## Component 12 - Unprofitability

This component accounts for 2.216% of the total variance and has two statements, out of which only one variable is considered. The statement Var23 is not considered for further study as it has the value of variance less than 0.5. Table 18 shows the factor loadings of the variable.

**Table 18.**   Component 12 - Significant Loadings of Variables

| Itemcode | Statement | Loading |
|---|---|---|
| Var11 | I get less salary in comparison to the quantum of my labor/work. | **.621** |

*Source:* Primary data and A. K. Srivastava and A. P. Singh, 'The manual of Occupational Stress Index', Manovaigyanic Parikshan Sansthan, Varanasi, 1984.

This component is named as "Unprofitability", as the above statement describes that the occupational stress is related with remuneration (increments and salaries).

Table 19 shows factor loadings based on factor analysis for the factors influencing occupational stress among Information Systems professionals.

**Table 19.**   Factor Loadings

| Components | Item | Factor Loading |
|---|---|---|
| Role Overload | I am unable to carry out my assignments to my satisfaction on account of excessive load of work and lack of time. | .751 |
| Role Ambiguity | I am unable to perform my duties smoothly owing to uncertainty and ambiguity of the scope of my jurisdiction and authorities. | .647 |
| Role Conflict | It becomes difficult to implement all of a sudden the new dealing procedures and policies in place of those already in practice. | .806 |
| Political Pressures | Sometimes it becomes complex problem for me to make adjustment between political / group pressures and formal rules and instructions | .478 |
| Persons Responsibility | The responsibility for the efficiency and productivity of many employees is thrust upon me. | .520 |
| Under Participation | Most of suggestions are heeded and implemented here. | .773 |
| Powerlessness | Our interests and opinion are duly considered in making appointments for important posts. | .744 |
| Poor Peer Relations | Some of my colleagues and subordinates try to defame and malign me as unsuccessful. | .819 |
| Intrinsic Impoverishment | My assignments are of monotonous nature. | .773 |
| Low Status | My higher authorities do not give due significance to my post and work. | .424 |
| Strenuous Working Conditions | I do my work under tense circumstances. | .641 |
| Unprofitability | I get less salary in comparison to the quantum of my labor/work. | .621 |

*Source:* Primary data and A. K. Srivastava and A. P. Singh, 'The manual of Occupational Stress Index', Manovaigyanic Parikshan Sansthan, Varanasi, 1984.

## LIMITATIONS

The present study has certain limitations like:
- This research was conducted only among 12 selected Information Technology companies. in Hyderabad, Telangana State.
- This study is based purely on the feelings/attitudes/opinions of the respondents which can change/vary from situation to situation, time to time while answering the questionnaire.
- Present research concentrates only on identification of occupational stressors experienced by the Information Systems professionals post COVID.

## CONCLUSIONS

In conclusion, a twelve factor model of occupational stressors was confirmed using factor analysis in the Information Systems Professionals in post COVID-19 which proves that the scale adopted for the present research has high analytical capability for measuring occupational stress and for identification of areas which require key focus in the Information Technology sector/industry.

Majority of Information Systems Professionals are adopting individual strategies to overcome the occupational stress post COVID-19 by reading books and newspapers, gardening, meditation and yoga, watching television and movies with families, spending time with family members, cooking etc., It is not only the individual strategies help in overcoming the occupational stress.

It is very important that the IT companies also understand the needs of its employees and provide what is best for them which can help the Information Systems professionals to overcome the stress in a better way during post COVID. Constant appraisal programs, challenging assignments, recognition, awards and rewards, proper definition of the job roles, providing job security, frequent town hall meetings and appreciation from the superiors should be provided to reinstate and motivate them to feel "work and home" instead of "work from home".

## REFERENCES

B. Prathyusha. (2021). The Effect of Demographic Variables Occupational Stress: A Study on Software Professionals. *Recent trends and Innovation in Business* (pp. 145–158). Hyderabad: KGRL College.

B. Prathyusha, C. P., & Reddy, S. (2016). A Quantitative Erudition of Occupational Stress in Information Technology Professinoals. *International Journal of Computational Engineering and Management*, 1–4.

B. Prathyusha, Prasad, C. S., & Reddy, M. S. (2014). Occupational Stress, Health Concerns ans Coping Strategies of software professionals-an empirical study. *NCESTM 2K14* (pp. 107–109). Hyderabad: Malla Reddy Engineering College.

B. Prathyusha, Prasad, C., & Reddy, M. S. (2014). Investigation of stress coping strategies in software professionals. *Stress Management Professional - An International Journal*, 35–40.

B. Prathyusha, Prasad, C., & Reddy, S. (2015). Professional Life Stress among Software Professionals in Hyderabad - An Evaluaton. *International Journal of Innovative Research in Science, Engineering and Technology*, 12371–12376.

Devi. T, U. (2011). A Study on Stress Management and Coping Strategies with reference to IT Companies. *Journal of Information Technology and Economic Development*, 30–48.

Drucker. P.F. (1954). *The pratice of management: A study of most important function in American Society.* New York: Harper.

Jayesh Ranjan, I. E. (2020). *Annual Report 2019-20.* Hyderabad: Government of Telangana.

K.D.V. Prasad, R. V. (2016). A Comparative analysis on the causes of Occupational Stress among Men and Women employees and its effect on performance at the workplace of Information Technology Sector. *International Journal of Management Excellence*, 797–807.

Misra, A. (2015). Globalisation and stress among computer professionals. *International Journal of Multidisciplinary Research and Development*, 288–291.

P.S. Manjula, P. (2015). Occupational Stress and its impact on Work Exhaustion-An Empirical Study among Information System Personnel. *International Journal of Appplied Business and Economic Research*, 6419–6431.

Rani, A. (2013). Workplace Stress among Women in IT Sector. *Gavesana Journal of Management*, 86–88.

Srivastava A.K., S. A. (1984). *Manual of the Occupational Stress Index.* Varansi: Banaras University.

Vimala Thomas, Y. K. (2019). Study on stress among software professionals in Madhapur area of Hyderabad. *International Journal of Management Excellence*, 4062–4066.

# CHAPTER FIVE

# Indian Life Insurance Market: The Liberalisation Experience and Emerging Dynamics

**Prof. K.V. Bhanu Murthy**
*Professor, Delhi Technological University*
*East Delhi Campus, Vivek Vihar II, Delhi*
*bhanumurthykv@yahoo.com*

**Dr. Manisha Choudhary**
*Assistant Professor, Govt. College*
*Rithoj, Gurugram, Higher Education Department, Haryana*
*manishachoudharydr2017@gmail.com*

**Abstract**—*The Indian life insurance market, after remaining a free market since its inception was nationalised in 1956 with the setting up of Life Insurance Corporation of India (LIC). LIC did fairly well in terms of spreading insurance culture and reaching out to the masses but under the nationalised regime, the market remained undertapped. To bring reforms, Malhotra Committee was constituted which recommended the opening up of the market to private players to induce competition and improve market performance.*

*This paper studies the impact of liberalisation over the 20 year period (2001 to 2020) through secondary data analysis (obtained from various IRDAI Handbooks on Indian Insurance Statistics) using semi-log regression model of growth rate and other descriptive statistics. Data analysis has revealed that there is negligible rise in life insurance penetration during the 20 year post-reform period whereas density has risen at the rate of 9% per annum. LIC still remains the dominant firm in terms of total premium, new business premium and number of new policies issued. In terms of surplus, after an initial shock due to entry of private players, LIC has recovered and adjusted itself to show a consistent rise but the private players are still struggling to have steady growth. Competition has resulted in market expansion and the market has become more dynamic - in terms of products, distribution channels, geographical spread, micro insurance, surplus and growth pattern. On the whole, liberalisation has partially succeeded in improving the market.*

**Keywords**—Indian Life Insurance Market, Liberalisation, LIC, Private Insurers, Malhotra Committee

## INTRODUCTION

Life insurance in India dates back to 1818 when the first life insurance company, named Oriental Life Insurance Company was set up. Since then, this market remained an open market till 1956. In 1956, it was nationalised keeping in view the social objective of life insurance. For this purpose, Life Insurance Corporation of India (popularly known as LIC) was set up in 1956. LIC did a fairly good job of spreading awareness about life insurance and making it popular amongst the masses. However, being a state monopoly, it had its own drawbacks and the market remained under-tapped. This led to the initiation of reforms in this market which started with the constitution of Malhotra Committee in 1993. Malhotra Committee gave its recommendations in 1994. One major recommendation was opening up of the sector to private players and also allowing foreign participation, with adequate regulation in place.

In 1999, Insurance Regulatory Development Authority of India (IRDA) was set up as the separate regulator for the insurance market. Also, the private players were allowed to enter the market. At present, there are 23 private life insurance companies along with the incumbent state veteran LIC, which makes it a total of 24. The way this market has behaved in the post-liberalisation period is really interesting to study. Liberalisation or reforms implemented in 1999 brought new hopes to improve the performance of this market. Here, it is pertinent to mention that market performance of life insurance is measured through two parameters- life insurance penetration and life insurance density. Life insurance penetration is expressed as a percentage of life insurance premium to Gross Domestic Product (GDP) of the country. Life insurance density is the per capita insurance. It was felt that by introducing competition, customers will get better products, better prices and the overall market performance (life insurance penetration and density) would go up.

This paper focuses on the impact of liberalisation on life insurance market. It has been 20 years now that the major reforms were introduced. Also, IRDA (now renamed as IRDAI), keeps bringing in necessary amendments and reforms from time to time keeping in view the changing national and international environment. Whether this entire reform process is able to yield the desired results is an important question. Through the analysis of this market over this 20 year period we intend to assess the efficacy of these reforms and the performance of Indian life insurance market in the post-reform period.

### Malhotra Committee: Major Recommendations

The Malhotra Committee submitted its report in 1994. As per the Law Commission of India (2003) Report, some of the major recommendations made by it were as under:-

(a)   "the establishment of an independent regulatory authority (akin to Securities and Exchange Board of India);

(b)   allowing private sector to enter the insurance field;

(c)   improvement of the commission structure for agents to make it effective instrument for procuring business specially rural, personal and non-obligatory lines of business;

(d)   insurance plans for economically backward sections, appointment of institutional agents;

(e)   marketing of life insurance to relatively weaker sections of the society and specified proportion of business in rural areas;

(f)   provisions for co-operative societies for transacting life insurance business in states."

## LITERATURE REVIEW

The literature review is focused on the studies that measure the impact of liberalisation on the life insurance market.

Gulati and Jain (2011) revealed that private sector has induced competition but is unable to affect the performance of LIC.

Bodla and Chaudhary (2012) studied the reasons why the private sector after initially capturing a significant market share is now struggling for a regular growth in business and market share.

Shah et al. (2011) recognized profitability as the biggest challenge for the industry. Private life insurers had accumulated losses of over 16,000 crores till March 2010.

Jain (2013) found that after liberalization, the life insurance industry of India witnessed marvelous growth but this growth declined after economic crisis in 2008.

Ansari and Fola (2014) did not find a significant difference in the new business premium of private and public life insurance companies.

Kulkarni (2017) through an analysis of the Indian life insurance sector revealed that after an initial growth in business (mainly led by ULIPs), the growth of private sector has slowed down and has been found to be lop-sided.

The above studies reveal that the reforms initiated in 1999 definitely led to increased competition and expansion of market but even now, the market hasn't realised its full potential. So, we want to contribute to the knowledge of impact of liberalisation on life insurance market by studying the impact of reforms over the entire 20 year period (2001-2020).

## OBJECTIVES

The objectives of this paper are to study the impact of opening up of the life insurance market and the emerging changes. These objectives are given below:

1. To study the density and penetration of life insurance in the post reform period.
2. To look at growth profile of LIC and private insurers.
3. To analyse the network of life insurance business – area wise spread of offices.
4. To study the pattern of growth of Micro-insurance business.
5. To study the growth of Agent base of LIC and private insurers.
6. To study the growth of life insurance products.
7. To analyse the growth pattern of Surplus/deficit of LIC and private insurers.

# DATA AND METHODOLOGY

## Data

To study the various indicators in line with the objectives, secondary data has been used. This data is obtained from the IRDAI website through the Handbook on Indian Insurance Statistics 2007-08, 2011-12, 2012-13, 2015-16 and 2018-19. The insurance Annual Reports 2001-02 to 2019-20 are also referred to fill some data gaps. The latest data released by IRDAI through its Handbook of Statistics on 12th March, 2021 has also been incorporated to present an upto date analysis.

## Methodology

1. To study the growth patterns of various indicators of life insurance market's performance, semi-log growth equations are used.

### Semi-Log Growth Equation

The natural log of each variable of life insurance, like life insurance penetration, density, total premium etc. (Y) is regressed on time ($t$). Therefore, the regression equation can be written as follows (1), in exponential form:

$$Y = e^{\alpha + \beta t} \qquad\qquad \dots (1)$$

Taking log of both sides and adding an error term;

$$Ln\ Y = \alpha + \beta t + \mu t \qquad\qquad \dots (2)$$

Where,     $Ln\ Y$ = Natural log of variable Y
            $\alpha$ = intercept term
            $\beta$ = slope of the regression equation (instant growth rate)
            $t$ = time
            $\mu t$ = error term

2. To study the growth pattern of surplus/deficit of LIC and private players, a set of descriptive statistics are used.

# DATA ANALYSIS AND INTERPRETATION

## Life insurance penetration and density

As discussed in the introductory section, life insurance penetration and life insurance density are two accepted parameters to measure the performance of life insurance market. Growth of these two parameters is shown in Table 1.

**Table 1.**   Life Insurance Density and Penetration

| Indicator | Period | Growth | Std. Error | t Stat | P-value |
|---|---|---|---|---|---|
| **Life Insurance Density** | 2001-2019 | **0.09** | 0.014 | **6.63** | **4.26E-06***** |
| **Life Insurance Penetration** | 2001-2019 | 0.00 | 0.010 | 0.31 | 0.76 |

| |
|---|
| *    Significant at 10% |
| **   Significant at 5% |
| ***  Significant at 1% |
| *Source:* Authors' Estimation |

After the coming of private players and liberalisation, there is a statistically significant growth of 9% per annum in the life insurance density over the period 2001 to 2019. However, if we see the growth rate of life insurance penetration from 2001 to 2019, there is no growth in the life insurance penetration, although the result is not statistically significant. This result points towards the unsatisfactory performance of life insurance market.

## Growth Profile: LIC vs Private Insurers

After looking at the overall market performance, now we wish to see the growth profile of LIC and the private players. The growth profile has been measured through three indicators- total premium, new business premium and number of individual new policies issued. These results are presented in Table 2.

**Table 2.**   Growth Profile in Life Insurance Business

| Indicator | Period | Entity | Growth | Std. Error | t Stat | P-value |
|---|---|---|---|---|---|---|
| **Total Premium** | 2001-2020 | LIC | **0.11** | 0.01 | 16.24 | 3.38E-12*** |
| | | Private | **0.36** | 0.06 | 6.01 | 0.00*** |
| **New Business Premium** | 2001-2020 | LIC | **0.13** | 0.01 | 12.83 | 1.69E-10*** |
| | | Private | **0.31** | 0.05 | 5.41 | 0.00*** |
| **Number of Individual New Policies Issued** | 2003-2020 | LIC | **−0.02** | 0.01 | −2.09 | 0.05** |
| | | Private | **0.06** | 0.03 | 2.09 | 0.05** |

| |
|---|
| *    Significant at 10% |
| **   Significant at 5% |
| ***  Significant at 1% |
| *Source:* Authors' Estimation |

Total premium of LIC has shown a statistically significant growth of 11% per annum over the period 2001 to 2020. Over the same period there is a statistically significant growth in the total premium of private players at the rate of 36% per annum. This shows that private insurers have been successful in expanding the market.

The second comparison is between the growth of new business premium of LIC and the private players. New business premium is the sum of premium of the new single premium policies and the first year premium of other policies. The new business premium of LIC has risen at a statistically significant rate of 13% per annum over the period 2001 to 2020. Over the same period, the new business premium of private players has risen at a statistically significant rate of 31% per annum. This shows that the market has expanded over this 20 year period.

In terms of the individual new policies issued, LIC has shown a statistically significant negative growth of 2% per annum over the period 2003 to 2020. Over the same period, private players have exhibited a statistically significant growth of 6% per annum in the number of individual new policies issued. This also points towards the expansion of the market.

But this comparison between the growth rates of private players and LIC should be read with caution. It should in no way be believed that private sector has outperformed LIC just going by the face value of these results. Private sector is showing a much higher growth in certain cases, just because it started from a very low base. LIC began with a large base in 2001 whereas the private players started from scratch. Secondly, it is a comparison of one company (LIC) with the entire private sector (comprising of 23 companies). This shows that these 23 private insurers even if taken together are not able to give a tough fight to the state veteran LIC.

## Network of Life Insurance Business

Network of life insurance business as reflected in geographical spread of life insurance offices is shown in Table 3.

**Table 3.**   No. of offices_Area-wise

| Indicator | Period | Entity | Growth | Std. Error | t Stat | P-value |
|---|---|---|---|---|---|---|
| No. of Offices (metro + urban) | 2007-2020 | LIC | 0.08 | 0.01 | 8.72 | 1.54E-06*** |
| | | Private | 0.0913 | 0.01 | 8.10 | 3.29E-06*** |
| No. of offices (unclassified) | 2007-2015 | LIC | 0.1065 | 0.01 | 8.37 | 0.01*** |
| | | Private | 0.0169 | 0.05 | 0.32 | 0.76 |
| Semi-urban | 2016-2020 | LIC | −0.004 | 0.00 | −1.05 | 0.37 |
| | | Private | −0.102 | 0.04 | −2.70 | 0.07* |
| Rural | 2016-2020 | LIC | 0.0316 | 0.00 | 14.07 | 0.01*** |
| | | Private | −0.5561 | 0.20 | −2.76 | 0.07* |

\*      Significant at 10%
\*\*     Significant at 5%
\*\*\*    Significant at 1%

*Source:* Authors' Estimation

Before presenting the analysis, the description of the geographic division is called for. So, first it is explained how the areas are divided into various categories. From 2007 to 2015, IRDA has given three-way classification of the area-wise distribution of offices namely, metropolitan, urban and unclassified. Metropolitan cities are those having a population of 10,00,000 or more; urban areas are those which have a population between 100,000 to 9,99,999. It implies that the areas referred to as unclassified had a population of less than 1 lakh, but it is not explicitly stated.

From 2016 onwards, the classification of areas given by IRDA changed to four, namely, metropolitan, urban, semi-urban and rural wherein semi-urban areas are those having a population of 10,000 to 99,999 and rural areas had a population upto 9,999.

**Metropolitan and Urban Areas:** For the purpose of our analysis, we have added the offices in metropolitan and urban areas (which represent a population of more than 1,00,000) and seen their growth rate for LIC and private insurers. In case of LIC, there is a statistically significant growth of 8% per annum in the offices situated in metropolitan and urban areas over the period 2007 to 2020. Over the same period, there is a statistically significant growth of 9% in the offices of private insurers situated in metropolitan and urban areas.

**Unclassified Areas:** The second analysis is done for the offices situated in unclassified areas which represent a population of less than 1,00,000. From 2007 to 2015, the number of offices of LIC situated in these areas with a population upto 99,999 have risen at a statistically significant rate of 10% per annum. However, the private companies' offices in these areas have grown at a meagre 1.6% per annum over the same period and this is also not statistically significant. Thus, it can be seen that the private life insurers do not have more offices in less populated areas and their offices are majorly confined to metropolitan and urban areas.

**Semi-urban Areas:** The third analysis is for the offices situated in semi-urban areas starting from the year when IRDA started releasing the data for this category i.e., 2016. From 2016 to 2020, the number of offices of LIC situated in semi-urban areas have shown a miniscule negative growth of 0.4 % per annum though it is not statistically significant. Over the same period, the number of offices of private insurers situated in semi-urban areas have fallen at a statistically significant rate of 10% per annum.

**Rural Areas:** The fourth analysis is for the offices situated in rural areas, again starting from the year 2016, which coincides with the release of separate data for these areas by IRDA. LIC has reported a statistically significant increase of 3% per annum in the number of offices situated in rural areas from 2016 to 2020. The private insurers have however shown a decline in the number of offices situated in rural areas over the same period, showing a statistically significant negative growth rate of 55.6% per annum which is quite high and points towards the dwindling presence of private life insurance offices in rural areas.

So, we also see the dynamics in the form of changing geographic spread of offices.

## Micro-insurance Business

IRDA notified the micro insurance guidelines on 10th November, 2005 which were revised in 2015. The main idea was to reach out to the poor and economically weaker sections through simpler and need based insurance products, including life insurance. Micro-insurance products have a sum assured of upto Rs 50,000. Table 4 reflects the performance of life insurers in terms of micro-insurance business.

**Table 4.**   Micro insurance business

| Indicator | Period | Entity | Growth | Std. Error | t Stat | P-value |
|---|---|---|---|---|---|---|
| Micro insurance (no. of lives covered) | 2009-2020 | LIC | −0.093 | 0.086 | −1.08 | 0.30 |
| | | Private | **0.379** | 0.074 | 5.06 | **0.00\*\*\*** |
| Micro insurance (premium) | 2009-2020 | LIC | −0.050 | 0.071 | −0.71 | 0.49 |
| | | Private | **0.470** | 0.093 | 5.08 | **0.00\*\*\*** |
| \*     Significant at 10% | | | | | | |
| \*\*    Significant at 5% | | | | | | |
| \*\*\*   Significant at 1% | | | | | | |
| *Source:* Authors' Estimation | | | | | | |

There are two types of micro-insurance products - individual and group. IRDA releases the data for both. In case of group insurance schemes, number of lives covered is also provided. The performance of micro insurance business is analysed through studying the growth of number of lives covered and the premium in this segment. To calculate the total number of lives covered, the individual policies and the lives covered through group insurance have been added. Similarly, the premium on individual policies and group policies is added to get the total premium from micro-insurance business.

LIC has shown a decline of 9% per annum in the number of lives covered through micro-insurance from 2009 to 2020, though it is not statistically significant. Over the same period, private life insurers have also reported a statistically significant growth of 37.9% per annum in terms of the number of lives covered through micro-insurance. In terms of premium underwritten through micro-insurance, LIC has again shown a negative growth of 5% per annum from 2009 to 2020, though it is not statistically significant. Over the same period, there is a statistically significant growth of 47% per annum in the premium underwritten by private insurers through micro-insurance business.

## Agent-base

Table 5 depicts the growth of agent base of LIC and private insurers across two categories- individual and corporate agents. Individual agents represent the traditional channel of distribution whereas the Corporate agents represent the newer ways of selling life insurance. Corporate agents include banks (popular as bancassurance) and non-banking institutions.

Individual agents of LIC have grown at a small but statistically significant rate of 1% per annum over the period 2002 to 2020. Over the same period, the growth rate of number of individual agents of private insurers is 13.4% per annum and is statistically significant. The number of corporate agents (Banks and others) of LIC has declined at a very small rate of 0.6% per annum from 2002 to 2020 but this decline is not statistically significant.

**Table 5.** Agent Base

| Indicator | Period | Entity | Growth | Std. Error | t Stat | P-value |
|---|---|---|---|---|---|---|
| Individual Agents | 2002-2020 | LIC | 0.0104 | 0.0049 | **2.12** | **0.05**\*\* |
| | | Private | 0.1343 | 0.0331 | **4.05** | **0.01**\*\*\* |
| Corporate Agents | 2002-2020 | LIC | −0.006 | 0.0333 | −0.19 | 0.85 |
| | | Private | −0.007 | 0.0341 | −0.21 | 0.83 |

\*     Significant at 10%
\*\*    Significant at 5%
\*\*\*   Significant at 1%

*Source:* Authors' Estimation

On the other hand, the number of corporate agents of private insurers has shown a decline of 0.7% per annum from 2002 to 2018, but again it is not statistically significant. This shows some underlying trend which is not statistically significant. It gives a hint that the corporate agency channel is less preferred by the insurers (both LIC and private players) and the traditional channel of individual agents still enjoys greater popularity.

## Life Insurance Products

Life insurance products have undergone a lot of variation with the coming of private players. Introduction of Unit Linked Insurance Plans (ULIPs) is largely attributed to the private insurers and also seen as a major contributor to their initial success. However, lately it is seen that ULIPs are becoming less popular. So, the total premium of life insurers can be divided into two broad categories- non-linked (traditional products not linked to market performance) and linked (ULIPs which are linked to market performance).

**Table 6.** Life Insurance Products

| Indicator | Period | Entity | Growth | Std. Error | t Stat | P-value |
|---|---|---|---|---|---|---|
| Non-Linked Premium | 2007-2020 | LIC | **0.105** | 0.0041 | 25.71 | **7.307E-12**\*\*\* |
| | | Private | **0.243** | 0.0148 | 16.42 | **1.373E-09**\*\*\* |
| Linked Premium | 2007-2020 | LIC | **−0.388** | 0.0354 | −10.96 | **1.321E-07**\*\*\* |
| | | Private | **0.039** | 0.021 | 1.91 | **0.08**\* |

\*     Significant at 10%
\*\*    Significant at 5%
\*\*\*   Significant at 1%

*Source:* Authors' Estimation

As shown in Table 6, over the period 2007 to 2020, there is a statistically significant growth of 10.5% per annum in the non-linked premium of LIC. Over the same period, there is a statistically significant growth of 24.3% per annum in the non-linked premium of private insurers. In the linked business category, the premium of LIC has fallen at a statistically significant rate of 38.8% per annum over the period 2007 to 2020. Over the same period, private insurers have reported a statistically significant 3.9% per annum growth in the linked premium. This is again an interesting result which shows that LIC has gradually moved out of the ULIP business as it was never its stronghold. Even the private players, who were the leaders in this category have reported a much lower growth as compared to the growth of their non-linked business. So, the initial charm of ULIPs generated by promises of higher return seems to be fading and there is a general trend of decline in the linked business, though more pronounced in case of LIC. So, we have also witnessed changes or dynamics in terms of popularity of different types of products.

## Surplus/Deficiency

Table 7 shows the year-wise surplus/deficit of LIC and the private insurers from 2002 to 2020. Surplus reflected through the Policyholders' accounts has been taken as measure of profitability to have comparable results. LIC has shown the highest surplus in the year 2002 whereas private sector has shown the highest surplus in 2018.

**Table 7.**   Surplus/Deficit Indices

| Year | Pvt. Surplus (in Lakhs) | LIC Surplus (in Lakhs) | Index of Pvt. Surplus | Index of LIC Surplus |
|------|-------------------------|------------------------|-----------------------|----------------------|
| 2002 | −33755.00 | 1215687 | −4.73 | 100 |
| 2003 | −19134.00 | 48810 | −2.68 | 4.02 |
| 2004 | 23095.00 | 54813 | 3.24 | 4.51 |
| 2005 | 2382.44 | 69660.17 | 0.33 | 5.73 |
| 2006 | 7670.89 | 62177 | 1.08 | 5.11 |
| 2007 | 19964.02 | 75780.57 | 2.80 | 6.23 |
| 2008 | 45465.10 | 82958.97 | 6.37 | 6.82 |
| 2009 | −24098.00 | 92912 | −3.38 | 7.64 |
| 2010 | 178089.38 | 103092 | 24.96 | 8.48 |
| 2011 | 271141.27 | 113761.71 | 38.01 | 9.36 |
| 2012 | 560655.61 | 128122.9 | 78.59 | 10.54 |
| 2013 | 619219.09 | 143638.18 | 86.80 | 11.82 |
| 2014 | 572383.83 | 163426.52 | 80.23 | 13.44 |
| 2015 | 564514.35 | 180305.19 | 79.13 | 14.83 |
| 2016 | 505222.43 | 249703.48 | 70.82 | 20.54 |
| 2017 | 534969.86 | 220033.36 | 74.99 | 18.10 |

| 2018 | 713403.61 | 242182.26 | 100 | 19.92 |
| 2019 | 141019.77 | 266060.00 | 19.77 | 21.89 |
| 2020 | 139003.77 | 269774.00 | 19.48 | 22.19 |
| *Source:* Authors' estimation | | | | |

LIC has never reported a deficit over this entire period whereas in case of private insurers, there are three years viz 2002, 2003 and 2009, where a deficit is reported reflected through the negative sign. Index of surplus/deficit is constructed taking the highest surplus as the base. For LIC, the base year is 2002 (year with highest surplus), thus the index for this year is 100. After an initial fall of 96 basis points in 2003, LIC gradually started picking up. After constant improvement till 2016, there was a slight dip in 2017 but thereafter it again picked up and has shown an impressive growth over the last three years i.e., 2018 to 2020. Private sector on the other hand, after initial ups and downs finally started showing a consistent upward trend in its surplus since 2010 till 2014, dipped in 2015 and 2016, then rose in 2017 and reached the maximum in 2018. After that, there is again a drastic fall of around 80 basis points during the last two years. It shows that LIC is more consistent in maintaining a positive surplus, which is not true for private insurers. These ups and downs in surplus also reflect the dynamics that have emerged through liberalisation. This is clearly reflected in Figure 1 given below.

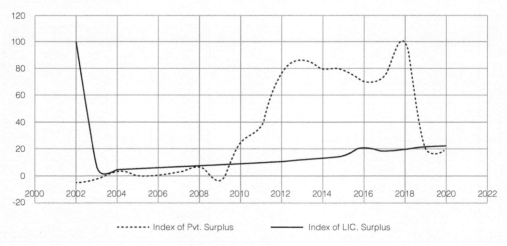

**Figure 1.** Index of Surplus
*Source:* Authors' own

Table 8 reflects certain descriptive statistics calculated using surplus of LIC and Private sector. The last column shows the ratio of private to LIC for each statistic and its interpretation is given below.

**Table 8.**　Surplus (LIC vs Private)

| | Private Surplus | LIC Surplus | Ratio of Private to LIC in %age terms |
|---|---|---|---|
| Mean | 253748.07 | 199099.91 | 127.45 |
| Standard Error | 62141.89 | 59059.47 | 105.22 |
| Median | 141019.77 | 128122.90 | 110.07 |
| Standard Deviation | 270870.21 | 257434.25 | 105.22 |
| Sample Variance | 73370668379.01 | 66272392187.91 | 110.71 |
| Kurtosis | −1.62 | 15.34 | −10.58 |
| Skewness | 0.44 | 3.76 | 11.76 |
| Range | 747158.61 | 1166877.00 | 64.03 |
| Minimum | −33755.00 | 48810.00 | −69.16 |
| Maximum | 713403.61 | 1215687.00 | 58.68 |
| Sum | 4821213.42 | 3782898.31 | 127.45 |
| Coefficient of Variation | 106.75 | 129.30 | 82.56 |
| *Source:* Authors' estimation | | | |

The mean surplus of private players is 27% more than LIC. But here it is important to mention that LIC is one company and private sector comprises of 23 companies. The median surplus of private players is also 10% higher than that of LIC. Half of the private companies have a surplus more than 141019.77 which is 10% better than LIC. Standard deviation reflects the volatility. Volatility of surplus is no different between private insurers and LIC. But if we look at the coefficient of variation, private sector is 18% less volatile than LIC because there is a spread in case of private companies because of which the volatility goes down. Also, since the mean is higher in case of private players, their coefficient of variation is less despite of the standard deviation being almost the same. Kurtosis in case of private players is negative or leptokurtic which shows that all the firms are getting average surplus over these years and in case of LIC, it is peaked which shows that most of the values are around the mean and high. Skewness is more in case of LIC which shows that LIC got an initial shock and its surplus fell down drastically but then it is rising consistently in the later years. It means that the dynamics of competition have gone down in favour of LIC whereas the private sector is variable. Minimum surplus of private players is much lower than LIC and is also negative (showing deficit). Maximum value of LIC surplus is also much higher (41% more) than private players. Therefore, the range of surplus is also 36% less in case of private players. Total surplus of private players over this entire period is 27.45% more than that of LIC because private sector represents 23 companies.

## CONTRIBUTION

This paper has contributed to the existing knowledge by providing an analysis of the growth of Indian life insurance market over the entire post reform period (2001 to 2020) and bringing out the emerging dynamics through various indicators- geographical spread, growth profile, products, channels of distribution, micro-insurance and surplus.

## CONCLUSION

Liberalisation of life insurance market ignited great hopes for improving this market by inducing competition. But it is clearly seen that there is negligible rise in life insurance penetration over the 20 year post-reform period, though density has risen at 9% per annum. LIC still remains the dominant firm in terms of total premium, new business premium and number of new policies issued. The growth rates across these categories are higher in case of private sector but this is primarily due to starting from a low base. Most of the private insurers' offices are concentrated in urban and metropolitan areas whereas LIC's offices are also growing in semi-urban and rural areas. Individual agents still enjoy greater popularity as a channel of distribution in comparison to the corporate agents. Linked business of LIC has shown a drastic fall and even in case of private players, it is receding. Private insurers have shown stupendous growth (much higher than LIC) in the micro-insurance business over the past few years which shows that private sector is trying to carve a niche as it is unable to directly compete with LIC. In terms of surplus, after an initial shock due to entry of private players, LIC has recovered and adjusted itself to show a consistent rise and even during the 2020 crisis, it has shown an impressive performance. Therefore, LIC has emerged as a hard rock and a seasoned player over this period but the private players are still struggling to have consistent growth. Competition has definitely resulted in market expansion and the market has become more dynamic- in terms of products, distribution channels, geographical spread, surplus and growth pattern. On the whole, liberalisation has partially succeeded in improving the market.

## REFERENCES

Ansari, V. A., & Fola, W. (2014). Financial soundness and performance of life insurance companies in India. *International Journal of Research, 1*(8), 224–254.

Ghosh, A. (2013). Does the insurance reform promote the development of life insurance sector in India? An empirical analysis. *Journal of Asia Business Studies, 7*(1), 31–43.

Gulati N.C., & Jain, C.M. (2011). Comparative Analysis of the Performance of All the Players of the Indian Life Insurance Industry. *VSRD International Journal of Management and Research, VSRD-IJBMR, 1*(8), 561–569.

IRDA (2009). Handbook of Indian Insurance Statistics 2007-08. Available at www.irda.gov.in. (accessed December 15, 2020).

IRDA (2013). Handbook of Indian Insurance Statistics 2011-12. Available at www.irda.gov.in. (accessed December 10, 2020).

IRDA (2015). Handbook of Indian Insurance Statistics 2013-14. Available at www.irda.gov.in. (accessed December 11, 2020).

IRDA (2017). Handbook of Indian Insurance Statistics 2015-16. Available at www.irda.gov.in. (accessed December 12, 2020).

IRDAI (2019). Handbook of Indian Insurance Statistics 2017-18. Available at www.irda.gov.in (accessed December 10, 2020).

IRDA (2021). Handbook of Indian Insurance Statistics 2019-20. Available at www.irda.gov.in (accessed March 13, 2021).

Jain, Y. (2013). Economic Reforms and World Economic Crisis: Changing Indian Life Insurance market place. *IOSR Journal of Business and Management (IOSR-JBM), 8*(1), 106–115.

Kulkarni, L. (2017). Liberalization of India's Insurance sector: An evaluation. *GIPE Working Paper 39*, Gokhale Institute of Politics and Economics, Pune (India).

Law Commission of India (2003). Consultation Paper on the revision of the Insurance Act 1938 and the Insurance Regulatory and Development Act 1999. [Online]. Available from: http://lawcommissionofindia.nic.in/consult_papers/ insurance %201-27.pdf (accessed October 30, 2013)

Shah A., Mehrotra, P., & Goyal, R. (2011). India-Insurance, Turning 10, going on 20. *The Boston Consulting Group*. Available at www.bcg.com (accessed March 15, 2014).

# CHAPTER SIX

# Pivoting business model as a strategic response to COVID-19: A study of select organizations in India

**A. Ramesh**
*Sr Assistant Professor*
*Vignana Jyothi Institute of Management, Hyderabad, Telangana, India*

COVID-19, a black swan event of the 21st century, has shocked the world and put the industry into a spin by forcing organizations to reinvent business models for survival and growth. The paper attempts to examine how several lesser-known Indian firms and reputed firms had pivoted their business models. Some of the measures of pivoting include launching new products and services which are highly relevant to existing and new markets, offering to digital experiences to name a few. The paper also attempts to examine pivoting actions and build a conceptual model based on the strategic responses made by few organizations in India.

## INTRODUCTION

Organizations need to change their business models in the event of extreme uncontrollable events. The invisible enemy of the world covid-19, had played havoc with the businesses and thereby impacting the economy of several countries. According to Mark W. Johnson, et al (2008), components of Business model include, Customer value proposition (CVP), Resources, and key processes, profit formula.

Several organizations how they have changed their business models in terms of dynamic capabilities. Organizations need to keep pace with the change in the environment and it may impact (Audia et al, 2000), The dynamic capabilities (DCs) explain how the competitive advantage can be sustained in dynamic markets (Teece et al., 1997).

In order to achieve competitive advantage, organizations can use two different but complementary strategies: fitting environmental demands and forming market change. Eisenhardt and Martin, 2000). Dynamic capabilities (The DCs) view helps in understanding how the organizations get and sustain competitive advantage in changing environments

(Teece et al., 1997; Peteraf et al., 2013) and is ingrained in the resource-based view of the firms (Eisenhardt and Martin, 2000; Zahra and George, 2002; Teece et al., 1997).

DCs are defined as "the capacity of an organization to purposefully create, extend or modify its resource base" (Helfat et al., 2007). Capacity implies acceptable level of performance, while a firm's resource base includes intangible and tangible and human resources and capabilities that a firm possesses, controls or to which it has preferential access (Helfat et al., 2007) which are important to the organization.

Organizational capabilities are classified into into DCs and operational capabilities. Operational capabilities allow an organization to perform basic functional activities (Collis, 1994) and help in day-to-day problem-solving (Zahra et al., 2006). Dynamic capabilities (Cs) are of higher order (Barreto, 2010), path dependent (Teece et al., 1997) and future oriented (Ambrosini and Bowman, 2009).

However, DCs do not directly result in marketable goods or services (Teece et al., 1997), but contribute to building, integrating and reconfiguring operational capabilities (Protogerou et al., 2012).

Marketing capabilities are important in DC's framework as generate customer knowledge, competing products and distribution channels. (Barrales-Molina et al., 2014). Marketing capabilities emphasizes customer value (Fang and Zou, 2009). Zou, 2009; Landroguez et al., 2011 and considered to be subset of DC's (Bruni and Verona, 2009). There is a relationship between Marketing capabilities and CVP, and resources and key processes. The dynamic marketing capabilities are important.

Bruni, D. S., & Verona, G. (2009) defined "Dynamic marketing capabilities" (DM's)  as indicating human capital, social capital, and the cognition of managers involved in the creation, use, and integration of market knowledge and marketing resources in order to match and create market and technological change. Market knowledge consists of customer and competitor areas (e.g., Kohli and Jaworski, 1990; Narver, and Slater, 1990); marketing resources are tangible and intangible assets such as products, brands, and distribution channels (Grant, 1991). Dynamic marketing capabilities involves middle management and enables organization to cope with the change.

According to Mark W. Johnson, Clayton M. Christensen, and Henning Kagermann (Harvard business review 2008), Business model components include, CVP, Resources, and key processes, profit formula.

India reported first laboratory-confirmed case of coronavirus disease 2019 (COVID-19) on 30 January from Kerala. As the cases spread across the country lockdown was imposed on March 25, 2020. The prevailing new conditions are referred as the new normal. The norms of social distancing, wearing mask and handwashing was advocated to fight against the Covid-19.

## OBJECTIVES OF THE PAPER

1. To explore the strategic responses made by select organizations in response to Covid-19.
2. The strategic responses are examined in the light of customer value proposition, resources, for the new and existing markets etc.
3. To build conceptual model to understand strategic responses made by the organizations.

### Suparshava Swabs

During March 2020, polyester swabs were not manufactured in India and were imported, and as the demand rose, but it was becoming expensive. It provided an opportunity to domestic market. A Delhi based organization, Suparshava Swabs came forward and successfully pivoted to manufacture personal hygiene products including swabs under Tulip's brand. It converted its 100% cotton processing unit at Ghaziabad factory to produce polyester-spun swabs required for covid 19 testing. It is important to note that these are validated by national reputed govt agencies such as ICMR & NIV.

### IHCL

IHCL launched Qmin, a mobile app in July 2020 to brings its collection of culinary experience online from restaurants to customers' homes in Mumbai, Delhi, Kolkata, Bengaluru, Chennai etc. The app was designed with Tata Digital in six weeks, which showcases customer centricity, resilience and sustainability. It offers guests a discerning delivery experience through a seamless interface which allows personalization of orders, curate menus, and track deliveries real-time."

### 10 by 10

The organization diversified portfolio by launching ISO.POD which is an instant room, a portable solution that protects people against infection and based on DIY methodology. ISO. POD comes in the size of 8' × 7' × 10', making it compact, modular, and easy to duplicate and scale. During the lockdown as hospitals are running out of beds, this product innovation which acts airtight enclosure comes as great rescue and priced at Rs 15,000.

### Shree Shakti Enterprises

Shree Shakti Enterprises, a kitchenware company during lockdown was forced to innovate for survival by launching new product portfolio comprising sensor-based sanitiser dispensers to hands-free hand wash systems, and automatic foot sanitisers, which are extremely useful during covid 19 crisis. These can be used at offices etc. Shree Shakti received large orders from public, and government institutions, and private organizations including Hero Moto Corp, Wipro, Mohalla Clinics, the Ministry of Home Affairs, CRPF, BSF, police stations, and political parties. This allowed the company to avoid job cuts and gross Rs 1.15 crore in sales through the lockdown. This enabled the company to stop job cuts and gross Rs 1.15 crore in sales through the lockdown.

## Boiline India

Indore-based Bioline India, founded in 2001, manufactures affordable and quality medical equipment. Hand sanitizers were slow moving category till pandemic struck, and it became most important item of the households and probably will remain for few years. The organization launched ULV Bio Fooger in 2005 and increased production to meet the full demand.

## Fabindia

Fabindia stores were shut during lockdown, but as the government allowed the sales of essential items and hygiene products, the organization decided to increase production. The hygiene products grew to 15 to 20 % of business from 2% to 3%. Teamwork and collaboration played key role in success of the new activity.

## Workshala

Established in 2013, Workshala started an initiative called Homescape to provide the tables, chairs and desks to individuals at homes. This provided comfort and ease of working for those who are working from home. This resulted in increase in productivity.

## Hula Global

Founded in 218, Hula Global is a Noida based organization manufactures apparel and also used to exports was badly hit by pandemic. It diversified its business into PPE kits, N95 masks, face shields. The company invested significantly to expand its manufacturing capacity from 10,000 coveralls a month to 10 lakh coveralls a month. From zero N95 masks in March, it is now producing 80,00,000 masks monthly. Very few organizations make all these products under one roof.

## Koko boost

Koko boost is a Bengaluru based small organization which manufactures millets and monga energy bars. Distributors were reluctant to stock during Covid-19, as the customers were not preferring to purchase. This affected the business badly and company decided to widen its product portfolio. The company decided to make innovative range of immunity-based products under brand name "Santrupt" made from the existing input and used social media for promotions.

## Homz

Homz is a construction company a Delhi based company started in 1989. It is a niche player in high end luxury residential projects, reached out to its customers by giving them digital experience, and closed sales.

## Parle-G

The brand had phenomenal success and achieved highest sales during covid-19, which is highest ever for eight decades. The brand Parle-G brand falls under the 'below-Rs100 per kg' affordable / value category, which holds one-third of the total industry revenues and accounts for over 50% of the volume sold. Getting permissions to run plant, manning people to work at factories and sales, and educating the labor and onboarding on the fact that it's just not mundane biscuit but providing food security for vast majority of the people by virtue of sheer size of consumption across the country. As govt placed it under essential commodities, the organization shifted to Digital strategy, advertising on OTT and social media for promotions. The other reasons include, there is increase in home consumption during lock down and some consumers also downgraded to Parle-G, buying whichever is available. Reduced workforce as per restrictions is also a challenge for the organization.

## Cavin care

CavinKare's launched hand sanitizer under its well-known personal care brands of Chik, Nyle, Raaga. It provided much needed accessibility and affordability to ensure safety of everyone. Everybody must regularly wash hands or use sanitizer for safety and to fight Covid-19.

## ITC

ITC' had launched Savlon Surface Disinfectant Spray as part of the ongoing fight against Covid-19. As the health stipulations have instructed two important facets to help protect against the deadly virus – hand hygiene and the hygiene of frequently touched surfaces. Savlon spray would disinfect frequently touched surfaces such as tables, doorknobs, chairs, and sofas, among others, which may have germs that can be transmitted and increase the chances of infection. See Table 1 for summary of the pivoting actions taken by organizations.

**Table 1.** Pivot actions taking by organizations

| Name of the firms | Challenges & opportunities, and other key issues faced by the organization | Pivoting actions |
|---|---|---|
| 1. Suparshva swabs | Regulation from ICMR and NIV | special swabs under the Tulips brand. |
| 2. IHCL | The lockdown period saw a significant increase in the time spent by people on their mobile devices, and food being an essential commodity was readily available at the doorstep. | An app that gives guests a differentiated delivery experience through a seamless interface that allows them to personalise their orders, curate menus, and track deliveries real-time. |
| 3. Bioline india | Targeting the same customers with different product | Bioline India finds itself playing a bigger role in the daily battle against bacteria with its ULV Bio Fogger. |
| 4. Fabindia | The government was allowing the sales of essential items and hygiene products during the lockdown | Decided to ramp up its organic foods production. |

| 5. Workshaala | As most people started working from home amidst the pandemic, furniture is required which gives comfort and ease in working. | Homescape' to provide furniture to people working from home. tables, chairs, and desks to individuals. |
|---|---|---|
| 7. Hula global | To meet the rising demand for such products in the country. | Diversified into manufacturing PPE kits, N95 masks, face shields, etc., |
| 8. Koko boost | To take care of the immunity | brand of immunity-boosting powders made from moringa |
| 9. Gulshan homz | Digitisation and virtual tours have been started by realtors, and this has helped them reach their target audience and close substantial sales even during the lockdown." | "Digitisation and virtual tours |
| 10. 10 by 10 | During Covid-19, the hospitals were running out of beds and ventilators. | ISO.POD — an instant isolation room solution that protects people against further infection. |
| 11. ITC | To protect families and remove germs from vegetables | Launch of safe veg wash |
| 12. DETTOL | To protect families and remove germs | Handwash and sanitizer |
| 13. Shree Shakti Enterprises | To meet the safety demand of corporate customers arising of covid -19 crisis | From sensor-based sanitiser dispensers to hands-free hand wash systems, and automatic foot sanitisers, |
| 14. Parle-G | To meet surging demand from at home, NGO' s and migrant and poor people segment. | Focus on production, distribution, getting permissions. |
| 15. Cavin care | low priced sanitize for the on-the-go segment | Chick sanitizer |
| 16. ITC | To meet safety demands arising out of the covid-19 | Surface disinfectant |

*Source:* Prepared by the author based on secondary data.

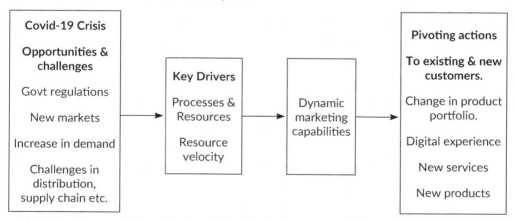

**Figure 1.** Proposed Conceptual model for Strategic response of Organizations to covid-19
*Source:* created by author

## CONCLUSION

The dreaded pandemic Covid-19, had forced the industry into turmoil which led to unprecedented challenges. These varied from, restrictions on labour availability, regulatory constraints and compliances, supply chain and promotion challenges to name a few. The organizations mobilized available resources at a fast pace (resource velocity), explored opportunities for new products, new services, create new customer experience offline or digital, at the same time ensuring employee safety. The organizations created new and strong value proposition, for new and existing market. They also widened product portfolio, sometimes giving impetus to the new product launches, increasing production, and using digital media for promotions etc. Most importantly these strategies had a positive bearing on top and bottom line of the organizations.

## REFERENCES

1. Bruni, D.S. and Verona, G. (2009), "Dynamic marketing capabilities in science-based firms: an exploratory investigation of the pharmaceutical industry", British Journal of Management, Vol. 20, pp. S101–S117

2. Barrales-Molina, V., Martínez-Lopez, F.J. and Gázquez-Abad, J.C. (2014), "Dynamic marketing capabilities: toward an integrative framework", International Journal of Management Reviews, Vol. 16 No. 4, pp. 397–416.

3. Fang, E.E. and Zou, S. (2009), "Antecedents and consequences of marketing dynamic capabilities in international joint ventures", Journal of International Business Studies, Vol. 40 No. 5, pp. 742–761.

4. Landroguez, S.M., Castro, C.B. and Cepeda-Carrion, G. (2011), "Creating dynamic capabilities to increase customer value", Management Decision, Vol. 49, pp. 1141–1159.

5. Zou, S., Fang, E. and Zhao, S. (2003), "The effect of export marketing capabilities on export performance: an investigation of chinese exporters", Journal of International Marketing, Vol. 11 No. 4, pp. 32–55.

6. Teece, D.J., Pisano, G. and Shuen, A. (1997), "Dynamic capabilities and strategic management", Strategic Management Journal, Vol. 18 No. 7, pp. 509–533.

7. Landroguez, S.M., Castro, C.B. and Cepeda-Carrion, G. (2011), "Creating dynamic capabilities to increase customer value", Management Decision, Vol. 49, pp. 1141–1159.

8. Collis, D.J. (1994), "Research note: how valuable are organizational capabilities?", Strategic Management Journal, Vol. 15 No. S1, pp. 143–152.

9. Eisenhardt, K.M. and Martin, J.A. (2000), "Dynamic capabilities: what are they?", Strategic Management Journal, Vol. 21 Nos 10/11, pp. 1105–1121.

10. Helfat, C.E., Finkelstein, S., Mitchell, W., Peteraf, M.A., Singh, H., Teece, D. and Winter, S.G. (2007), Dynamic Capabilities: Understanding Strategic Change in Organizations, Blackwell, London.

11. Bruni, D. S., & Verona, G. (2009). Dynamic marketing capabilities in Science-based firms: An exploratory investigation of the pharmaceutical industry. British Journal of management, 20, S101–S117.

12. Nohria, N. (2020). What organizations need to survive a pandemic. Harvard Business Review: Boston, MA, USA, 30.

14. Nitin Nohri (2020) observed the ability to sense continuously and develop response capabilities are key aspects of organizations preparedness in the light of the covid-19 pandemic.

15. Fang, E.E. and Zou, S. (2009), "Antecedents and consequences of marketing dynamic capabilities in international joint ventures", Journal of International Business Studies, Vol. 40 No. 5, pp. 742–761

16. Audia, P.G., Locke, E.A. and Smith, K.G. (2000), "The paradox of success: an archival and a laboratory study of strategic persistence following radical environmental change", Academy of Management Journal, Vol. 43 No. 5, pp. 837–853

17. Zahra, S.A. and George, G. (2002), "Absorptive capacity: a review, reconceptualization, and extension", The Academy of Management Review, Vol. 27 No. 2, pp. 185–203.

18. Peteraf, M.A., Di Stefano, G. and Verona, G. (2013), "The elephant in the room of dynamic capabilities: bringing two diverging conversations together", Strategic Management Journal, Vol. 34 No. 12, pp. 1389–1410

19. Johnson, M. W., Christensen, C. M., & Kagermann, H. (2008). Reinventing your business model. Harvard business review, 86(12), 57–68.

20. Kholi, A. and B. Jaworski (1990). 'Market Orientation: The Construct, Research Propositions, and Managerial Implications', Journal of Marketing, 57, pp. 53–70.

21. Grant, R. M. (1991). 'The Resource-based Theory of Competitive Advantage: Implications for Strategy Formulation', California Management Review, 33, pp. 114–134.

22. Narver, J. C. and S. F. Slater (1990). 'The Effect of a Market Orientation on Business Performance', Journal of Marketing, 54, pp. 20–35.

22. https://www.dnaindia.com/business/report-parle-g-records-best-sales-in-8-decades-during-covid-19-lockdown-2827364

23. https://www.businessinsider.in/advertising/brands/article/how-parle-g-continues-to-exceed-its-sales-record-despite-a-recession/articleshow/77489835.cms

24. https://yourstory.com/smbstory/indian-brands-pivot-persist-covid-19-economic-challenge?utm_pageloadtype=scroll

25. https://yourstory.com/smbstory/indian-brands-pivot-persist-covid-19-economic-challenge?utm_pageloadtype=scroll

26. https://yourstory.com/smbstory/covid-19-testing-india-polyester-suparshva-swabs-business

27. https://yourstory.com/smbstory/taj-hotels-covid-19-ihcl-travel-tourism-hospitality

28. https://www.product.10by10.co/isopod

29. https://yourstory.com/smbstory/small-industry-day-india-smbs-covid-19

30. https://yourstory.com/smbstory/msme-bioline-india-indore-medical-equipment-covid-19-ulv-bio-fogger

31. https://www.thehindubusinessline.com/companies/cavinkare-extends-its-beverages-portfolio-launches-fruit-based-carbonated-drinks/article33675271.ece

32. https://brandequity.economictimes.indiatimes.com/news/business-of-brands/cavinkare-launches-sanitizers-under-chik-nyle-and-raaga-brands/74910875

33. https://www.itcportal.com/ReturnViewImage.aspx?fileid=1451

34. https://www.thehindu.com/news/national/indias-first-coronavirus-infection-confirmed-in-kerala/article30691004.ece

# CHAPTER SEVEN

# A study on Marketing Strategies of Banking Services during Covid times

**Dr. Sheeja R**
*Associate Professor*
*CMS Institute of Management Studies, Coimbatore, Tamil Nadu, India*
*Email: sheeja.ramakrishnan@gmail.com*

**Mrs Namitha Krishnan**
*MPhil Scholar*
*Nehru College of Management, Coimbatore, Tamil Nadu, India*
*Email: namiz8@gmail.com*

**Abstract**—*The main intent of this paper is to assess the prevailing literature on marketing of banking services in Kerala. The Indian banking system, by custom and practise, considered deposit growth as the business objective and other parameters such as productivity, profitability, beneficiary satisfaction, etc. were considered less important. Banks today are functioning in a highly competitive and briskly changing environment. In the fluctuating economic scenario, a professional approach to business development is vital and the persistence of a banking institution depends on its capacity to take up challenges coming up in the environment. Developing business through marketing of bank's services is one of the crucial areas which need attention of the bankers to ensure profitable survival. A marketing strategy, in general, is a systematic, appropriate and feasible set of concepts and actions through which the institution strives to achieve its goal of beneficiary satisfaction and profitable survival. Strategy should be designed after taking into account the strengths and weaknesses of the organisation. The operational aspects of strategies for marketing contain actions such as development of Relationship Banking, designing of effective delivery system, ensuring beneficiary-oriented services and modifying the system into a personal selling organisation. In western banking, officials assigned the job of personally contacting the beneficiaries and offering the services at doorsteps was been able to make a significant impact on the development of business for their organisations. The importance and role of personal selling and beneficiary contacts in* *the marketing efforts of a banking institution stem from the success of such efforts in many banking institutions all over the world.*

**Keywords**—Indian Banking System, Relationship Banking, Marketing Mix, Product/ Service Mix, Promotion Mix, Beneficiary Satisfaction

# 1. INTRODUCTION

Banks are the most important constituents of the financial infrastructure of a country. They play a vital role in bringing about desired change in the economic development of the country. The size and composition of banking transactions mirror the economic happenings in the country. Banks provide a convenient avenue for investment of surplus funds, and to the investor a source to finance. Thus, they, as 'Repositories of People's Savings', mobilise small and scattered savings of the community and as 'Purveyors of Credit' channelize the savings so mobilised into the production of capital goods and thereby facilitate capital formation[3]. By providing cheap and timely credit to the best of the schemes, they help in optimum utilisation of scarce productive resources and in keeping the production cost low. Further, by providing remittance facility with their vast branch network help free flow of funds over different parts of the country wherever there is a need for it instead of allowing them to lie dormant in stagnant pools. They help in the implementation of various welfare programmes of the Government and are also of tremendous help to the Government in meeting plan objectives by directing the resources through desired channels.

Market development and Market penetration were the focus in 1970s when banks expanded their area of operation by opening more branches. Banks developed new products and services in the 1980s to cater to the various needs of increasing number of customers. With the advent of banking sector reforms in the 1990s the scenario of banking has totally changed. In order to bring efficiency, accountability and high degree of customer services, competition has been induced by granting license for banking business to new operators like private banks, regional rural banks and cooperative banks. In such a competitive environment the ability of a bank to achieve growth rate depends on how well the needs of customers are identified and effective Marketing strategies evolved. This involves developing new and improved products and services, providing better amenities and facilities, exploring new distribution channels, and evolving effective Marketing strategies so as to continuously meet the changing customer needs. During 1990s the financial sector and implicitly the banking sector experienced a significant growth in the developed countries.

During the 21st century, the banks act in a dynamic environment, where the Market and the other factors (components of the political, economic, social, juridical, cultural, demographical and technological environment) frequently raise problems, forcing them to additional efforts or offering them opportunities that need to be fructified as well as possible; they need to integrate their current actions to their long term objectives which were previously determined by the bank Marketing policy. Adapting the banking institutions activity to the environment requires a continuous tracking of the structural quality and quantity changes which the environments register or will register. In order to successfully achieve the purpose of the Marketing process the banks should perform analysis in order to know the bank customers to the highest possible extent, so that the offered banking products/services match their needs and the sale is ensured, systematically analyse the financial Market identifying the profitable Markets, the new agencies, intermediaries and entrepreneurs acting on these Markets and efficiently using their own resources in order to create new banking products/services and to diversify them according to the consumers' wishes and expectations. Hallowell Roger conducted a research on customer satisfaction, loyalty and profitability and found that as compared to public sector, private sector bank customer's level of satisfaction is higher.

Today banks can look back with satisfaction by having responded effectively to the challenges put before them from time to time – whether of social control or of reforms. In future, the banks will have to adjust their system of functioning, venturing into new areas, improve efficiency levels by inclusion of trained and skilled manpower and restructure their organizations. Then only they can face the challenges of the future more confidently and proactively.

## 2. LITERATURE REVIEW

Marketing by service industries is yet to gain momentum, especially when it comes to marketing by commercial banks. Marketing orientation of banks is imperative for survival and success. Marketing of financial services by banks is under active and extensive discussion among academicians and bank personnel survey and research have been conducted by both academic researchers and practitioners on the various aspects of services marketing in general and financial services marketing by banks in particular both in India as well as abroad.

Leorge William R and Hiran C Barksdale studied the marketing activities in the service firms and discovered that services' marketing is generally on the low ebb. Service firms tend to be less marketing oriented less likely to have marketing mix activities carried out in the marketing department; less likely to perform analysis in the area of service product more likely to undertake advertising internally rather than go to specialized advertising agencies less likely to have overall sales plan less likely to develop sales training programmes less likely to utilize the services marketing consultants and marketing research firms and less likely to spend much on marketing, as a percentage of gross sales'.

Bessom, Richard M and Donald W Jackson jr referred that 400 service and marketing firms revealed that service firms are less likely to have marketing departments, to make use of sales planning and training, and to employ marketing professionals like consultants, advertising firms and market research agencies. Today, the banking sector is changing in terms of providing the customer with what he wants, when he wants and where he wants. Thus, the element of marketing which was unheard of in earlier days of banking has assumed great significance in today's world of stiff competition. As such, no bank today can do without marketing its services.

Sarkar, Kaptan and Sagane reveal that most of the work in the area of marketing of financial services has been undertaken in countries like USA and U. K. This area of research has not received much attention of the researchers in India. A few studies which have been conducted in India reveal that no comprehensive study has been carried out to make a comparative analysis of marketing strategies of the public, private and foreign banks in India.

B. N. Bhattacharya, Koparkar, Sreedar have dealt with marketing in commercial banks. They have emphasized motivation research, marketing research and promotional aspects in marketing of services and suggested to improve the marketing strategies to cope with the changing environment. Nascenzi pointed out that though bankers use market segmentation they were yet to identify and locate their best customers. He suggested that market segmentation must be used to define profitable target customers.

R.M. Chidambaram and K. Alamelu enunciated the measures to face the challenges in marketing of services in view of proliferation of financial services. They emphasized the need for learning about the customer and developing strategies for future. Berry, Kehoe and Lindgreen's found that most frustrating aspects of bank marketing were 1) lack of management support 2) lack of interdepartmental co-operation 3) crisis management 4) government intrusion 5) advertising and media problems.

Zeitham and Bitner identified that one of the most basic concepts in marketing is the marketing mix, defined as the elements of an organisation controls that can be used to satisfy the customers unlike marketing of products. The services also have four elements in the marketing mix, viz. product, price, place and promotion. Apart from that, there are three more elements, people, process and physical evidence, in the marketing mix for service marketing. A combination of these seven Ps makes marketing offers of the service provider. Kaptan studied marketing aims not only at delivering (selling) whatever products (schemes and services) banks have but also creating products as per customer needs.

# 3.  OBJECTIVES OF THE STUDY

- To investigate into the marketing process
- To understand the banking behaviour
- To study the present banking scenario
- To analyze the 7p's of marketing mix

# 4.  STRUCTURE OF BANKING INDUSTRY

The organised banking system in India can be broadly divided into three categories, viz., the central bank of the country known as the Reserve Bank of India, the Commercial banks and Cooperative banks. Another and more common classification of banks in India is between scheduled and non – scheduled banks. The Reserve Bank of India is the supreme monetary and banking authority in the country and has the responsibility to control the banking system in the country. It keeps cash reserves of all scheduled banks and hence it is known as the "Reserve Bank".

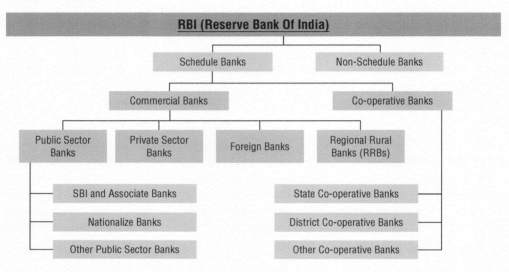

## 5. TYPES OF BANKS IN INDIA

A. **Commercial Banks:** Commercial Banks in India consist of Public Sector Banks, Private sector Banks and Foreign banks in India.

    **i.** **Public Sector Banks:** Public Sector Banks include State Bank of India and its associate banks called the State Bank group, 20 nationalized banks and Regional Rural Banks mainly sponsored by Public Sector Banks.

    ii. **Private Sector Banks:** Private Sector Banks includes Old generation private banks and new generation private banks in India.

    iii. **Foreign banks:** The foreign banks were referred as "Exchange banks" as their transactions primarily related to foreign exchange and foreign trade. The 'Indian Central Banking Enquiry Committee Report' (1931) pointed out that the entire foreign exchange was virtual monopoly of these banks.

B. **Cooperative Banks:** Cooperative Banks in India consists of State Co-operative Banks, Central Co-operative Banks, Primary Agriculture Credit Societies, Land Development Banks, Urban Co-operative Banks, Primary Agricultural Development Banks, Primary Land Development Banks and State Land Development Banks.

C. **Development Banks:** Development Banks in India are Industrial Finance Corporation of India (IFCI), Industrial Development Bank of India (IDBI), Industrial Credit and Investment Corporation of India (ICICI), Industrial Investment Bank of India (IIBI),

Small Industries Development Bank of India (SIDBI), SCICI Ltd, National Bank for Agriculture and Rural Development (NABARD), Export Import Bank of India and National Housing Bank.

# 6. NATIONALIZATION OF BANKS

Nationalization of banks began with the passing of the Reserve Bank (Transfer of Public Ownership) Act 1948, which became law on the 3rd September, 1948. It was thought desirable to nationalize the bank to ensure greater co-ordination of monetary, economic and Fiscal policies. The nationalization of the Reserve Bank was, indeed, necessary in the interests of large–scale planning upon which the Union Government had embarked. The objective of this nationalization was to enhance the ability of the banking system to meet more effectively the needs of the development of the economy and to promote the welfare of the people more adequately. The nationalized banks play a new and pioneering role in helping the public sector get on its feet. If banks do not function effectively, nationalization may promote serious dislocations and distortions in the economy, and a transfer of deposits may take place from the nationalized banks to the smaller banks which are still in the private sector.

## 6.1 Reasons for Nationalization

The important reasons for the nationalization of major banks in India can be enumerated as follows:
* Equitable distribution of economic power
* To provide finance to neglected sectors of agriculture, small-scale industries etc.
* Removal of malpractices
* Expansion of banking facilities

## 6.2 Objectives behind Nationalization of Banks

The main objectives behind the nationalization of banks are as follows:
* Social Welfare
* Controlling Private Monopolies
* Expansion of Banking
* Reducing Regional Imbalance
* Priority Sector Lending
* Developing Banking Habits

# 7. ECONOMIC REFORMS OF THE BANKING SECTOR

Indian banking sector has undergone major changes and reforms during economic reforms. Though it was a part of overall economic reforms, it has changed the very functioning of Indian banks. This reform has not only influenced the productivity and efficiency of many of the Indian Banks, but has left everlasting footprints on the working of the banking sector in India. Some of the important reforms in the banking sector in India are:

- Reduced Cash Reserve Ratio (CRR) and Statutory Liquidity Ratio (SLR)
- Deregulation of Interest Rate
- Fixing prudential Norms
- Introduction of Capital to Risk Weighted Asset Ratio
- Operational Autonomy
- Banking Diversification
- Emergence of New Generation Banks
- Improved Profitability and Efficiency

# 8. CHALLENGES FACED BY INDIAN BANKING INDUSTRY

- **Rural Market:** Banking in India is generally fairly mature in terms of supply, product range and research even though reach in rural India, still remains a challenge for the private sector and foreign banks.
- **Management of Risks:** With gradual deregulation, banks are exposed to different types of risks. Banks face various market risks like Interest rate risk, Liquidity risk, Exchange risk etc.
- **Growth of Banking:** As the Indian banks move gradually beyond universal banking and position themselves as financial service providers, banking business is getting redefined. The structure of Indian banking system may be expected to undergo a transformation, the main drives of which will be consolidation, convergence and technology.
- **Market Discipline and Transparency:** Banks are expected to be more responsive and accountable to the investors.
- **Human Resource Management:** On account of introduction of certain advanced technology, there would also be a strong case for recruiting fresh talent with attractive pay and perquisites.
- **Global Banking:** It is practically and fundamentally impossible for any nation to exclude itself from world economy. Therefore, for sustainable development, one has to adopt integration process in the form of liberalization and globalization
- **Financial Inclusion:** Financial inclusion has become a necessity in today's business environment. Whatever is produced by business hours, that has to be under check from period with continuous net losses for over 6 years, erosion of entire net worth, adverse media publicity, consequent low morale of staff, and a throttled decision making process.
- **Employee's Retention:** Long time banking employees are becoming disenchanted with the industry and are often resistant to perform up to new expectations. The diminishing employee morale results in decreasing revenue.
- **Environmental Concerns:** The object is to assist in enhancing the public and political awareness of the actions that could have a significant impact on global emissions growth and to disseminate the message that it is time to act.

- **Social and ethical aspects:** There are some banks which proactively undertake the responsibility to bear the social and ethical aspects of banking.
- **Customer retention:** In India, currently, there are two types of customers – one who is a multichannel user and the other who still relies on a branch as the anchor channel. The primary challenge is to give consistent service to customers irrespective of the kind of the channel they choose to use.

## 9. BANKING MARKETING PERIOD

It is also known as modern period. The frantic pace of branch expansion and credit disbursement during the development banking period has direct impact on the health of public sector banks. The real outcome was the proliferation of loss-making branches. The problem of communication and transport network in the countryside, rising customer dissatisfaction with banking services, and resultant apathy of bank staff towards developmental work are the basic reasons for this. The RBI urged commercial banks to take stock of the state of affairs, to consolidate their gains and go slow on branch expansion, thus ushering in the period of consolidation. The bank visualises the risk inherent in continuing to do business as before. So there is a growing awareness that marketing was an essential tool in the hands of the banker, an inescapable necessity without which perhaps survival itself might become difficult in future.

Bank Marketing is defined as "identifying the most profitable markets now and in future, assessing the present and future needs of customers, setting business development goals and making plans to meet them, managing the various services and promoting them to achieve the plans – all in the context of a changing environment in the market". Marketing thus aims not only at delivering whatever products banks have but also creating new products as per customer needs. As far as India is concerned, the position of marketing in the banking industry has been quite dismal.

Banks essentially deal in services and not products. "Financial service is any act or performance that one party can offer to another; it is essentially intangible and does not result in ownership of anything. It broadly includes investment activities in terms of investment management, investment advice and investment arrangement. Berry has contrasted services from goods by defining "a good as an object, a device or a thing. A service is a deed, a performance and an effort. When goods are purchased, something tangible is acquired. When a service is purchased, there is generally nothing tangible to show for it. Services are consumed but not possessed.

According to Federal Express, the giant express delivery organization, services have been redefined as all actions and reactions which customers perceive they have purchased. The above definitions clearly show that services do have certain specific characteristics which make them different from goods. These are broadly defined as intangibility, perishability, heterogeneity and inseparability of production and consumption.

## 10. MARKETING MIX FOR BANKING SERVICES

The formulation of marketing mix for the banking services is the prime responsibility of the bank professional who based on their expertise and excellence attempt to market the services and schemes profitably.

The bank professionals having world class excellence make possible frequency in the innovation process which simplifies their task of selling more but spending less. The four sub mixes of the marketing mix, such as the product mix, the promotion mix, the price mix and the place mix, no doubt, are found significant even to the banking organizations but in addition to the traditional combination of receipts, the marketing experts have also been talking about some more mixes for getting the best result. The "People" as a sub mix is now found getting a new place in the management of marketing mix. It is right to mention that the quality of people/employees serving an organization assumes a place of outstanding significance. This requires a strong emphasis on the development of personally-committed, value-based, efficient employees who contribute substantially to the process of making the efforts cost effective. In addition, we also find some of the marketing experts talking about a new mix, i.e. physical appearance. In the corporate world, the personal care dimension thus becomes important. The employees re supposed to be well dressed, smart and active. Besides, we also find emphasis on "Process" which gravitates our attention on the way of offering the services. It is only not sufficient that you promise quality services. It is much more impact generating that your promises reach to the ultimate users without any distortion. The banking organizations, of late, face a number of challenges and the organizations assigning an overriding priority to the formulation processes get a success. The formulation of marketing mix is just like the combination of ingredients, spices in the cooking process.

## 11. THE 7 P'S OF MARKETING MIX

The marketing mix is a key foundation on which most modern marketing strategies and business activities are based. The concept of the 'Marketing Mix' came about in the 1960s when Neil H. Borden, professor and academic, elaborated on James Culliton's concept of the marketing mix. Culliton described business executives as 'mixers of ingredients': the ingredients being different marketing concepts, aspects, and procedures. However, it's now widely accepted that Jerome McCarthy founded the concept. After all, it was McCarthy who offered the marketing mix as we know it today; in the form of 'The 4Ps of Marketing': Product, Place, Price, & Promotion. The 4Ps then paved the way for two modern academics, Booms and Bitner, who, in 1981, brought us the extended version of the marketing mix: the '7Ps'. The 7Ps comprise McCarthy's 4 original elements, and extend to include a further 3 factors: Physical Evidence, People, & Processes.

## 11.1 Product / Service

Product/service define the core offering of a business. In banking industry, managers must strive to satisfy customers as customers are after value and benefits. Kotler and Armstrong (2013) define product as anything tangible or intangible offered to a market for attention, use and consumption with aim of satisfying needs and wants of customers. In this definition, they consider product to include services. Products in banks includes different accounts for customers to use for example current accounts, savings accounts, save for children, other products are investment advice, loans and agencies. Researches have established relation between product and customer satisfaction. Banks must encourage customers to open account and increase the service quality with different product innovation in order to achieve competitive advantage. Therefore, the relationship between service and customer satisfaction has been established.

The main products of Banks are Saving Account, Current Account, Forex Department, Salary Accounts and Demat Account. The other products are Home loan, personal loan, Insurance, Credit cards, etc.

## 11.2 Price

Bank offers an assortment of financial services to its esteemed customers. It has a very clear-cut pricing policy. It deals in a competitive market and so it has a policy that involves improvisation at each level. The bank's value added strategies are made keeping in mind and analysing the customer's mind set and economic changes happening in the market. It has also started an aggressive pricing policy that involves acquisition through low-cost funds. The bank's main aim is to eliminate competition in the banking field. The bank offers loans and schemes to attract its customer. The rates are evaluated at regular periods and changed to suit the needs and demands of both the bank and the customer. The price of the product depends upon the services provided by the Bank on the respective product to the customers.

## 11.3 Place

Place plays an important role in tangibilizing service offerings. Quality of service is perceived by many customers in the form of place of delivery - locational appeal, interiors, ambience, etc. If a bank is located in a crowded market the place or location will be a negative tangibilizes. Providing excellent tangibles in the form of place or location and interiors is particularly important for appealing to the customers segment. More recently, some of the private banks in India are providing very attractive tangibles in the form of their locations, exteriors and interiors.

The places acts as a distribution channel for the banking facilities where services are provided anytime 24*7.The concept of Internet banking and using of technology for any kind of services is encouraged. All its branches are equipped with modern facilities. The bank has opened various information centres where all the related queries can be answered.

## 11.4 Promotion

The promotion strategy of Banks comprises of direct and indirect communication to the customers. Besides emphasizing on the modernization of its banking facilities stress is also laid on the benefits one gets on using the banks services. The benefit of each product is highlighted so that the clients become impressed and they are forced to grasp the services of this bank. Promotion can tangibilize services in different forms:

- Visualization
- Association
- Physical representation
- Documentation.

Visualization tangibilizes services through hoardings, TV and print campaigns or advertisements. Physical representation in services has a good promotional appeal to customers like use of colours to symbolize wealth and status. Service providers use documentation in their promotions in support of their claims for dependability, popularity and responsiveness

## 11.5 People

People, refers to those involved in service delivery. Their level of training, interpersonal behaviour, discretion in rendering the service and appearance matters a lot in customer satisfaction in banking industry. Thorsten (2004) opines that customer orientation of service employees is a key driver of customer satisfaction. The interaction of employees and customers create good customer satisfaction. Customers rely on bank employees for advice, complaint and direction towards some of the banks' products and channel of distribution. Interaction quality is an important factor when customers evaluate service quality.

People are a common factor in every service. And people tangibilize services. Good people (means good performance) make good or successful services. Bad performers deliver bad services.

## 11.6 Process

Process shows procedure of rendering services. Banks should create a good service process to maintain satisfied customers and attract potential customers. Banks are constantly taking initiatives to offer the best in class service that seek to enhance customer experience.

## 11.7 Physical Evidence

This deals with environment where business operates. It includes reducing of paper usage, gives higher standard of services through product innovation, Satisfies the diverse need of individual and corporate clients, customer centric, and service oriented.

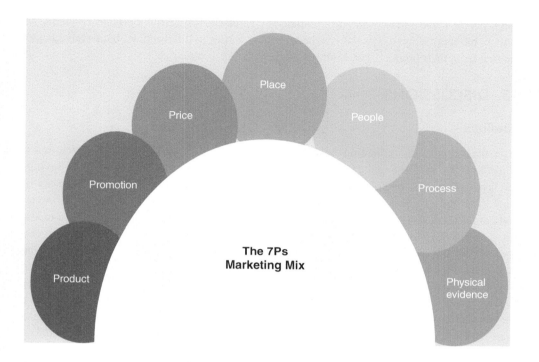

The 7Ps
Marketing Mix

## 12. PERCEPTIONS OF BENEFICIARIES

With the current change in the functional orientation of banks, the purpose of banking is being redefined. The main driver of this change is changing beneficiary needs and expectations. Beneficiaries in urban India no longer want to wait in long queues and spend hours in banking transactions. This change in beneficiary attitude has gone hand in hand with the development of ATMs, phone and net banking along with availability of service right at the beneficiaries door step. Further, the world class banking experience provided by private and multinational banks with their ever evolving products and services has raised the bar of beneficiary expectations.

With the emergence of universal banking, banks aim to provide all banking product and service offerings under one roof and their Endeavour is to be beneficiary centric. The Indian banking industry is also embracing technology rapidly. Big players among the private and public sector banks are reengineering and automating their core banking processes.

Beneficiary Satisfaction is a key indicator of the operational and financial performance of a bank. Due to an increase in the number of beneficiaries, traditional one-to-one beneficiary interaction has become unsustainable. This sets the goal for the financial services sector to use sector insights to understand how to create an effective multi-channel beneficiary experience that is personalized and relevant, differentiated by value and respectful of privacy concerns. As global competition increases and products become harder to differentiate, banks have begun moving from their product centric attitude to beneficiary-centric one.

# 13. DISCUSSIONS

## Findings

From the inception of civilization the banking sector has dominated the economic development of a country by mobilizing the savings from the general people and channelling those savings for investment and for economic development and growth of the country. The issues of marketing and promotion in the banking sector are becoming more and more important and complicated as internationalization of financial services continues to increase. In recent years, India has emerged as an attractive market for many western countries and several banks have started their operation here. So, the industry has become competitive and the banks essentially need to look for unique and competitive promotional activities in order to stay in competition and to retain prospective beneficiaries. To keep itself up-to-date banking industry is adopting these new services in their portfolio. For success it is important to make the beneficiaries aware of the new products. So it becomes the duty of the commercial banks to provide more information to their target beneficiaries about themselves & their products. Here comes the need for introducing marketing strategy in banking industry. For this aspect banks are now adopting different promotion activities to make their products acceptable and familiar in the market.

The present study falls under the area of marketing. The theme in broad is to analyse the marketing mix and how far this tool useful in the present situation. The objective for which this research has been undertaken is to investigate into the marketing process. i.e. 7P's of services marketing. In present day context banking industry is mainly focusing on marketing practices to attract the beneficiaries.

The scope of the present study extends to the attitude and perceptions of bankers and beneficiaries towards bank marketing and is confined to the bankers and beneficiaries of commercial banks operating in Thrissur District, Kerala. For this purpose it is proposed to elicit the perceptions from managerial and non-managerial staff of the banks. An attempt has been made to elicit the opinions from beneficiaries, because they are having their own banking behaviour.

The preliminary limitation of this study relates to the behavioural sciences. The basic limitation of behavioural sciences is that they would deal with attitudes. These attitudes differ from individual to individual. The preliminary limitation of this study relates to the behavioural sciences. The basic limitation of behavioural sciences is that they would deal with attitudes. These attitudes differ from individual to individual.

Today, the banking sector in India is fairly mature in terms of supply, product range and reach. As far as private sector and foreign banks are concerned, the reach in rural India still remains a challenge. In terms of quality of assets and capital adequacy, Indian banks are considered to have clean, strong and transparent balance sheets relative to other banks in comparable economies in its region. The Reserve Bank of India is an autonomous body, with minimal pressure from the government. The stated policy of the Bank on the Indian Rupee is to manage volatility but without any fixed exchange rate. Till now, there is hardly any deviation seen from this stated goal which is again very encouraging. With passing time, Indian economy is further expected to grow and be strong for quite some time-especially in its services sector. The demand for banking services, especially retail banking, mortgages and investment services are expected to grow stronger.

## Suggestions

The following are some of the suggestions made to the branch managers and employees of the banks.

**Technology:** Banks need to continue their focus on the innovation required to compete and grow while coping with the instability engendered by reform. Banks will need to rethink their strategies as they respond to the sweeping changes in their markets and the regulatory environment.

**Knowledge Management:** The value of the knowledge must be recognized in order to successfully implement knowledge management measures in the banks. Banks have to emphasize on information technology and the dissemination of information. Banking industry must strengthen their research and development work encourage flow of ideas, develop new non-conventional strategies, introduce more professional human resources management policies which can address all the issues.

**Expansion & Diversification:** Expansion and diversification by a bank leads to increase in operational risk. However, higher risk leads to higher returns so long as the bank has adequate systems in place to handle such risks.

**Marketing Strategy:** Banks have to market their products and services by giving the proper knowledge about the product to beneficiary or by awarding the beneficiary about the products. Bank should literate the beneficiaries. In the wake of the changing dynamics in the financial services sector, banks in the region have the uphill task of retaining their existing beneficiaries, acquiring new beneficiaries, building beneficiary confidence and maintaining a robust financial performance. For these challenges, the Indian banks need to adopt and implement innovative relationship marketing strategies to maintain the competitive edge in the market place.

**Increased competition:** The liberalised policies of RBI and Govt. of India relating to Indian Banking have set the stage for a competitive banking. The banks should add intense competition; all the banks are increasingly subjected to severe regulatory and prudential measures that are intended to ensure the viability and substance of the business as well as the safety of its stakeholders.

**Banking Ethics:** The performance of Indian banks has to be judged on the basis of growth, credit quality, strength, soundness, efficiency and profitability. The ethics of banking is based on the trust of the depositors and the borrowers. The measure of this trust is the strength and soundness of a bank.

**Human Resources:** HR plays a pivotal role at the Bank, by implementing the strategy for recruiting, developing and retaining the talented people needed to deliver against its objectives. Human Resource Management is important for banks because banking is a service industry.

**Customer Relationship Management:** The marketing strategy consists of a very clear definition of prospective beneficiaries and their needs and the creation of marketing mix to satisfy them. A recent development in this regard in banks is Customer Relationship Management (CRM). It is a business strategy to learn more and more about customer behavior in order to create long term and sustainable relationship with them. It is a comprehensive process of acquiring and retaining selective beneficiaries to generate value for the bank and its beneficiaries.

**Build Customer Trust:** Provide beneficiaries with required information for making financial decisions. Build loyalty through superior banking service and consistent messaging. Expend bank's share of wallet by providing innovative financial products, value pricing and having a clear understanding of individual financial goals.

## 14. CONCLUSION

This project is all about identifying the Role of marketing in banking industry. Use of marketing mix in banking sector is increasing day by day with 7'Ps. Thus, marketing concept is very important for every bank. The main purpose of this study is to get an overview of bank marketing and to find out the role of marketing in the banking industry and see how marketing mix (product, price, place, & promotion) is most important for a bank. Use of 4 p's for banks and implementation of that in bank's marketing concept and finding out why marketing is important for a bank. And combination of extra 3'Ps (people, process, Physical evidence) are also very important for a bank in the present scenario. To summarize all these, the project comprises detailed study of the role of marketing in banking sector. Bank Marketing has become a necessary survival weapon and is fundamentally changing the banking industry worldwide. The rise of Bank Marketing is redefining business, relationships and the most successful banks will be those that can truly strengthen their relationship with their beneficiaries. Technology innovation and fierce competition among existing banks have enabled a wide array of banking products and services, being made available to retail and wholesale customer through an electronic distribution channel, collectively referred to as e-banking. Technology is altering the relationships between banks and its internal and external beneficiaries.

# 15. REFERENCE

Chawla, A.S., "Nationalisation and Growth of Indian Banking" Deep and Deep Publications, New Delhi, 1988

Ghosh Roy, D., "Marketing, A Hand Book for Branch Bankers" BDP Publishers, Pune, 1994

Ghoshroy, D., Bank Marketing a Hand Book for Branch Bankers, BDP Publishers, Pune, 1994, P. 33

James F Engel, Roger D Blackwell and Paul W.Miniard, Consumer Behaviour, 8th Edition, (The Dryden Press, Harcourt Brace College Publishers, 1995) Pp. 362–363.

Adrian Palmer, "Principles of Services Marketing", McGraw Hill International Edition, 3rd Ed, 2001m pp. 249

Adrian Payne, "Essence from Service Marketing", PHI, 1993: pp. 32

Kotler, P., "Principles of Marketing" Prentice-Hall of India Pvt. Ltd., New Delhi, 1983

Kotler Philip, Marketing Management: Analysis, Planning and Control, New Delhi, Prentice Hall of India Pvt. Ltd

Baker, Michael The Strategic Marketing Plan Audit 2008. ISBN 1-902433-99-8 P. 3

Homburg, Christian; Sabine Kuester, Harley Krohmer (2009): Marketing Management A Contemporary perspective (1st ed.), London.

Aaker, David Strategic Market Management 2008 ISBN 978-0-470-05623-3

Hausman Marketing Letter Definition of Marketing Series

Kotler, P. Marketing Management, New Delhi, Prentice Hall, 2004.

Madhukar, R.K., "Dynamics of Bank Marketing," Sri Sudhindra Publishing House, Bangalore, 1990

Mehra, M., "Bank Advertising in India," IBA, Bombay, 1976

Meidan, A., "Bank Marketing Management," MacMillan Publishers Ltd. Hong Kong, 1984.

Anchal Singh "Marketing of Banking services A case study of Varanasi District", Marketing Master Mind, October 2009, Pp. 21–24

Baker, M. "Introduction", in Marketing: Critical Perspectives on Business and Management, London, Routledge, 2001, Pp. 1–25

Bhattacharya, B. N, "Marketing Approach to Promoting Banking Services": Viklpa, Ahmadabad, Vol. 14, No. 2, April-June, 1989.

Kaptan, Sanjay Shankar (1994), "Marketing of Bank Services," Indian Journal of Marketing, Pp. 14–20.

Kaptan, Sanjay and Nilkanth V. Sagane (1995), "Customer Service in Banks: Some Points to Ponder," Business Analyst, Vol. 15, No. 1, Pp. 20–26

Levesque, T and Mc.Dougall, G.H.G, "Determinants of Customer Satisfaction in retail Banking" International Journal of Bank Marketing, 14(7): 1996, Pp. 12–20.

Levitt, T. "Marketing Intangible Products and Products Intangible", Harvard Business Review, March-June 1981, P. 94

Usha Arora "marketing of Banking Services", Marketing Master Mind, June 2010, Pp. 17–21

https://www.onlinesbi.com/

https://www.federalbank.co.in/

https://www.axisbank.com/

https://www.icicibank.com/

https://www.hdfcbank.com/

https://www.southindianbank.com/

# CHAPTER EIGHT

# An Understanding of the Emerging Dynamics in the Luxury Ecosystem

**Raghupriya. A**
*Full-time PhD scholar*
*Department of Management Studies, CEG, Anna University, Chennai*
*Email id:raghurpiya28.sa@gmail.com*

**Dr. Thiruchelvi. A**
*Associate Professor*
*Department of Management Studies, CEG, Anna University, Chennai*
*Email id:thiruchelvi_y@annauniv.edu*

**Abstract**—*The year 2020 is the most challenging period in the history marked with the intense humanitarian crisis topped with the deepening economic crisis.COVID19 pandemic has affected the consumers' everyday aspects of life. Like many sectors, the luxury fashion sector is also facing unprecedented shift in their ecosystem. According to McKinsey GFI analysis (2021), the fashion companies will post a 90% decline in economic profit in 2020 after a rise of 9% in 2019. For the luxury industry the pandemic will accelerate the revamping trends that were in action prior to the crisis such as more digitization, customer empowerment and social responsibilities.*

*Currently a lot of research related to the luxury fashion industry is available, but through this study we aim to collate our understanding of the emerging dynamics in the luxury fashion industry and provide an outline of the revamped luxury ecosystem and recommend business strategies with focus on agile, flexible, ethical, culture-sensitive, omni-channel presence and enhanced use of data and analytics and customer-centric. Though there is no one strategy that fits for the whole sector, the business should tailor their strategies based on their operational resilience and capabilities for being relevant and to emerge from this unexpected crisis.*

**Keywords**—Luxury industry, COVID19, Consumption trends, Digitization, Data analytic, Agile SCM

# INTRODUCTION

The concept of luxury has been continuously evolving. "What one generation sees as a luxury, the next sees as a necessity." (Anthony Crosland). The global personal luxury industry has seen a steady trajectory at a pace of 6% CAGR since 1990's and was worth over $308 billion as of 2019 with China accounting for 90% of the market's growth in 2019 (Bain & Co., 2020). The Covid-19 pandemic has hit all the industries and luxury is no exception. With social distancing, rise in unemployment and consumers becoming more conscious than conspicuous, the personal luxury market witnessed a decline of 23% in 2020, the largest since recorded (Bain & Co., 2020), with some iconic luxury retailers becoming bankrupt. The companies that have already experiencing distress have had a harder impact because of the pandemic. The survey of GLEN members by the Luxury Institute highlights the current luxury environment and predicts varying degrees of projections for 2021 across the categories with rise in sectors such as consumer wellness and technology, home appliances; fall for retail and flat level for travel and hospitality, automotive and fashion apparels and accessories. Relevance being the new legacy, the future fashion industry should focus on digitization and sustainability (McKinsey & Co., 2020). The luxury retailers must be ready to embrace the disruptive technologies, adapt the omni-channel strategy, understand the changing roles of consumers and align their business models and value proposition according to the changing ecosystem.

Currently a lot of researches are available for both the impact of pandemic across various fields and also the trends in luxury industry. In this conceptual paper, we present our understanding of the luxuryy market scenario by collating secondary qualitative data obtained from the relevant journals and reports from global consulting firms. The aim of this article is to present the new age luxury ecosystem and propose the need for business to strategize on the relevant trends which serve as silver linings to gain brand momentum to revamp from the pandemic impact.

# THEORETICAL FOUNDATION

In Emergency Committee meeting, the Director-General, WHO stated that "The COVID pandemic is an unanticipated rare health crisis, the effects of which will be felt for decades to come."This immense and prolonged epidemic led to unexpected and unprepared economic shock with different industries affected in varying degrees in three major areas: financial, supply value chain, consumer market, each of which is inter-linked.

## The impact of pandemic on the consumer behaviour

The Covid-19 has led to a perceived anxiety related to health and income patterns which has led to a decrease in the quality of life and emotional state of the consumers (Lai, 2020). This resulted to broader repercussions of fear and this is reflected in their uncertainty in spending decisions (Loxton, M et al., 2020). There is a shift in buying behaviour with more focus on essential and safety items than on emotional and hedonistic goods as anticipated by the Maslow's Hierarchy of needs. These behaviours were exhibited even during the past crisis and was reflected in the form of panic buying, herd mentality and discretionary spending (Loxton, M et al., 2020). In the time of crisis, customers tend to closely watch how companies cope throughout in terms of employees and social responsibility (Buheji & Ahmed, 2020). The 2020 Edelman Trust Barometer signifies the fact that during the crisis brands can either build a new level of connection with customers or lose the relationship forever. There has been a slow transformation by the sector but a growing demand for digital presence by the luxury consumers even before the crisis (Kim & Ko, 2012). This crisis will only increase the customers' expectations as they are more addicted to convenience and omni-channel experience (Klaus & Zaichkowsky, 2020) which has led to certain industries adapting the disruptive innovative technology to enhance the customer experience (Klaus, 2020a). Though the pandemic has affected the luxury sector economically, it provides an unique opportunity to the industry if they focus on employment, emotions and expectations of the consumers (Klaus et al., 2020)

## The luxury industry

The notion of luxury has been evolving over a longer term on the basics of several value terms related to the consumers' perspectives(Cabigiosu,2020).Traditionally, luxury   was defined with elegant  shops and luxurious aesthetics with digitization and customization never a part of brand strategy. Some of the players in this sector were hesitant about introducing customization owing to the fear of brand dilution; it is the consumers who prefer to experience engagement, entertainment and interactive shopping though online. The study by Yoo, J and Park, M (2016) adopted  the "Consumer-Perceived Value Tool" (CPVT) identified that through mass customization the luxury brands could build a better customer relationships by providing hedonistic, utilitarian, uniqueness, self-expressive, and creative achievement value with no negative impacts on their brand image. Also the branding literature states that though there have been clear distinction between luxury and mass products in the past, the boundaries are getting blurred since the recent past and every product has a piece of luxury in it. The decrease in household size, increased income and change in lifestyle influenced by education, technology and travel has resulted in consumers 'trading up' and the brands 'trading down' to welcome and retain the new affordable consumers. Even before the crisis the luxury sector was going through the changes but was slow and not able to fulfil customers' desire to buy luxury products and services online. Even though, McKinsey report (2018) states that by 2025, luxury good purchase online will be 20%  and influence by online channels on all the purchases will be 80%, it has been identified that the online channels of some luxury brands do not deliver the experiences that the customers desire. The epidemic has now defined digitization as the strategy for the future and luxury brands should embrace and enhance their digital presence and shopping facilities for customers (Bain&Co., 2020). The retailers need to adapt the online technology  to enhance their supply chains and can use the communication platform to show how the brands act and care for the society, this would lead to an increased brand loyalty (Sender, T, 2020). In an attempt to handle the crisis and to recover from heavy losses, the brands are developing strategies to emotionally connect with their customers (Siddiqui, B. & Ganjoo, M. 2020) and communicating the responsible actions, product innovations and the price adjustments to gain the brand trustworthiness and loyalty (Xie, J. & Youn, C., 2020). The performance analysis in the second quarter of 2020 signifies that the luxury brands are open to more digital marketing and the level of online sales will rise in the future (Peiyu,W., 2020).

The luxury industry had witnessed some economic downturns in the past starting from the recession due to World War II, 1990s Gulf oil crisis, the dot.com, 9/11 and the 2008 recession. Despite the fact that there was a decline in the luxury spending during crisis, the trajectory is not linear or uniform and each of these times, the industry has not only emerged but strengthened by re-aligning and re-focusing on the outstanding quality, fostering customer experience, improving marketing channels, product innovation and capital investment (Reyneke, M. et al, 2020).

Recently the luxury market is gaining more attention among the scholars and lots of articles related to various evolving concepts are available. Even as we present this study we expect some evolution in the industry. Based on the existing literature, we have attempted to represent a model of the new luxury ecosystem of the millennial marked by more empowered and engaged consumers who prefer casual than glam, online than offline, product value than price, sustainability and responsibility, local culture and heritage. We recommend the significance of digitization, co-creation and sustainability, measurement of brand value equity considering the whole omni-channel as part of business strategy to sustain in an era of "Luxury 4.0" term from 'The Age of Digital Darwinism" (McKinsey, 2020)

## THE NEW LUXURY ECOSYSTEM

In this study, we have presented a framework for the new luxury ecosystem and will discuss each arena in detail in the following sections.

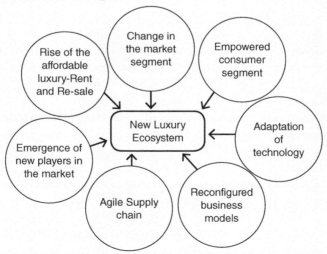

**Figure 1.** The New Luxury Ecosystem

## Change in the market segment

The UN's COVID-19 Immediate Socio-Economic Response framework warns that "Even though the global health is mainly affected, the core society and economy are also affected." The impact varies from developed to developing countries. There is a pressing need to focus on the social consequences related to job losses, depression, stress, domestic violence and so forth (Aneja, R. & Ahuja, V., 2020). This results in immediate focus on SDGs by the governments and UN, as the development trajectories mainly depends on the countries' measures. The UN has extended its full capacity to its 131 countries and supporting 162 territories in developing mitigation plans.

In the economy sector the effect on migrants, job losses and poverty varies disproportionately globally. Like many sectors, the luxury is also facing unexpected economic crisis. In the BoF and McKinsey, 'State of Fashion survey 2021', the business executives had a divided outlook on the pandemic recovery across the sector and geography with 45% of the respondents stating that COVID19 and the economic crisis being the biggest challenge in 2021.Increased unemployment, inequality, lockdown and travel restrictions has heavily influenced consumers psychologically resulting in reduced buying behaviour and constrained spending power leading to diminished demand. Owing to which the global sales is expected to go below 2019 level by as much as 15%. The recovery timeline is expected to vary between third-quarter of 2022 to third-quarter of 2023 based on government trade and travel regulations, improvement in the geographical markets led by China followed by Europe and USA.

## Adaptation of technology

According to 'The Age of Digital Darwinism', the digital trajectory leads to an emergence of Luxury 4.0. The pandemic has led the lackadaisical move towards online innovation to a sprint as brands started focusing on their only source of revenue: e-commerce. The global fashion e-commerce market is expected to grow from $549.55 bn in 2020 to $668.1 bn in 2021 at a CAGR of 21.6% mainly because the sector has adapted the new normal in their operations and resuming from the pandemic impact. This growth is also attributed to the rise in use of internet and smartphones (Digital 2019 Global Overview Report). Digital is seen by a third of executives as a silver lining that presents the biggest opportunity in 202 (McKinsey & Co., 2020)

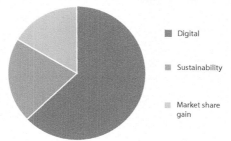

**Figure 2.** Top Three Answers of the Fashion Executives

*Note:* Adapted from BoF-McKinsey State of Fashion 2021 Survey

It is expected that by 2025, one-fifth of the personal luxury sector will happen online with variations in purchase across products. Luxury shoppers of all age groups are embracing digital as a consumption channel moving from laptop to smart phones. The main challenge lies in how the marketers could translate the art of story-telling through a smart device. The acceptance of digital reality is happening in the luxury sector which is seen through the change in brands promotion investments and adopting of new technologies such as AI, scanners, VR outfits and automation tools which provides highly relevant and personal consumer experience (Fashion E-commerce Global Market Report 2021, Business Research Company) Fashion shows, 3D virtual exhibitions and interactions, conversational bots serve as a powerful tool for digital communication. The e-luxury business models are evolving with e-retailers (Matches Fashion), marketplaces (Farfetch) and tech companies (Stitch Fix) (McKinsey, 2020). The most forward looking brands use consumer data and adapt AI in enhancing the front and back-end operations. According to CEO, CFDA; this pandemic has also introduced Phygital as the future of fashion weeks which is evident from the virtual fashion shows organized in the main fashion cities with live audiences owing to the travel ban of luxury tourists. Though these virtual fashion weeks worked for lot of brands, some still need a physical presence.

Apart from creativity, digital storytelling and omni-channel, there is a rise in the use of influencer marketing which has proved itself more important than ever in this year. Still, measuring the value of brand visibility across social media is a primary challenge for brands to estimate ROI. The Media Impact Value is a key global strategy to determine brand's ROI and rank among competitors. According to Launchmetrics, brands make hefty investments in the following channels: Influencers, Celebrities, Partners and Media (Paid, Earned and Own). As online penetration accelerates and shoppers demand ever-more sophisticated digital interactions, fashion players must optimize the online experience and channel mix while finding persuasive ways to integrate the human touch.

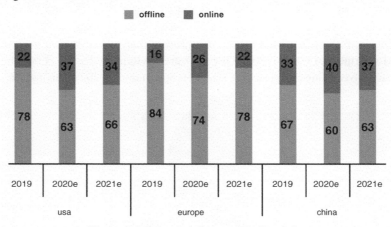

**Figure 3.**  Expected Share of Online Sales

*Note:* Adapted from BoF-McKinsey State of Fashion 2021 Survey

## Empowered consumer segment

The luxury industry is witnessing a trend in their consumer segment: demographically (millenials, GenZ, HENRYs), geographically (rise in the Asian market), psychologically (social media influencers, KOLs) and behaviourally (focus on brand value, sustainability, social ethics, purchase behaviour). For the marketers, this pandemic has amplified the need to focus and capitalize on the segment patterns. In the global battle with pandemic, the everyday aspects of the consumers have changed drastically making them a conscious spender than a conspicuous consumer. There was a slow shift towards digital shopping which has increased to 60% or more during the quarantine. Even in a typical brick and mortar market like Hong Kong, the consumers quickly moved to e-commerce apps. In the Asian region, social media also served as a platform for COVID19 updates.

During the crisis, there is an increase in demand for social responsibility and sustainability from the luxury brands and their involvement are being carefully assessed. The top luxury brands are also contributing to the fight against COVID through product or monetary donations. These socially responsible measures by the brands will increase the consumers brand trust, loyalty and emotional bond for a longer time post the turmoil (Bain, 2020) and these are communicated via digital channels (paid, earned and owned).Nearly two-thirds of the consumers expect their brands to be responsible towards their employees during this crisis and state that they would either stop or significantly reduce their purchase with brands mistreating the employees (McKinsey & Co., 2020).

The new age luxury market is dominated by the millennial and Gen Z who will make up for a 40% market share by 2025.There is also a rise in the medium and medium-higher groups (HENRYs-High Earners Not Rich Yet)who are affordable and aspirational and view luxury as an investment. The luxury brands try to attract and retain them through the premium entry products (McKinsey & Co., 2020). The millennial HENRYs especially, are tech-savvy, with better purchasing power and use social media for buying decisions. The BCG study stated, this new segment appreciate collaboration of KOLs and brands, consider re-sale value, focus on 'silent luxury' (craft and heritage rather than glam)and prioritize sustainability (McKinsey & Co., 2020). A study from Nielsen states that nearly three-quarters of the millennial are willing to spend more for products that comes from a sustainable and social responsible brands. With digital presence, sustainability along with process transparency will gain brand trust from consumers. Brands are competing for this new age mindshare and focussing on engaging with influencers who are in line with their brand values. The spike in TikTok popularity during lockdown, has spurred a new thought for luxury to engage with this audience via this channel.

All luxury consumers are going digital; this trend is not just linked with millennial. Baby boomers spend 16.4 hours in the Internet and 75% of them use social media as compared to 17.5 hours and 98% use by the millennial (McKinsey & Co., 2020). With increased online purchase the customer wants to engage via multiple digital points and experience the product customization

(De Keyser et al, 2020). In the past 5 years, the number of touch-points influencing consumers purchase journey have become thrice. In case of Chinese luxury consumers the points are estimated to be around 15. The customer also expects this continuous and coherent brand relationship via these digital points, even as they travel from one geography to the other. This is still a challenge for brands who are organized around channels and geographies. Daigou, the act of shoppers outside China market buying luxury goods for consumers back home, is an indication of the consumers' willingness towards digital touch points across boundaries. The use of WeChat by Chinese consumers for the entire purchase journey is another example of the rise in digital luxury shopping.

The luxury brands should be willing to accept the concept of co-creation not only in production development but also in brand content generation without affecting the core brand identity. The brands have to develop strategies to make the consumers the brand ambassadors. The digital luxury is turning into a C2C economy with the greater engagement and empowerment of consumers who are not just a purchaser but a creator, meta-voice and a propagator (Liu-Thompkins et al, 2020).

**80% of sales are influenced by online**
Sales of personal luxury goods[1], € billions

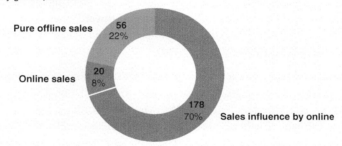

**Figure 4.**  Sales Influenced by Online

*Note:* Retrieved from Euro-monitor, Forrester, McKinsey Annual Reports

The impact of digital experience makes consumer set expectations on online shopping and also the same in the physical store. It is time for reverse omni-channel where stores are expected to match the level of online experience. Digital is no longer a medium of mere sales or communication but a source of inspiration to re-design the store and re-focus on the customer experience.

Another dynamically and fast-growing trend in luxury sector is the "Experiential luxury" which along with social media influencers are gaining momentum. Social distancing and lockdown had made popular brands like Louis Vitton, Saint Laurent, Versace and Burberry to name a few use nostalgic marketing campaigns via social media channels (instagrammable moments) and develop product designs based on nostalgic theme to attract the boomers and the millennial equally.

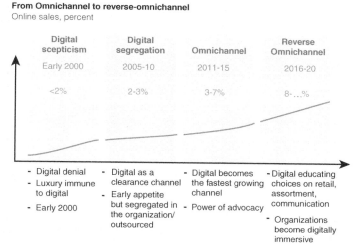

**From Omnichannel to reverse-omnichannel**
Online sales, percent

| Digital scepticism | Digital segregation | Omnichannel | Reverse Omnichannel |
|---|---|---|---|
| Early 2000 | 2005-10 | 2011-15 | 2016-20 |
| <2% | 2-3% | 3-7% | 8-...% |

- Digital denial
- Luxury immune to digital
- Early 2000

- Digital as a clearance channel
- Early appetite but segregated in the organization/ outsourced

- Digital becomes the fastest growing channel
- Power of advocacy

- Digital educating choices on retail, assortment, communication
- Organizations become digitally immersive

**Figure 5.** Reverse Omni-channel

*Note:* Retrieved from Euro-monitor, Forrester, McKinsey Annual Reports

The lockdown has resulted in revenge spending which is observed in the China market as the situations are settling down. The consumers have started to resume their shopping behaviours with the alleviation of the situation and we foresee a higher spending than before from China, given the fact that travelling is still restricted. With big data and machine learning, the luxury brands can improve the authenticity and customer relationship. In early days, Louis Vitton used to send personalized product suggestions to their customers, the same unique personalized recommendation can now be achieved using Big Data analytic and this marks the era of contextual marketing where each customer is unique in each situation.

The new age luxury consumers embrace ethics, crafts, heritage, technology and prefer casual over glam. This pandemic has created an opportunity for the industry to reconsider 'rest of the world' strategy to focus on other emerging markets than China and focus on engaging and empowering consumers.

## Rise of the affordable luxury-Rent and Re-sale

The re-sale or re-commerce market for the fashion goods were booming even before the pandemic. Consumers started valuing their once purchased luxury items as not only a style factor but a trade-able asset. The online retail site such as The RealReal, Poshmark, Depop and ThredUp are boosting of a growing amount of consumers in this sector which serves as a means of financial security especially during the time of this epidemic. The luxury apparel and accessories market reached $24 billion in 2019 and is expected to reach $53 billion by 2023. Even though the millenials and GenZ dominate this sector; Boomers and GenX are also embracing this market as a means to clear-up their closets. The RealReal holds the authenticated designer brands such as Chanel, LV and Valentinno. While the ThredUp holds the consignment of around 45,000 brands from Gap to Gucci, the sites like Poshmark and Depop provide a C2C transaction platform. According to ThredUp report 2020, over the three years the resale business grew at a speed of 21 times as that of new apparels business with millenials and Gen Z holding a market size which is 2.5 times that of the boomers and GenX. This pandemic has led to a 50% increase in the business size. Also, the legacy retail players have tapped into the resale market to attract the young consumers which is witnessed by the tie-up of retailer Macy with ThredUp.

The re-sale market has also been hit by the pandemic. According to Founder of Luxury Institute, the supply of the consignment has been increasing with consumers ready to sell their used fashion goods but the demand is far less leading to difficulties in inventory management. The RealReal is witnessing a downward slope and the resale business also looks for way to re-model their business and is connecting with their customers virtually. But there is a viability of resale business in European and Asian markets and the big brands like Gucci and Chanel will invest in pre-owned business to avoid counterfeits in the market.

With environment and economy conscious consumers on the rise, another viable option to experience luxury is through renting. Renting becomes the new owning. There is an increasing number of online apps and platforms which offer an option for renting luxury items for a subscription. With this the consumers can flaunt the luxury for a specific period with less investment and maintenance. Renting is extended across various sectors of luxury from homes (AirBnb, Homeaway), clothing (Rent n Flaunt, Le Tote), Accessories (Bag, Borrow or Steal), Cars (Rolls-Royce Drophead, Turo) etc...

## Emergence of new players in the market

The introduction of Amazon's Luxury Stores and the Farfetch China are two notable entrants to the luxury industry in the pandemic era.

The launch of a section on Amazon's mobile app called the Luxury stores in the fashion sector on September 2020, has been an opportunity for the already struggling fashion department stores, as it serves as a new channel for distribution. The Amazon luxury stores provide an efficient gateway for designers who find it difficult to connect with the consumers and the retailers who are facing bankruptcy. The Amazon's luxury stores will provide a 360-degree interactive window for shoppers to view items on different body types and skin tones. It has also stated it provides the retailers the option for independent decision regarding product assortment, price, delivery and service options. With its strong customer database and technology adoption, the Amazon luxury stores will play a dominant competitive role in the luxury business.

Another new entrant in the luxury industry amidst the pandemic is the creation of online marketplace Farfetch China, the most high profile luxury e-commerce deal with $1.1 billion venture between Richemont, Alibaba,Artémis and Farfetch and a joint investment of $600 million by Alibaba and Richemont in Farfetch resulting in a quarter percent stake in Farfetch's operations in China.

During the period of extended lockdown with increased consumers purchase through smart devices and reduced store footprints, Farfetch's e-commerce share of the global luxury market nearly doubled from 12%–23%. This resulted in a staggering market capitalization rise by 475% with its first ever profit during the fourth quarter of 2020. This deal has led to dedicated Farfetch shopping channels on Alibaba's Tmall Luxury Pavilion, Luxury Soho online and cross-border marketplace Tmall Global. For Richemont, this is an opportunity to tap the China market and emerge as a global digital competitor to its rival LVMH who has a strong digital presence, 24S and Lyst, since 2017. For Alibaba, who have been tapping the US market with its B2B selling program and the use of Western influencers in social media promotions, this deal would make it a global competitor to Amazon in the luxury space. Farfetch would benefit from Alibaba's strong data capabilities and mark a footprint in the East and South-east Asia.

## Reconfigured Business Models

The business models are focusing more on vertical integration and omni-channel strategy to emerge victoriously from the pandemic. From Gucci to Hermes and fast fashion retailers like Zara and H&M were slowly moving towards vertical integration even before the pandemic to avoid bankruptcy and better value chain management. Though this sector is composed of consolidation by big players, the pandemic has proven that there is still opportunity for young independent and local players. The focus on serving the local market with the local supplies and not tourist dependent is gaining momentum as this serves as a best recovery from the pandemic. The elite and the millennial are getting inclined more towards local artisans and craftsmanship. So the luxury models should focus on culturally relevant and building up of local community craftsmanship (Luxe Digital, 2020). The marketers should work collaboratively with the Chinese market experts and incorporate brand value aligned KOLs,Asia Weibo and Douykin to make domestic communication to be successful in the Eastern market (Julia, C., 2020). The JIT management of Industry 4.0 along with digital enhancement will lead to an agile and responsive operations of the luxury sector without diluting the brand identity resulting to Luxury 4.0 offering 3D printed products to their consumers in the next five years as stated by McKinsey survey report. Also, Sustainability growth strategy is gaining momentum which is emphasized by the Forbes report which signifies millenials concern about environment (42%), animal welfare (26%) and baby boomers primary concern for ethical manufacturing (32%).

## Agile Supply chain

The risks due to disruptions (natural or man-made) have a significant impact on supply chain. The disruption in one link of the supply chain will move downstream if there are no proper buffers and adequate lead times leading to a ripple effect. In an era of globalization, a small epidemic arising out of a geographical area will disperse across regions. Ivanov (2020) identifies three characteristics of an epidemic outbreak: (1) unpredictable disruption period, (2) the ripple effect and (3) consequent disruptions followed in the logistics, demand and supply. With asynchronous nature of epidemic spread and variation in disaster management followed by countries, we observe a unique angle of disruption with varying levels of period and intensity in various countries either as a ripple effect or as a lockdown. With China being the dominant player on the global luxury industry, the supply chain of this sector was temporarily impacted during the rise of the pandemic. This highlights the complex and interdependent nature of this sector. Also, we identify that there has been a disturbances in the supply and demand with consumers changing or canceling the demands of the non-essential fashion goods. This reflects the impact of epidemic on the upstream and downstream supply chains. The business should strategize on implementing agile SCM with adequate inventory management for an effective value creation (McMaster et al. 2020).

## DISCUSSIONS

This study highlights the following trends for the luxury brands to rebuild its business post the pandemic:
- Brands should focus on brand momentum
- Measure brand equity value by considering all the omni-channels
- Build upon Sustainable Ethical Growth strategy
- Develop agile and flexible supply value chain
- Emphasize on local crafts and heritage
- Communicate with consumers for a better exchange of data and improved sales and improve emotional connect
- Collaborate with brand value aligned influencers
- Embrace technology and data analytics
- Even though the market witnesses mergers of big players, there are opportunities for young independent local players
- Diversify the market portfolio by considering the rest of the world strategy

## CONCLUSION

According to Altagamma foundation, "The year 2021 will be the beginning of recovery from recession and we can expect a pre-crisis return from 2022. An average growth of 14% across all luxury sectors, with 22% increase in online and 18% from Chinese market has been predicted."There is a greater scope for the use of Artificial Intelligence and Big Data and the brands who are early adaptor of this technology will gain better customer-relationship and emerge a stronger player in the market. Through this framework of the new luxury ecosystem this study identifies the key trends for an evolutionary future. Digitization and Sustainability are the silver linings to overcome this global crisis era. The luxury sector will be more dynamic, reactive, adaptable and push their creative limits to emerge stronger.

# REFERENCES

Aneja, R., & Ahuja, V. (2020). An assessment of socioeconomic impact of COVID-19 pandemic in India. *Journal of Public Affairs*, e2266. https://doi.org/10.1002/pa.2266

Bain & Company. (2020). Luxury after Covid-19: Changed for the Good? https://www.bain.com/ insights/luxury-after-coronavirus

Buheji, M., & Ahmed, D. (2020). Foresight of Coronavirus (COVID-19) Opportunities for a Better World. *American Journal of Economics*, 10(2), 97–108. https://doi.org/10.5923/j.economics.20201002.05

Cabigiosu, A. (2020). An Overview of the Luxury Fashion Industry. In: *Digitalization in the Luxury Fashion Industry*. Palgrave Advances in Luxury. https://doi.org/10.1007/978-3-030-48810-9_2

De Keyser, A., Verleye, K., Lemon KN, Keiningham TL, Klaus P. (2020) Moving the Customer Experience Field Forward: Introducing the Touchpoints, Context, Qualities (TCQ) Nomenclature. *Journal of Service Research*, 23(4):433–455, doi:10.1177/1094670520928390

Ivanov, Dmitry., & Ajay Das. (2020). Coronavirus (COVID-19/SARS-CoV-2) and supply chain resilience:A research note. *International Journal of Integrated Supply Management*, 13(1):90–102. Inderscience Enterprises Ltd. https://doi.org/10.1504/IJISM.2020.107780

Julia, C (2020, December 28). The 12 Trends and Predictions for 2021 From Fashion, Luxury and Beauty Experts. https://www.launchmetrics.com/resources/blog/2021-trends-predictions

Kim, A.J,. & Ko, E. (2012). Do social media marketing activities enhance customer equity? an empirical study of luxury fashion brand. *Journal of Business Research*, 65(10):1480–1486. doi:10.1016/j. jbusres.2011.10.014

Klaus, P,. & Manthiou, A. (2020). Applying the EEE customer mindset in luxury: re-evaluating customer experience research and practice during and after corona. *Journal of Service Management*, 31(6):1175–1183. https://doi.org/10.1108/JOSM-05-2020-0159

Klaus, P. (2020a). Customer experience, not brands will be on the iron throne. *International Journal of Market Research*, 62(1):6–8. https://doi.org/10.1177/1470785319858570

Klaus, P,. & Zaichkowsky, J. (2020). AI voice bots: a services marketing research agenda. *Journal of Services Marketing*, 34(3):389–398. https://doi.org/10.1108/JSM-01-2019-0043

Lai, A. (2020). A snapshot of US consumers' attitudes and behavior during COVID-19. https:// go.forrester.com/blogs/a-snapshot-of-us-consumers-attitudes-and-behavior-during-covid-19/

Loxton, M,. Truskett, R,. Scarf, B,. Sindone, L,. Baldry, G,. & Zhao, Y. (2020). Consumer Behaviour during Crises: Preliminary Research on How Coronavirus Has Manifested Consumer Panic Buying, Herd Mentality, Changing Discretionary Spending and the Role of the Media in Influencing Behaviour. *Journal of Risk Financial Management*, 13(8):166. https://doi.org/10.3390/jrfm13080166

LuxeDigital. The Future of Luxury: 6 Trends To Stay Ahead in 2021. https://luxe.digital/business/ digital-luxury-trends/luxury-future-trends/

McKinsey & Company. (2018). Luxury in the age of digital Darwinism. https://www.mckinsey.com/ industries/retail/our-insights/luxury-in-the-age-of-digital-darwinism

McKinsey & Company. (2020). The State of Fashion 2021. https://www.mckinsey.com/industries/retail/ our-insights/state-of-fashion

McMaster, M,. Nettleton, C,. Tom, C,. Xu, B,. Cao, C,. & Qiao, P. (2020). Risk Management: Rethinking Fashion Supply Chain Management for Multinational Corporations in Light of the COVID-19 Outbreak. *Journal of Risk Financial Management*, 13: 173. https://doi.org/10.3390/jrfm13080173

Reyneke, M,. Sorokáčová, A,. & Pitt, L. (2012). Managing brands in times of economic downturn: How do luxury brands fare? *Journal of Brand Management*, 19:457–466. https://doi.org/10.1057/ bm.2011.53

Sender, T. (2020). Strategies for UK fashion to adapt to the pressures of Covid19. https://www.mintel. com/blog/retail-market-news/covid-19-is-putting-huge-pressure-on-the-uk-fashion-sector/

Siddiqui, B,. & Ganjoo, M. (2020). Impact of Covid-19 on Advertising: A Perception Study on the Effects on Print and Broadcast Media and Consumer Behavior. Purakala.Com, 31(28):52–62.

Wen Peiyu (2020). Analysis on the Different Response of Fast Fashion Brands and Luxury Brands to the Epidemic. *Proceedings of the 2020 2nd International Conference on Economic Management and Cultural Industry (ICEMCI 2020)*, 15-1, Atlantis Press.

Xie, J,. & Youn, C. (2020). How the Luxury Fashion Brands Adjust to Deal with the COVID-19. *International Journal of Costume and Fashion*, 20(2):50–60.

Yoo, J,. & Park, M. (2016). The effects of e-mass customization on consumer perceived value, satisfaction, and loyalty toward luxury brands. *Journal of Business Research*, 69(12):5775–5784. https://doi.org/10.1016/j.jbusres.2016.04.174

Yuping Liu-Thompkins,. Ewa Maslowska,. Yuqing Ren,. & Hyejin Kim. (2020). Creating, Metavoicing, and Propagating: A Road Map for Understanding User Roles in Computational Advertising. *Journal of Advertising*, 49(4):394–410. https://doi.org/10.1080/00913367.2020.1795758

# CHAPTER NINE

## Trends in ICT Management for Faster Adoption to Gain Competitive Advantage

**Sameer Kulkarni** *
*Department of Technology Management*
*Defense Institute of Advanced Technology [DU], Girinagar, Pune*
* *sameer.kuls@gmail.com, 9667149111 (first author)*

**Dr. Sumati Sidharth** **
*Department of Technology Management*
*Defense Institute of Advanced Technology [DU], Girinagar, Pune*
***sumatisidharth@gmail.com, 9689903672 (corresponding author)*

**Abstract**—*The paper presents analytical explanation and integrated solution in trends and best practices in Technology Management in ICT domain with specific focus on critical sectors. The paper reviews key technologies in ICT domain, their trends and future directions in meeting existing challenges as well as envisaged future challenges. ICT technologies are the key enablers in almost every facet of human life. It plays even vital role in diverse fields towards improving the situational awareness and providing valuable innovative solutions for issues in unthinkable ways. ICT plays a key role in enhancing productivity and efficiency in any organizations be it public or private, critical or otherwise. The value of ICT assets like computer systems, communication networks, hardware, software, media technologies coupled with latest technologies like Artificial Intelligence & Machine Learning, Big Data Analytics, IoT, Blockchain becomes a formidable force multiplier to drive modern developments, innovation and knowledge management in any organization. ICT technologies also make the management of information, critical factor in modern day, more effective and efficient. Technology Management entails all management activities involved in planning, management of resources, application of appropriate technologies to improve processes and outcomes. The major challenges faced in application of Technology Management in ICT domain are Formulating the use cases, Selection of appropriate technologies, Assimilation of requisite information resources ready for exploitation, Garnering top management support for using ICT in strategic thinking, Reengineering existing process and change management in organization,*

*Managing the hardware resources (public or private cloud) and more importantly Monitoring and auditing for enhanced customer experience. In this ever-evolving ICT technology domain, it is important to keep pace with latest developments and this is a critical factor in adopting ever changing applications / processes as existing human force is not ready for such fast pace. However, this has changed significantly during the current Covid scenario. The paper aims to delve in to these realms to exploit latest development in ICT domain for its fast adoption and implementation in critical sectors for future ready business processes.*

**Keywords**—ICT; Use cases; Reengineering processes; Public or Private Cloud; IMPLEMENT

The Information and Communication Technologies (ICT) cover two distinct domains including Information Technology covering Computers (Hardware / Software), Cyber aspects, and Communication Technology covering networking, voice, video, data communication over wired or wireless media. The ever-changing nature of these technologies makes a visible impact on every facet of human life be it social, personal, Govt or corporate affairs. These fields are evolving at a faster pace than envisaged by Moore's laws. It is important to keep the pace of implementation as fast as the technology is evolving, to extract maximum benefits for competitive advantage. It is normally seen that the implementation of projects in ICT domain in any sector typically takes 4-5 years, whereas the technology changes in same period, making the implementation infructuous or irrelevant. However, if you evolve with the ICT advances, it definitely gives competitive advantage.

## METHODOLOGY

This paper discusses the semi-systematic review of the literature to deal with the issues and challenges in faster adoption of the ICT technologies. A detailed literature review is envisaged to get the nuances of the ICT technologies, their applicability in current processes, and issues faced during their implementation. Thereafter, a qualitative analysis of the implementations of ICT technologies in certain companies will be covered to extract meaningful perspectives for faster adoption and implementation in specific time frame.

## ANALYTICAL LITERATURE REVIEW OF KEY TECHNOLOGIES IN ICT DOMAIN

According to Soumaya El Kadiri, et al., as business conditions change rapidly, the need for integrating business and technical systems calls for novel ICT frameworks and solutions to remain concurrent in highly competitive markets. Accordingly, for all critical sectors, it is imperative that ICT technologies and trends therein need to be integrated in the existing process to evolve in more effective systems in specific timeframes. Gabriel Kabanda (2019) argues that ICT Management is heavily dependent upon the alignment of technology and business strategies, and includes considering the value creation that is created through technology. As per T. H. AlBalushi and S. Ali (2015), with the development of a greater number and variety of e-services, citizens have higher expectations and demands and they only quest for those government e-services that are high in quality (i.e., as far as performance, security, availability, etc. are concerned). This is made possible with converged ICT domains. Even the quality factors can be improved with latest AI&ML, Big Data Analytics tools towards customer delight.

According to Esther Le Rouzic, et al, with one third of the world population online in 2013 and an international Internet bandwidth multiplied by more than eight since 2006, the ICT sector is a non-negligible contributor of worldwide greenhouse gases emissions and power consumption. The advances in ICT domain are driving efficient energy solutions as well as contributing to green resolutions. From energy efficient IoT devices, to smart grids, to intelligent monitoring solutions, ICT plays a key role in energy efficient networks.

The ICT Roadmap is to align with contemporary technologies and corresponding Digital roadmap. There has to be continuous steps to remain updated in ICT domain and incorporate the latest technology in the ongoing projects. Existing ICT resources itself are changing the effectiveness and productivity in areas like Operations, Maintenance management, Administration, Hospital management, Accounting, Supply chain management etc. In the normal functioning of any critical sector, these ICT resources are paving the way for improvement in overall productivity and responsiveness. ICT has enabled data collection, transmission and storage of information for subsequent analysis. This is providing a background for better utilization of the available resources and the advances in ICT are evolving just to ensure its effectiveness. However, the ICT is evolving at a much faster pace than adoption by Organizations. The advancements in ICT domain are enormous. We are going to focus on following key technologies from the perspective of their relevance for current processes, relative availability of implementable solutions and feasible adoption in critical sectors:

(a)  Cloud Computing
(b)  Artificial Intelligence and Machine Learning
(c)  Big Data Analytics
(d)  Blockchain
(e)  Robotics Process Automation
(f)  Software Defined Networking
(g)  5G
(h)  Cyber Security, encompassing all above aspects

## Cloud Computing

Cloud computing technology definitely minimizes the usage cost of computing resources while optimizing the resource utilization. The advances in hyper converged infrastructure make the fit case for exploiting cloud computing for migrating old systems to the cloud computing systems.

The private cloud or public cloud options are there to explore. A flexible and cost-efficient cloud deployments are integrating newer concepts of load balancing, integrated monitoring, secure storage etc. The need based dynamic allocation of resources, easy implementation of roles, secure access and orchestration makes it the right infrastructure for adoption. Cloud Computing optimally allocates both processing ability and bandwidth as well as works on optimized electric power capacity with latest advancements.

## Artificial Intelligence and Machine Learning

Artificial Engineering (AI) and Machine Learning (ML) have arrived in the market and have the potential to transform the processes than ever before. Massive volumes of data are getting generated across the globe. AI is complementing human intelligence and it enables greater insight from data for helping human experts making better decisions and providing better advice. All the facets of thinking, perceiving, learning, problem solving and decision making are enabling the AI implementations.

The Natural Language processing can be effectively utilized to find anomalies even in multilingual architecture. D. Mujtaba and N. Mahapatra (2019) clearly states that several datasets and knowledge representations for question answering, coreference resolution, and inference tasks have been discussed and built upon in the NLP community.

The facial recognition technology is another important facet of AI&ML evolving at faster rate aiding in monitoring and auditing. The tracking of facial activities from video is an important and challenging problem as brought out by Prem Chand Yadav, et al (2016). This paper clearly brings out that AI&ML have facilitated lot of advances in facial action tracking for Fatigue Detection, Real Time 3D Face Pose Tracking from an Uncalibrated Camera, Simultaneous facial action tracking and expression recognition using a particle filter and Simultaneous Tracking and Facial Expression Recognition using Multi-person and Multiclass Autoregressive Models. These are key advancements which can be exploited in avoiding accidents, enhancing performance of individuals and avoiding emotional aspects in key decision-making scenarios.

## Big Data Analytics

Every application begins with large amounts of data. Even though various data analytics are used in primitive or advanced forms, still there are instances which prevent the analytics to be used for enhancing the human intelligence. With the aid of AI&ML, this can be overcome and Big Data Analytics can provide meaningful insights in the data by correlating, corroborating and analyzing with advanced algorithms. As rightly put by O. Baker and C. N. Thien (2020), business data are originating in various kinds of sources with different forms from conventional structured data to unstructured data, it is the input for producing useful information essential for business sustainability. The advanced algorithms and a host of resources are paving the way for extracting meaningful insights towards effective knowledge management. It also utilizes the distributed data architectures to better assimilate data from disparate sources. This makes it easy for storing the information like IoTs storing in edge servers. This can greatly enhance the application development and decision-making processes.

## Blockchain Technology

Blockchain technology has evolved and is already changing traditional financial systems. It is a Distributed-ledger technology which is most commonly used for Cryptocurrency. However, the technology has immense benefits in carrying forward secure financial transactions and associated functions like auditing. Blockchain is an important tool enabling critical distributed applications without requiring centralized trust over untrusted network. Harsh Desai, et al, (2019) clearly brings out that private blockchains have been proposed to allow more efficient and privacy-preserving data sharing among pre-approved group of nodes / participants. H. Yoo and N. Ko (2020), also brings out that smart contract mechanism based on blockchain can guarantee the automatic and secure trading. Blockchain technology can be used for securing scores of technology domains like 5G, Communication channels used for sensitive information exchange.

## Robotics Process Automation

As per Y Hao, et al, recent advances in Information and Communication Technologies (ICTs) have allowed manufacturing enterprises to improve business collaboration both within an enterprise and among enterprises, for achieving mutual benefits. This can be possible due to advances in Robotics Process Automation which is revolutionizing the manufacturing as well as Supply Chain Management. Already Businesses are exploiting Virtual Factory (VF), in MSME sector through cloud-based data exchanges. These cloud-based messaging platforms are ensuring that the process automation is in line with the strategic requirements of those entities.

C. Balaguer (2004) has been vocal in bringing out research trends in robotics and automation in construction industry. RPA efforts are concentrated more in the software integration, sensory data acquisition and processing, safety and secure systems, sensor-based process control and construction industrialization. Such advancements in Robotics Process Automation can be effectively exploited in host of automation requirements especially in Manufacturing industries.

## Software Defined Networking

J Bhatia, et al, states that evolving mega-trends such as mobile, social, cloud, and big data and correspondence innovations (ICT) are identifying new difficulties to evolving technologies, for which omnipresent availability, high data transmission, and dynamic management are essential. Software Defined Networking (SDN) has emerged as the default networking solution for converged infrastructure including wired as well as wireless networks, including 5G. SDN also brings in paradigm networking shift in the way we communicate information. The distinct layers for data and control planes, orchestration made possible with SDN is making seamless exchange of information across disparate platforms possible. The practical applications of SDN coupled with load balancing provides right mix of communication flexibility for running any application be it web based, app based or stack based. The nature of all new generation networks (NGN), wireless technologies, and broadband access is IP-based which ensures ease of access through any device or from any region in the world. SDN makes this functionality even more feasible due to its orchestration and management / monitoring functionalities.

## 5G

Y. Tan et al (2019), states that with the burgeoning of the Internet of everything, 5G network gradually attracts people's attention. After passing the technology hype around the 5G implementations, it is truly evolving in next generation of communication network capable of supporting low power endpoints with relatively high bandwidth and seamless connectivity across smart devices and other wired and wireless technologies. The advancements are making it possible for storing the data from end devices in edge devices itself, which was considered a major issue in explosion of IoT devices. The migration is in implementation stage in developed world, but surely it has the potential to bring in paradigm shift in connecting smart devices and extracting data from them.

## Cyber Security

With ICT technologies breaking the glass ceilings and becoming pervasive, there is a constant cyber threat. ICT thrives on connected world and cyber agents have a sneak peak in to these connected devices be it hardware, software, firmware or communication devices. The advances in ICT are getting automated and so are the cyber weapons as well. The enormous powers of ubiquitous computing, easy access to resources and host of new tools with AI&ML, automation makes it potent force to reckon with. When the adversary is getting more powerful, there is a need to be aware and prepared for the worst. This has been evident during the Covid scenario, when most of the working is remote and ICT driving the economy and society, there has been substantial increase in cyber-attacks as well, which is alarming. There are serious concerns about data protection, financial frauds, attacks on communication technologies including IoT, wired or wireless. World Economic Forum (WEF) has rightly enlisted cyber-attacks as the third biggest concern in Covid times only after recession and bankruptcy. All the domains covered above, Cloud / Edge computing, AI&ML, Big Data Analytics, Robotics Process Automation, Software Defined Networking and 5G, where disruptive innovation has taken place, remains sub-servient to cyber threats.

Having seen the literature about the importance of these cutting-edge ICT technologies, it is worthwhile to see their implementations to draw meaningful insights.

## Implementation Case Studies

FFF Enterprises, a pharma entity, tried to migrate their SAP ERP application system to private cloud in 2016, however, due to scalability issues of hardware as well as networking devices, they had to adopt cloud computing. They migrated their entire system to Google Cloud in limited timeframe to ensure their critical pharma business is not affected. They experienced 80% improvement in speed vis a vis cost. With this migration to the cloud, the FFF managed to concentrate on innovation and support, instead of worrying about outages in their systems, which was handled by the cloud providers. A host of cloud solutions are provided from Google, Microsoft, IBM, AWS etc. for seamless migration of services and providing secure, reliable and uninterrupted services.

Cisco suffered its worst ever inventory write-down worth $2.2b in 2001. The Cisco business and IT teams worked in unison in adopting the ICT advancements to streamline their Supply Chain Management world over. They adopted innovative RPA, 3D printing, single database instance across the world to seamlessly integrate Suppliers, Manufacturers and customers alike to ensure their Supply Chain Management system becomes the best and contribute to their success stories. Cisco promptly identified the use cases, adopted best in class ICT technologies, and reengineered their processes in time to reap the benefits.

Renowned banks are embracing AI&ML for fraud detection, customer service, credit service and loan decisions and meeting regulatory compliance. There have been numerous success stories in EdTech industry, especially in Covid scenario, to adopt the ICT developments like AI&ML, BDA in formulation of courses, student behavior analysis, assimilation of results etc. This is helping improve retention of students which had been the key concern. AI&ML are being extensively utilized by Human Resources to screen the applications and improve the employee retention with analysis of employee behavior on real time basis.

Retail industry also adopted ICT technologies and most of the e-tailers like Naykaa, Amazon, Flipkart etc. could improve customer satisfaction to delight by improving their delivery schedules, supply chain aspects and analysis of customer requirements on real time basis.

A leading middle east-based refinery adopted the ICT technologies including cloud, big data analytics, AI&ML to focus on value addition in planning & scheduling, refinery operations, process engineering, maintenance & reliability and safety environment. The gap analysis was done and the processes were reengineered with ICT resulting in increase in refining margins, reliability of plant and reduction in annual maintenance costs to the tune of $2m.

In a latest adoption of Blockchain technology, a critical problem of vaccine tracking and distribution of Covid vaccines is being tried out. Distribution across the world, with short supply, batching process and need to keep it under strict environmental conditions, poses complex problems which are being addressed by IoT and Blockchain technologies. In recent instances across the world, the social media could filter out outliers, unwanted objectionable content through effective use of AI&ML and big data analytics. Though the very ICT technologies are enabling hackers to automate attacks, make it possible from distributed sources, the same technologies provide effective ways through AI&ML, BDA to counter them in real time. A score of such cyber-attacks were detected and counter measures were deployed to further stop the damages caused.

The biggest proponent of Cloud technologies, Microsoft was at one time lagging behind in the market after creating behemoths like Google, Facebook etc. due to culture in adopting to latest ICT developments. Microsoft, after realizing lack of profits, and competition from IBM, AWS, ventured in to Cloud technologies with their Azure framework and concentrated on AI&ML, Power BI, Mobile ready OS and Office solutions. This paved the way for Microsoft to be back in to the market.

There have been instances of businesses being wrapped up because of non-adoption of technologies in right earnest. Kodak, despite developing first digital camera in 1975, could not see the digital wave, advances in ICT technologies like storing, transmission of digital images, and went bankrupt. Similarly, Blockbuster, most prominent video on rental service provider in 2004, could not adopt ICT technologies and filed for bankruptcy in 2010.

## Analysis

The ontological qualitative analysis of all these implementation case studies clearly brings out the enormous advantages of adopting the technologies in ICT domain in right earnest. It also brings out some common issues being faced in the implementations like

(a)     There is a clear requirement for technology forecasting and identifying appropriate use cases for adoption in right earnest. The earlier it is realized, the faster will be the adoption. The use cases and implementations can be forward looking.

(b)     Though there are no clear timelines available in the implementations in case studies, it can be deducted from the open-source information available, that the ICT technologies were adopted in a span to two to three years. For large organizations, adoption by multiple entities will take time, however, it is pertinent to note that the solutions made available by the ICT vendors outweighs the resistance to change management.

(c)     Clear implementation plans are the key to faster adoption. Clear objectives, definite timelines and efficient implementation by all stakeholders was key to timely completion of the ICT projects.

(d)     Documenting the process also was found to be important to take forward the advantages.

# IMPLEMENT MODEL FOR FASTER ADOPTION OF NEW TECHNOLOGIES IN ICT DOMAIN

Having seen the analysis of latest key technologies in ICT domain, it is imperative to exploit these technologies to the best of their abilities for improvement in productivity and performance of systems. It is extremely important to take a lead in identifying and implementing latest developments as they become available. The stability is one of the issues for rapid transition, however, same can be effectively managed with careful planning, Technology road mapping and following the path to the hilt.

There is an urgent need to adopt these latest developments in ICT domain in right earnest to extract maximum benefits. Following IMPLEMENT model is proposed to actually put the process in action in a time-bound manner. IMPLEMENT stands for:

| I | Identify innovative use cases |
|---|---|
| M | Manipulation of appropriate ICT technologies |
| P | Provide top management support for using ICT in strategic thinking |
| L | Leverage requisite information resources for exploitation |
| E | Ensure availability of hardware and software resources (public or private cloud) |
| M | Managing transition of existing process through change management |
| E | Ensure effective monitoring and auditing for enhanced customer experience |
| N | Negotiate feedbacks |
| T | Transfer knowledge to requisite teams |

The implementation strategy covered herein is the key to adopting the latest ICT advancements in almost every facet of functioning. The details of the model are covered below: -

# I

Innovation is the key to any improvement and ICT can aid in furthering the innovation, be it new product development or processes improvement. When any application / process is aligned to the business vision, then it would substantially enhance the decision support of the organization's management. Towards this aim, anyone in the organization can identify innovative use cases while undergoing technology forecasting itself. AI & ML based chatbots and voice powered assistants can be used with centralized exchanges to enhance the user experience. AI and BDA can be utilized to search through vast data sets to cull out outliers / objectionable content from ecosystems. SDN and 5G can be used to store information at the edge and use it for effective decision making at centralized locations. Be it education, supply chain management, operational activities, maintenance management, accounting, monitoring and auditing, scores of use cases can be identified to seamless migration.

# M

Manipulation of appropriate ICT technologies is the key for sustainable growth. Even in AI & ML or BDA, which algorithms to use, how to customize options provided by these latest technologies, the key answer is to manipulate these technologies to meet the use case requirements. Choosing the right communication technology from SDN to 5G considering the cost implications and ease of deployment is the core need to manipulate. The complex nature of these developments can be overcome with thorough analysis of use cases vis a vis available ICT facet. It is important to note that the beginning is to be done to ensure effective contribution of these developments.

# P

Provide top management support for using ICT in strategic thinking. Without this step, it is impossible to progress in any adoption process. The organizational culture will be decided by the top management and then it becomes easy for acceptance of the changes required. The same AI&ML, BDA can give better advice to top management for growth-oriented decision making. Even the change management process covered later will be easy after acceptance by the top management. The strategic thinking can include adoption of ICT developments reaping the benefits of innovation from these advancements.

# L

Leveraging requisite information resources for exploitation of ICT advancements is a key to adoption. Organizing the information is the right thing to do to manage and support the decision-making. It is important to note that the data is available in abundance and multiple formats structured, unstructured or semi-structured. However, the ICT advancements in cloud computing, Big Data Analytics with Hadoop, Mango DB, Spark etc., AI&ML algorithms can organize these vast amounts of data with SDN, 5G.

# E

Ensure availability of hardware and software resources (public or private cloud). Data being the sole driver for AI&ML, BDA, RPA, Blockchain, the capacity for storing and processing can be the best driver for implementation. Storage infrastructure and huge computing resources have become commoditized and easily available from various vendors in the market. Only requirement is to identify right mix of converged infrastructure for the organization. In case of software as well, customized solutions are available for every activity. Redundancy and diversity in hardware and software must be ensured. Right mix of public and private cloud, considering the criticality of the data and its envisaged confidentiality, can be identified. AI can be utilized to analyze the data content and plan future compute / storage procurements.

# M

Managing transition of existing process through change management is the next important step in adoption. This becomes easier with top management support and direction. It is important for the individuals and teams to accept the development in ICT domain with a positive outlook. Some of the tasks of individuals / teams will become redundant with RPA, AI&ML, BDA, but ultimately, the decision making with empathy has to be done by individuals. Everyone has to unlearn and re-learn to update themselves to be relevant with adoption of new technologies.

The better the involvement in the change management, earlier and successful will be the adoption of ICT advancements. The advantages of the new technologies will far outperform the individual issues / concerns towards overall organizational objectives.

# E

Ensure effective monitoring and auditing for enhanced customer experience. Network monitoring and management will be another important step in successful management of new technologies. This will also contribute to quality in every aspects of the process as every step can be corrected / consolidated with better inputs. AI&ML, BDA will provide much needed tools to efficiently monitor and audit the systems automatically. Be it applications, network or hardware, monitoring and auditing will not only aid in better situational awareness but will also provide necessary inputs for further procurement of resources which is key for competitive advantage.

# N

Negotiating feedbacks is the key to improvement. The feedbacks can be positive or negative. But the essence of accepting feedbacks about any process during or after the adoption will improve the adoption. AI&ML can provide great deals of feedback based on the training data, contributing to removing the biases. The BDA algorithms also can be tweaked to extract meaningful feedback from the volumes of data available through scatter analysis, factor analysis etc. The feedback can then be used to correct RPA processes as well as network bandwidth management efficiently.

# T

Transfer knowledge to requisite teams is the last and most critical step in adoption of new ICT domain technologies. AI&ML, BDA, RPA, Blockchain implementations can give great deal of knowledge management resources throughout the process. Cyber security aspects will also provide valuable inputs for ensuring secure adoption of key technologies. SDN and 5G will make it easier to assimilate and use the knowledge from any region on any kind of device, which is key for better adoption by masses. It is extremely important to capture the tacit knowledge and make it available for further innovation and modernization.

All these technologies in ICT domain like Cloud Computing, AI&ML, Big Data Analytics and Blockchain are being offered as a service framework also, which will pave the way for their immediate adoption. The IMPLEMENT framework covered above can be seen in every case study. The organizations could see the possible use cases, analyze the available options for reengineering their processes, the top management drove the change process, the changes were embraced by the employees to letter and spirit, monitoring and auditing were ensured with these technologies, feedbacks were efficiently analyzed and finally these are all available for use to take the lessons learnt forward. These adoptions of latest developments in ICT domain have resulted in increased productivity, profits, responsiveness, reduction in costs, losses and overall improvement in customer satisfaction which encouraged the organizations to innovate further. It is extremely important to keep tab on the latest developments and ensure continuous improvement is carried out. A key to maintain such a tempo is improving the skill levels and enhance the knowledge management aspects across the spectrum of our society.

## CONCLUSION

It is important to harness the new developments in ICT domain and IMPLEMENT them in right earnest to gain maximum. It is imperative that latest developments in ICT domain can be implemented with collaborative efforts amongst agencies including public and private. ICT must be used to enable and deliver the envisaged changes towards improved productivity. The IMPLEMENT framework can be adopted with common ICT infrastructure, thereby enabling reducing concerns and fostering growth. This ICT adoption strategy will not only strengthen the governance but also provide adequate growth opportunities to individuals and organizations alike. The adoption of IMPLEMENT ICT strategy will enable the business venture in future with requisite resources and wherewithal to excel while maintaining safe cyber security posture.

The competitive advantage will accrue in terms of militaries gaining upper hand over adversaries, hospitals getting more aware about pandemic spread or patient behavior, HR having more insights in employee retention and enhancement, individuals getting more self-development opportunities, companies gaining more in new product development and launches, with faster and continuous adoption of latest developments in ICT domain. Early adoption of these latest developments in ICT domain will surely ensure meeting the sustainable development goals of the world.

## IMPLICATIONS FOR THE SOCIETY AND FUTURE RESEARCH PROSPECTS

The advances in ICT domain have revolutionized the society in multitude of ways. Especially after the Covid pandemic, ICT have ensured that the functioning of all sectors, especially education, healthcare sectors spearhead the societal changes. The current advances and implementable solutions in ICT domain will not only enhance the end user experience but will also aid in improving business processes, providing enormous growth opportunities.

The time factor analysis for effective implementation of ICT technologies can be taken forward to further streamline faster adoption. Thorough analysis needs to be done to migrate existing system with ICT technologies in time bound manner, without affecting the operations. Correlation analysis need to be undertaken for establishing impact of ICT technologies on societal needs, especially impact of AI&ML on learning effectiveness, impact of cyber security on adopting any of these ICT technologies, impact of Big Data Analytics on productivity and efficiency, etc.

# REFERENCES

Gabriel Kabanda (2019). Trends in Information Technology Management.

CATALIN, P., and Alina, P., (2010). Information Technology Management, Journal of Knowledge Management, Economics and Information Technology, http://www.scientificpapers.org.

T. H. AlBalushi and S. Ali, "Evaluation of the quality of E-government services: Quality trend analysis," 2015 International Conference on Information and Communication Technology Research (ICTRC), Abu Dhabi, United Arab Emirates, 2015, pp. 226–229, doi: 10.1109/ICTRC.2015.7156463.

E. Le Rouzic et al., "TREND towards more energy-efficient optical networks," 2013 17th International Conference on Optical Networking Design and Modelling (ONDM), Brest, France, 2013, pp. 211–216.

Y. Hao, P. Helo and A. Shamsuzzoha, "Cloud-based data exchange and messaging platform implementation for Virtual Factory environment," 2015 IEEE International Conference on Industrial Engineering and Engineering Management (IEEM), Singapore, 2015, pp. 426–430, doi: 10.1109/IEEM.2015.7385682.

J. Bhatia, R. Govani and M. Bhavsar, "Software Defined Networking: From Theory to Practice," 2018 Fifth International Conference on Parallel, Distributed and Grid Computing (PDGC), Solan, India, 2018, pp. 789–794, doi: 10.1109/PDGC.2018.8745762.

H. Desai, M. Kantarcioglu and L. Kagal, "A Hybrid Blockchain Architecture for Privacy-Enabled and Accountable Auctions," 2019 IEEE International Conference on Blockchain (Blockchain), Atlanta, GA, USA, 2019, pp. 34–43, doi: 10.1109/Blockchain.2019.00014.

H. Yoo and N. Ko, "Blockchain based Data Marketplace System," 2020 International Conference on Information and Communication Technology Convergence (ICTC), Jeju, Korea (South), 2020, pp. 1255–1257, doi: 10.1109/ICTC49870.2020.9289087.

D. Mujtaba and N. Mahapatra, "Recent Trends in Natural Language Understanding for Procedural Knowledge," 2019 International Conference on Computational Science and Computational Intelligence (CSCI), Las Vegas, NV, USA, 2019, pp. 420–424, doi: 10.1109/CSCI49370.2019.00082.

P. C. Yadav, H. V. Singh, A. K. Patel and A. Singh, "A comparative analysis of different facial action tracking models and techniques," 2016 International Conference on Emerging Trends in Electrical Electronics & Sustainable Energy Systems (ICETEESES), Sultanpur, India, 2016, pp. 347–349, doi: 10.1109/ICETEESES.2016.7581407.

O. Baker and C. N. Thien, "A New Approach to Use Big Data Tools to Substitute Unstructured Data Warehouse," 2020 IEEE Conference on Big Data and Analytics (ICBDA), Kota Kinabalu, Malaysia, 2020, pp. 26–31, doi: 10.1109/ICBDA50157.2020.9289757.

C. Balaguer, "Soft robotics concept in construction industry," Proceedings World Automation Congress, 2004., Seville, Spain, 2004, pp. 517–522.

Y. Tan, J. Liu, H. Wang and M. Xian, "The Development Trend Analysis of 5G Network," 2019 International Conference on Communications, Information System and Computer Engineering (CISCE), Haikou, China, 2019, pp. 382–385, doi: 10.1109/CISCE.2019.00090.

EJIAKU, S.A., (2014). "Technology Adoption: Issues and Challenges in Information Technology Adoption in Emerging Economies", Journal of International Technology and Information Management, Vol. 23, Issue. 2, Article 5.

# CHAPTER TEN

## No more TOP SECRET to wellbeing of Engineering Educators: A theoretical model during Covid-19

**Dr. Poonam Jindal**
*Assistant Professor, Vignana Jyothi Institute of Management*
*Dr.poonamjindal@vjim.edu.in*

**Dr. Yamini Meduri**
*Assistant Professor, Vignana Jyothi Institute of Management*
*yaminimeduri@vjim.edu.in*

**Abstract**—*Covid-19 pandemic has brought the unprecedented conditions for the whole wide world. Education world is no different in terms of getting impacted because of the covid-19 pandemic. The overnight shift to online teaching is the new normal for every education institute. The bigger challenge arises for the engineering institutions after observing the fast-changing technological challenge taking place everywhere. This article is an attempt to understand the well-being states of engineering educators. The relationship among perceived organisational support, workplace friendship and well being was the main objective of the study. By using these three constructs a theoretical model is designed and different items of the constructs help in developing a framework named as TOP SECRET (TS). Study is an effort of understanding how these TS parameters are no more TS for educators and institutions. Article is based on the literature review of the three constructs. Various seminal works in the area are taken into consideration for describing the TS parameters. To test the model, an empirical study is suggested for future research scope.*

## 1. INTRODUCTION

When Engineering, an area buried under practical learning cloud, moved online due to Covid-19 pandemic, the challenges the situation has uprooted have outnumbered when compared to other STEM disciplines. Being the domain specific professionals, the engineering faculty and students were expected to be the know-it-all when it came to virtual learning through a digital platform. The reality was quite the opposite, the faculty of engineering suffered more in moving to online platforms specially with the practical learning. With the sudden disruption in the household help, schools, care centers etc., the situation added on to the professional stress leading to higher differentials in academic productivity.

Inspite of the AICTE directives to the colleges to pay salaries on time, engineering faculty faced a nightmare in managing through their salary cuts. This further added on to the anxiety leading to a deeper impact of the pandemic. With the professional and personal lives in a mess, the engineering faculty experienced stress at different levels during the lockdown and later too. This resulted in extreme psychological impact of the educator on student learning as well. Institutions have created different platforms to ensure that the teaching learning does not get effected but the stressed teachers had to bear the brunt of the situation. This drastically effected the productivity of the engineering faculty with respect to research, consulting etc. and the situation is much deeper with the female employees (Krukowski, Jagsi & Cardel, 2020).

A survey report by QS IGAUGE, which rates colleges and universities in India with complete operational control held by the London-based Quacquarelli Symonds (QS), which comes out with coveted global university rankings in the Faculty Academic Review for Excellence (FARE) survey in 2020 highlighted as high as 45% of the engineering faculty are finding it difficult to cope with the stress and burnout experienced in the wake of Covid-19 pandemic and the digital transformation of the education process in the engineering domain. The report also highlighted that the online teaching as a reason for almost 60% of the faculty for moderate to high increase in their anxiety levels.

The scenario might have been different when the institutions provided the necessary support by creating an empathy driven environment to support the educators not only with the necessary technology required for online teaching but also with the necessary psychological support for better well-being. A study conducted by Evanoff, et. al. (2020) on university employees showed a significant and positive impact of the supervisory support on the emotional wellbeing of the employees in the wake of pandemic. This was also highlighted by a study by Lee, et. al. (2021) which suggested that the organizational support improved wellbeing and pointed out a significant impact on the self-efficacy.

From the times immemorial, it has been stressed on building workplace relationships and strengthening workplace friendships can develop organizational citizenship behaviour that denotes the sense of belongingness of the employees towards the organization which can positively impact job performance (Ong, 2013; Kleine, Choi & Ko, 2020). In the wake of the pandemic, the relationship further strengthened showing a positive impact on the emotional wellbeing of the employees (Polizzi, Lynn & Perry, 2020; Zhuang, et. al., 2020).

The covid-19 pandemic has drastically modified the workplace behaviours and employer expectations that every initiative to support and take care of the employees has resulted in positive results. The current study, therefore, attempted to study the relationship between the emotional well being, perceived organizational support and workplace friendship.

A further analysis of the current studies in the wake of the pandemic on stress and wellbeing focused on the health care workers (Rossi, et. al. 2020; Kinman, Teoh & Harriss, 2020; Gavin, et. al., 2020), students (Bono, Reil & Hescox, 2020, Charles, et. al, 2021), Information Technology employees (Prasad, Vaidya & Mangipudi, 2020); high school teachers (Košir, et. al. 2020) and very less focus was on engineering educators. The current study attempted to understand the state of wellbeing of engineering educators during the pandemic.

The further sections of the article explain the theoretical framework underlying the foundation for the study. The constructs are defined, and the hypothesized relationships are established through a detailed review of literature. The methodology section explains the review framework and inferences drawn. Based on the findings, the final sections propose the recommendations for the management of engineering colleges which can improve the educator wellbeing which can in-turn improve the effectiveness of the teaching learning process and educator productivity.

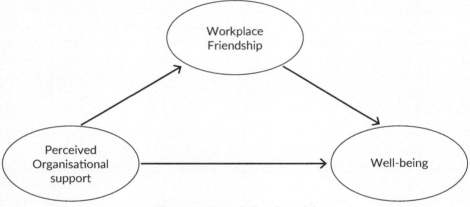

**Figure 1.**  Foundational Model

## 2. REVIEW OF LITERATURE

Based on a basic foundational evidence from the existing literature, it is understood that there could be a possible relationship better the three variables considered for developing the model i.e., Perceived Organizational Support, Workplace Friendship and Wellbeing. This section explains each of these variables through a decent review of existing literature.

### Perceived Organisational Support (POS)

POS has taken a very important role in various organisational context research studies since its emergence around three decades ago. Studies on employees performance, stress, well-being, turnover intentions, commitment, job satisfaction and many more construct have found the place for POS. Perceived Organisational Support (POS) is defined as the extent organisation supports and appreciates the efforts of employees and care about them. POS integrates the employee's conviction that appreciation for efforts is conveyed through acknowledgement, job enhancement, supervisor's support, compensation, other benefits, and Human resource management practices. According to Eisenberger (2002), more that 275 studies are published using POS as construct (Rhoades & Eisenberger, 2002; Cropanzano, Howes, Grandy & Toth, 1997; Moorman, Blakely & Niehoff, 1998; Settoon et al., 1996; Wayne et al., 1997; Allen, Shore & Griffeth, 2003; Eisenberger et al., 1999 to cite a few).

Studies concentrating on measuring perceived employer commitment, which was called a survey of Perceived Organisational Support suggested that perceived organizational support (POS) is an initiator of organisational commitment (Eisenberger, Hutchinson, Hutchinson, and Sowa, 1986). The social exchange idea was used to explain this phenomenon. An employee's perception about organisation's commitment towards oneself builds the employee's commitment to the organisation in return. The results of the study suggested that the social exchange idea fits well with the POS idea (Eisenberger et al., 1986).

The social-exchange literature suggests that organizational commitment reflects employees' perceptions about the nature of the relationship that exists between themselves and the employing organization. According to Eisenberger et al. (1986), "employees develop global beliefs concerning the extent to which the organization values their contributions and cares about their well-being" (p. 501).

There are various research studies indicating that employees having high level of POS receive their job experience as more positively showing increased job satisfaction, reduced stress and positive attitude. Such employees have shown more interest in new learning and invest more in organisation and work increasing the level of affective commitment and ultimately increasing their performance (Rhoades & Eisenberger, 2002).

A study that investigated the relationship of impact of POS on individual and group withdrawal behaviour found that, in groups where employees observe other peers withdrawing from work, the desire of the entire group to take part in withdrawal would be increased. In such situations, high POS may prevent this contagious effect of withdrawal behaviour (Eder & Eisenberger, 2008). If employee is valued in organisation, that leads to better career growth, salary, trust and respect, and access to information. He gets better situation to carry out his job and withdrawal may not happen. There are negative relationship aspects between better POS and intent to leave, that guides to management to create better environment for their employees to retain them (Makanjee et al., 2006).

A meta-analysis carried out on POS research (Rhoades and Eisenberger, 2002) indicates that there are three level of favourable conditions which employees perceive as POS are fairness of treatment in the system, manager's support, and reward and benefits including job support. Research has focused on the POS and career development opportunities for knowledge workers employees for taking decision about turnover. POS becomes big reason for employee's perception about their wellbeing at workplace.

Developing a supportive environment is the beneficial investment for organisations. The positive relations are established among POS and employee well-being, employee engagement (Caesens et al., 2016). Research has also indicated the negative relationship of POS and stress and burnout among employees (Walters & Raybould, 2007). Apprehension regarding employee well-being is seen through the organisational policies and human resources practices that expedite fulfilling work and life demands (Worley, Fuqua, & Hellman, 2009).

Taking cue from multiple studies, a good eleven variables are observed to better define POS. The variables are Value to work, Appreciation, Goals and values, Interest, Helping and transparent, Well-being, Satisfaction, Concern, Opinion and expression, Accomplishment, and Interesting Job. These variables present a deeper understanding of POS and how much organizations should be considering them for better productivity.

## Workplace Friendship

People develop profound relationships with others because of their social need (Robbins, 2018), which is a psychological need of getting affiliated with others in any context. Hence, they develop workplace friendships. Friendship is defined as a deliberate, individual, and personal relationship usually offering warmth and support (Fehr, 1999). Friendships can be on various levels and forms of intimacy (Spencer & pahl, 2006) and is mostly about sharing similar interests and experiences at workplace or any other context, and providing support in different ways (Pedersen & Lewis, 2012). The definitions of workplace friendship are though changed from common kinds of friendship. It mainly focuses on friendship that occurs in the workplace (Song, 2005).

Workplace friendship is a different form of friendship that occurs among coworkers and includes mutual trust, commitment, socialisation and sharing common interest and values (Berman, West, Maurice, & Richter, 2002). In workplace friendship people share instrumental and emotional support with each other by providing practical assistance and empathy. It is not merely acquaintances. Workplace friendship has two dimensions, opportunities of friendship at workplace and friendship prevalence (Nielsen et al., 2000). The validated scale is used to measure these two dimensions. Opportunities for friendship means the chances of getting to know your colleagues and communicating with them in an organisational setup and friendship prevalence is a feeling of trust, confidence and need to interact with others at workplace. Workplace friendship is not formal workplace relationship and are two different phenomena. Workplace friendship is more of voluntary relation and not bound with any formal actions. Employees choose to be friends or not (Marrison, 2004; Sias, Smith, & Avdeyeva, 2003).

The variables defining workplace friendship are Trust, Confinement, Interest in work and Socialisation.

## Well-being

Well-being often defined as hedonic and eudaimonic well-being in literature. Hedonic well-being is maximising the experience of pleasure and minimising pain (Ryan & Deci, 2001), and eudaimonic well-being is when individual take the responsibility of their happiness and use their full potential for that (Waterman, 2008). Hedonic and eudaimonic wellbeing are defined in different ways in literature but a recent research (Longo, Coyne, Joseph, & Gustavsson, 2016) found that there is a high correlation between the variables of these two. This shows that the difference is not really scientific and probably only philosophical. In the current study the well-being is used as general mental well-being rather than as hedonic or eudaimonic. There are various research studies on well-being that show the direct relationship with other construct like productivity (Heffernan & Dundon, 2016), work related stress (Ilies et al., 2015), employee resilience (Huang et al., 2019), family and social support (Huang et al., 2019), workplace income (Mokhtar et al., 2015) responsiveness, efficiency and friendliness in services are the core prescriptions to enhance the competitiveness of one's country. Financial well-being and employees are two aspects that consequently related with each other that have received substantial deliberation from researchers, employers and financial advisor. Financial well-being can affect both direct and indirectly towards an individual, team and also organization. Changes in employee's financial well-being level whether it becomes high or low will affect their job performance. The purpose of this study is to discuss the level of public employee's financial well-being in Malaysia as well as to examine the determinants of financial well-being. A total of 73 questionnaires have been distributed through e-survey (email based. A research with quasi-experimental group indicates the effect of job crafting on employee's wellbeing (van Wingerden et al., 2017) highlighting that job crafting has a positive relation with employee well-being with reference to Job demand-resource theory. Meanwhile people's personality also play role in their wellbeing (Traits & Theories, 1998) this also reflects that the attitude one have for developing relations with others will impact their well-being. At workplace it becomes the responsibility of human resource management and supervisors to investigate into the matter which are related with stress and absenteeism and may have impact on employee well-being (Kuehnl et al., 2019). These studies show that there are various constructs that may have influence on employee well-being. Consequently, organisations should be interested in promoting and maintaining their employees' well-being. Employees who experience positivity and express high levels of positive psychological functioning are valuable assets to any organisation. It is, therefore, imperative to analyse organisational and personal factors that contribute to employee well-being.

The variables used to define Wellbeing are Purposeful, Meaningful and engaging, Supporting and rewarding, Happiness for others, Competent and capable, Good life, Optimistic and Respect from others.

Having defined each of the study variables, an attempt to understand them from the engineering educators' perspective was undertaken. The business organizational strategies have been re-designed to suit the engineering educational institutions.

## Methodology

The main objective of the study is to design a framework for engineering educators during covid-19 times. This study is based on the literature review of three main constructs - POS, Workplace friendship and well-being. The comprehensive literature review helps in developing a theoretical framework and finally contributes to the body of knowledge.

## Theoretical Framework

Covid-19 has disrupted the lives of many and the engineering educators were affected no less. With a sudden disruption of the classrooms due to Nation wide lockdown, and the regulated 'new normal' conditions, students and teachers suffered the new and complex learning environment with almost no prior training. Though known for their development and use of technology, engineering educators were very less inclined towards online teaching learning process making the pandemic more complex for students and themselves.

An observation of the engineering colleges with the best of the accreditation scores also suffered during the pandemic halting the learning process for a few months before slowly opening it up. It was observed that most of the first colleges which started online teaching, have enjoyed a good institutional support to the educators. However, the educators opined that the process was difficult mainly because of the emotional stress that employees were already experiencing because of the pandemic.

A finer understanding of the variables in discussion, Perceived Organisational Support, Workplace Friendship and Wellbeing, has helped understand the defining constructs better. Table 1 illustrates the defining variables of the three constructs.

**Table 1.**   Defining variables

| POS | Workplace friendship | Well-being |
|---|---|---|
| • Value to work | • Trust | • Purposeful |
| • Appreciation | • Confide | • Meaningful and engaging |
| • Goals and values | • Interest in work | • Supporting and rewarding |
| • My interest | • Socialisation | • Happiness for others |
| • Helping and transparent | • Opportunity | • Competent and capable |
| • Well-being | • Collective problem solving | • Good life |
| • Satisfaction | • Informal Communication | • Optimistic |
| • Concern | | • Respect from others |
| • Opinion and expression | | |
| • Accomplishment | | |
| • Interesting Job-Engagement | | |

A further analysis of relevant research further reduced these generic variables to more specific variables to focus on. These variables shall help organizations, in general and engineering institutions in particular, to promote the importance of employee wellbeing and how much the formal and informal parts of the organization can play a role.

## TOP SECRET Model

The specific variables identified through the model which can help the institutions to take the necessary actions to promote and uplift the engineering educators wellbeing which can inturn lead to better teaching learning. The 'TOP SECRET' model is an acronym for the specific variables retained out of the generic variables. The 'TOP SECRET' variables are Trust, Optimistic, Purpose, Support, Engagement, Competent, Rewards, Expression & Transparency. The 'TOP SECRET' model is illustrated in Table 2.

**Table 2.** TOP SECRET Model

| Variable | Specific variables | Reference |
|---|---|---|
| Trust | Clarity<br>Compassion<br>Connection | Horsager (2012) |
| Optimistic | Positive Work Environment<br>Hygiene Factors<br>Collaborative goals & growth | Murphy (2015) |
| Purpose | Identify and connect to people purpose<br>Recognize the need for authenticity<br>Environment to find Meaning for work | Quinn, & Thakor (2018) |
| Support | Supervisory support<br>Improving perceptive social support<br>Reducing Stressors | Taylor (2008) |
| Engagement | Explicit Support<br>Solicit Feedback<br>Commit to Employee's employment | Jones & Kober (2019) |
| Competent | Capability enhancement<br>Career development support<br>Opportunity to diversify | Latha (2020) |
| Rewards | Recognition of good quality<br>Salary Commitment<br>Career progression opportunities | Hafiza, Shah, Jamsheed, & Zaman (2011) |
| Expression | Open Communication<br>Voice their dissent<br>Participative decision making | Kassing (2000) |
| Transparency | Quality of intentionally shared information<br>Coherence and comprehensibility<br>Timeliness | Schnackenberg & Tomlinson (2016) |

The 'TOP SECRET' variables can help educational institutions to work on core principles that help organizations survive and sustain during and after the pandemic. With the educators being the core of any educational institution and it's the faculty that help institutions gain sustainable competitive advantage, it has become more crucial for the institutions to manage them well during a crisis.

Horsager's research at Trust Edge Leadership Institute has identified eight key qualities to focus on, but three of these elements have seen to have a higher impact on faculty commitment which are Clarity, Compassion and Connection. It is important that the institutions work towards bringing role clarity for the faculty and define clear expectations from them. Enabling the leadership to show compassion towards the faculty can set an example for the faculty to empathize with the students which ultimately leads to Connection which is the major factor contributing to the success of an institution. Such an environment of trust when coupled with optimistic environment can help to explore personal and organizational purposes with a right alignment leading to astonishing results. An optimistic environment can trigger and increase intrinsic motivation which can ultimately lead to better performance and work collaboration. Developing the essence of trust and optimism through a sense of purpose and connecting faculty to that ultimate purpose of the institution and their profession can unleash a variety of positive energizers. The three aspects of Trust, Optimistic and Purpose factors of the 'TOP SECRET' model are more environment, culture and leadership driven factors which show a positive impact on the teaching learning process.

The next six factors of the 'TOP SECRET' model are more structural and process driven factors which when taken care of can drive results. There is a possibility that though there is a good environment, culture and leadership influence, if the structural and process driven factors are not taken care of, the idea of performance still lags behind. As important are the first three 'soft' factors, so are the next six 'hard' factors.

Most of the engineering educators have found it difficult in the earlier days of the pandemic is with the infrastructural support provided by the institutions. It is definitely the responsibility of the institutions to provide the space and personnel support for carrying on with the online education model which was new to both the educators and the students. It is the perception of this support which makes a big difference to all the efforts of the institutional leadership. The idea of engagement in educational institutions is more basic than any other aspect of people management. There are a lot of implied support systems which are less focused by the institutions. However, the pandemic has mandated that efforts have to be explicitly made to support the educators so they remain motivated and engaged during the complex situations. It is more important for the institutions to solicit feedback and ask employees to freely share information, both frustration and ideas for development in a productive way. Beyond all, it is important for the leadership to communicate upfront with the employees to ensure better communication and ultimately lead to better performance.

Covid-19 pandemic has thrown different set of challenges to the educators who lost jobs as the admission numbers faltered the plans. It is needless to say that engagement and commitment can only be sought from the employees when the institution commits to the employee's employment. The pandemic has also thrown up a lot of opportunities to upskill and reskill one's employees. Institutions should work towards capability development and support career development which can show a positive support for the employees during the complex times. With a lot of technological advancements seen due to the pandemic, institutions must encourage the educators to diversify and design new outlets to deliver such diversity in content.

One of the major aspect of people management that got affected by the pandemic is the rewards and recognition phenomenon. It is also an opportunity to redesign the reward strategy through a good non-financial benefits policy which can not only recognize the efforts but also help the institution to gain the faculty commitment. Empowerment, job crafting and challenging tasks through job enrichment can be a booster to educator commitment along with the regular increments and fringe benefits.

Creating an open environment for expression letting employees voice their dissent and share open feedback and/or opinions can bring in a sense of participation in decision making and take up a sense of responsibility and ownership towards institutional decisions. All of these can yield positive results when the quality of intentionally shared information shows transparency. The educators' awareness, coherence and comprehensibility of the information shared through a systematic information sharing mechanism can influence the perception of 'openness' in the system. It is important that the institutions should ensure the openness, timelines, availability and accessibility of the information to keep them connected to the core purpose of the organization.

## CONCLUSION

The covid-19 pandemic has drastically modified the workplace behaviours and employer expectations that every initiative to support and take care of the employees has resulted in positive results. The current study, therefore, attempted to study the relationship between the emotional well being, perceived organizational support and workplace friendship. The analysis of the existing literature helped develop a theoretical model which can help the engineering educational institutions to accelerate their teaching learning process.

Engineering educators have see a mix of opportunities and challenges during the pandemic and have been the most effected area of education with the highest expectation on delivery. The TOP SECRET model suggested in the current study can help the educational institutions to take care of the wellbeing of the educators who can highly influence the teaching learning process. With the accelerated changes in the technological advancements, it is important that the teaching learning process yields better innovations that the world is in need of currently and the institutions play an important role in the same.

# REFERENCES

1. Allen, D. G., Shore, L. M., & Griffeth, R. W. (2003). The role of perceived organizational support and supportive human resource practices in the turnover process. *Journal of management, 29*(1), 99–118.

2. Berman, E. M., West, J. P., & Richter, Jr, M. N. (2002). Workplace relations: Friendship patterns and consequences (according to managers). *Public Administration Review, 62*(2), 217–230.

3. Bono, G., Reil, K., & Hescox, J. (2020). Stress and wellbeing in urban college students in the US during the COVID-19 pandemic: Can grit and gratitude help? *International Journal of Wellbeing, 10*(3).

4. Caesens, G., Marique, G., Hanin, D., & Stinglhamber, F. (2016). The relationship between perceived organizational support and proactive behaviour directed towards the organization. *European Journal of Work and Organizational Psychology, 25*(3), 398–411.

5. Charles, N. E., Strong, S. J., Burns, L. C., Bullerjahn, M. R., & Serafine, K. M. (2021). Increased mood disorder symptoms, perceived stress, and alcohol use among college students during the COVID-19 pandemic. *Psychiatry research, 296*, 113706

6. Choi, Y., & Ko, S. H. (2020). Roses with or without thorns? A theoretical model of workplace friendship. *Cogent Psychology, 7*(1), 1761041.

7. Cropanzano, R., Howes, J. C., Grandey, A. A., & Toth, P. (1997). The relationship of organizational politics and support to work behaviors, attitudes, and stress. Journal of Organizational Behavior, 22, 159–180.

8. Eder, P., & Eisenberger, R. (2008). Perceived organizational support: Reducing the negative influence of coworker withdrawal behavior. *Journal of management, 34*(1), 55–68.

9. Eisenberger, R., Huntington, R., Hutchison, S., & Sowa, D. (1986). Perceived organizational support. *Journal of Applied psychology, 71*(3), 500.

10. Evanoff, B. A., Strickland, J. R., Dale, A. M., Hayibor, L., Page, E., Duncan, J. G., ... & Gray, D. L. (2020). Work-Related and personal factors associated with mental well-being during the COVID-19 response: survey of health care and other workers. *Journal of medical Internet research, 22*(8), e21366.

11. Fehr, B. (1999). Stability and commitment in friendships. In *Handbook of interpersonal commitment and relationship stability* (pp. 259–280). Springer, Boston, MA.

12. Gavin, B., Hayden, J., Adamis, D., & McNicholas, F. (2020). Caring for the psychological well-being of healthcare professionals in the Covid-19 pandemic crisis. *Ir Med J, 113*(4), 51.

13. Hafiza, N. S., Shah, S. S., Jamsheed, H., & Zaman, K. (2011). Relationship between rewards and employee's motivation in the non-profit organizations of Pakistan. Business Intelligence Journal, 4(2), 327–334.

14. Heffernan, M., & Dundon, T. (2016). Cross-level effects of high-performance work systems (HPWS) and employee well-being: The mediating effect of organisational justice. Human Resource Management Journal, 26(2), 211–231. https://doi.org/10.1111/1748-8583.12095

15. Horsager, D. (2012). The trust edge: How top leaders gain faster results, deeper relationships, and a stronger bottom line. Simon and Schuster.

16. Huang, Q., Xing, Y., & Gamble, J. (2019). Job demands–resources: a gender perspective on employee well-being and resilience in retail stores in China. International Journal of Human Resource Management, 30(8), 1323–1341. https://doi.org/10.1080/09585192.2016.1226191

17. Ilies, R., Aw, S. S. Y., & Pluut, H. (2015). Intraindividual models of employee well-being: What have we learned and where do we go from here? European Journal of Work and Organizational Psychology, 24(6), 827–838. https://doi.org/10.1080/1359432X.2015.1071422

18. Jones, M. D., & Kober, J. J. (2019). Employee engagement in difficult times. World Class Benchmarking.

19. Kassing, J. W. (2000). Exploring the relationship between workplace freedom of speech, organizational identification, and employee dissent. Communication Research Reports, 17(4), 387–396.

20. Kinman, G., Teoh, K., & Harriss, A. (2020). Supporting the well-being of healthcare workers during and after COVID-19.

21. Kleine, A. K., Rudolph, C. W., & Zacher, H. (2019). Thriving at work: A meta-analysis. *Journal of Organizational Behavior*, *40*(9–10), 973–999.

22. Košir, K., Dugonik, Š., Huskić, A., Gračner, J., Kokol, Z., & Krajnc, Ž. (2020). Predictors of perceived teachers' and school counsellors' work stress in the transition period of online education in schools during the COVID-19 pandemic. *Educational Studies*, 1–5.

23. Krukowski, R. A., Jagsi, R., & Cardel, M. I. (2020). Academic Productivity Differences by Gender and Child Age in Science, Technology, Engineering, Mathematics, and Medicine Faculty During the COVID-19 Pandemic. Journal of Women's Health.

24. Kuehnl, A., Seubert, C., Rehfuess, E., von Elm, E., Nowak, D., & Glaser, J. (2019). Human resource management training of supervisors for improving health and well-being of employees. Cochrane Database of Systematic Reviews, 2019(9). https://doi.org/10.1002/14651858.CD010905.pub2

25. Latha, S. (2020). Vuca in engineering education: Enhancement of faculty competency for capacity building. Procedia Computer Science, 172, 741–747.

26. Lee, T. C., Yao-Ping Peng, M., Wang, L., Hung, H. K., & Jong, D. (2021). Factors Influencing Employees' Subjective Wellbeing and Job Performance During the COVID-19 Global Pandemic: The Perspective of Social Cognitive Career Theory. *Frontiers in Psychology*, *12*, 455.

27. Longo, Y., Coyne, I., Joseph, S., & Gustavsson, P. (2016). Support for a general factor of well-being. *Personality and Individual Differences*, *100*, 68–72.

28. Lopes Morrison, R. (2005). *Informal relationships in the workplace: Associations with job satisfaction, organisational commitment and turnover intentions* (Doctoral dissertation, Massey University

29. Lynch, P. D., Eisenberger, R., & Armeli, S. (1999). Perceived organizational support: Inferior versus superior performance by wary employees. *Journal of applied psychology*, *84*(4), 467.

30. Makanjee, C. R., Hartzer, Y. F., & Uys, I. L. (2006). The effect of perceived organizational support on organizational commitment of diagnostic imaging radiographers. Radiography, 12(2), 118–126. https://doi.org/10.1016/j.radi.2005.04.005

31. Mokhtar, N., Husniyah, A. R., Sabri, M. F., & Abu Talib, M. (2015). Financial well-being among public employees in Malaysia: A preliminary study. Asian Social Science, 11(18), 49–54. https://doi.org/10.5539/ass.v11n18p49

32. Moorman, R. H., Blakely, G. L., & Niehoff, B. P. (1998). Does perceived organizational support mediate the relationship between procedural justice and organizational citizenship behavior? Academy of Management Journal, 41, 351–357

33. Murphy, S. (2015). The optimistic workplace: Creating an environment that energizes everyone. Amacom.

34. Nielsen, I. K., Jex, S. M., & Adams, G. A. (2000). Development and validation of scores on a two-dimensional workplace friendship scale. *Educational and Psychological Measurement*, *60*(4), 628–643.

35. Ong, L. D. (2013). Workplace friendship, trust in coworkers and employees' OCB. *Актуальні проблеми економіки*, (2), 289–294.

36. Pedersen, V. B., & Lewis, S. (2012). Flexible friends? Flexible working time arrangements, blurred work-life boundaries and friendship. *Work, employment and society*, *26*(3), 464–480.

37. Polizzi, C., Lynn, S. J., & Perry, A. (2020). Stress and coping in the time of covid-19: pathways to resilience and recovery. *Clinical Neuropsychiatry*, *17*(2).

38. Prasad, K. D. V., Vaidya, R. W., & Mangipudi, M. R. (2020). Effect of Occupational Stress and Remote Working on Psychological Wellbeing of Employees: An Empirical Study during Covid-19 Pandemic with Reference to Information Technology Industry around Hyderabad. *Indian J. Commer. Manag. Stud*, *2*, 1–13.

39. Quinn, R. E., & Thakor, A. V. (2018). Creating a purpose-driven organization. Harvard Business Review, 96(4), 78–85.

40. Rhoades, L., & Eisenberger, R. (2002). Perceived organizational support: a review of the literature. *Journal of applied psychology*, *87*(4), 698.

41. Robbins, R. M. (2018). *Evaluating the Impact of a Cross-Group Friendship Intervention on Early Adolescents* (Doctoral dissertation, UC Berkeley).

42. Rossi, R., Socci, V., Pacitti, F., Di Lorenzo, G., Di Marco, A., Siracusano, A., & Rossi, A. (2020). Mental health outcomes among front and second line health workers associated with the COVID-19 pandemic in Italy. *medRxiv*.

43. Ryan, R. M., & Deci, E. L. (2001). On happiness and human potentials: A review of research on hedonic and eudaimonic well-being. *Annual review of psychology*, *52*(1), 141–166.

44. Schnackenberg, A. K., & Tomlinson, E. C. (2016). Organizational transparency: A new perspective on managing trust in organization-stakeholder relationships. Journal of Management, 42(7), 1784–1810.

45. Settoon, R. P., Bennett, N., & Liden, R. C. (1996). Social exchange in organizations: Perceived organizational support, leader–member exchange, and employee reciprocity. Journal of Applied Psychology, 81, 219–227

46. Sias, P. M., Smith, G., & Avdeyeva, T. (2003). Sex and sex-composition differences and similarities in peer workplace friendship development. *Communication Studies*, *54*(3), 322–340.

47. Song, S. H. (2005). *Workplace friendship and its impact on employees' positive work attitudes: A comparative study of Seoul City and New Jersey state government public officials*. Rutgers The State University of New Jersey-Newark.

48. Spencer, L., & Pahl, R. (2018). *Rethinking friendship*. Princeton University Press.

49. Taylor, S. E. (2008). Fostering a supportive environment at work. The Psychologist-Manager Journal, 11(2), 265.

50. Traits, A. P., & Theories, P. (1998). SUBJECTIVE WELL-BEING. 311–312.

51. van Wingerden, J., Bakker, A. B., & Derks, D. (2017). Fostering employee well-being via a job crafting intervention. Journal of Vocational Behavior, 100, 164–174. https://doi.org/10.1016/j.jvb.2017.03.008

52. Walters, G., & Raybould, M. (2007). Burnout and perceived organisational support among front-line hospitality employees. *Journal of Hospitality and Tourism Management, 14*(2), 144–156.

53. Waterman, A. S. (2008). Reconsidering happiness: A eudaimonist's perspective. *The Journal of Positive Psychology, 3*(4), 234–252.

54. Wayne, S. J., Shore, L. M., & Liden., R. C. (1997). Perceived organizational support and leader-member exchange: A social exchange perspective. Academy of Management Journal, 40, 82–111

55. Worley, J. A., Fuqua, D. R., & Hellman, C. M. (2009). The survey of perceived organisational support: Which measure should we use? *SA Journal of Industrial Psychology, 35*(1), 112–116.

56. Zhuang, W. L., Chen, K. Y., Chang, C. L., Guan, X., & Huan, T. C. (2020). Effect of hotel employees' workplace friendship on workplace deviance behaviour: Moderating role of organisational identification. *International Journal of Hospitality Management, 88*, 102531.

# CHAPTER ELEVEN

## Impact of Expert System in Detecting Breast Carcinoma among Women Worldwide with Anxiety due to COVID-19

**Jaya Lakshmi Vakiti***
*Assistant Professor*
*Department of Management Studies*
*Nalla Malla Reddy Engineering College, Hyderabad, Telangana, India*
*(Email: jayalakshmivakiti@gmail.com)*

**Abstract**—*Breast carcinoma is one of the most often detected cancer in female, every year there we can see more than two million new diagnoses throughout the world. The anxiety with Breast cancer is one of the deadliest and COVID-19 catastrophe has now annexed yet another level to this anxiety. Breast cancer detection is difficult when the woman is in her thirties' and has just began planning a future for herself. Women are generally treated at a later, more advanced stage with poor diagnosis. If it continues then by 2030, this dangerous disease will cause most deaths among women in world than any other disease. The Breast Cancer Detection and medicament Technologies industry has expertise astonishing advancements in 2020 with different crucial techniques and improvements boosting the digital health market. Machine learning and Artificial Intelligence predict disease risk from Breast Carcinoma. There are different methods used in detecting carcinoma at early stages with expert systems such as Computed tomography laser mammography, computer-aided detection, Magnetic Resonance Imaging, Microwave Imaging, Electrical Impedance Scanning, Digital Tomosynthesis Mammography, Sonography, Digital Infrared Imaging etc. An extensive advance in healthcare practice is the incorporation of Clinical Decision Support Systems (CDSSs) to help and assist medical workforce in clinical decision-making, hence developing the quality of decisions and complete patient care while reducing costs. The utilization and operation of CDSSs in Breast Carcinoma care in present situation is gradually increasing. Although there may be variation in how certain CDSSs are developed, the decisions they suggest, and how they are used in medical practice. The Expert System which helps decision-making in Breast Carcinoma treatment is provided along with certain advantages, risks and Challenges for development.*

**Keywords**—Breast Carcinoma, anxiety, Expert System, Artificial Intelligence, Digital Mammography, COVID-19.

## 1.0 INTRODUCTION

Expert Systems can study how human brain envisage, grasp, choose and work, when it attempts to solve problems. Various tools and techniques are used in Expert Systems like artificial neural networks, psychology economics statistics, mathematics probability computer science, information engineering etc. Novel technologies are being developed and are more advanced in the detection and diagnosis of breast carcinoma. Medical expert-based systems are computer systems that have been instructed and trained with actual cases to perform sophisticated tasks. Some notable systems include Mycin for infectious diseases, and Internist-1, QMR and DXplain, Oncoin Quantx, e-morph koios medsol, IASST-IHC for general internal medicine.

Breast cancer testing programs are presently executed in most advanced countries and have been shown to rise earlier stage breast carcinoma recognition leading to developed diagnosis and reduction in death rates. Mammography is the most important screening tool for breast cancer for decades with more than billion women being scanned each year around the world.

The use of artificial intelligence (AI) in medical imaging, various innovative algorithms based on deep learning have been established and applied to digital mammography. Initial investigations have proved that the use of expert systems or AI systems as contemporaneous readers for analysing mammograms can increase efficiency of the doctors in terms of sensitivity and time. Medical expert systems usually include a knowledge base and rule based inference to generate a differential diagnosis.

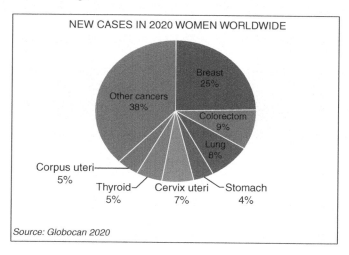

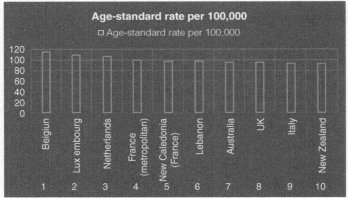

*Source: Globocan 2020*

## 2.0 TYPES OF EXPERT SYSTEM IN BREAST CARCINOMA HEALTH CARE

**Breast Cancer Detection**

| | |
|---|---|
| ▲ DIGITAL MAMMOGRAPHY | ▲ SONOGRAPHY |
| ▲ COMPUTER TOMOGRAPHY LAYER MAMMOGRAPHY | ▲ ELECTRONIC PALPATION |
| ▲ DIGITAL TOMO SYNTHESIS | ▲ DIFFRACTION ENHANCED IMAGING |
| ▲ DIGITAL INFRARED IMAGING | ▲ POSITRON EMISSION TOMOGRAPHY |
| ▲ OPTICAL IMAGING | ▲ DIGITAL TOMOSYNTHESIS |
| ▲ IMAGE GUIDED BIOPSY | ▲ MAGNETIC RESONANCE SPECTROSCOPY |
| ▲ MAGNETIC RESONANCE IMAGING | ▲ THERMO-RHYTHMOMETRY |
| ▲ ELASTOGRAPHY | ▲ ELECTRICAL IMPEDANCE SCANNING |
| ▲ ELECTRICAL POTENTIAL MEASUREMENT | ▲ MICROWAVE IMAGING |

*Source:* The National Center for Biotechnology Information

## 2.1 Digital Mammography

It is a method for storing x-ray images in digital format contradiction to x-ray film. The images are shown on a computer screen to identify the Carcinoma. The digital images may give better results when compare to regular mammography.

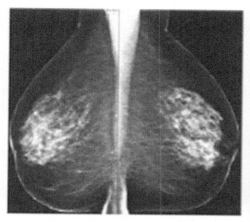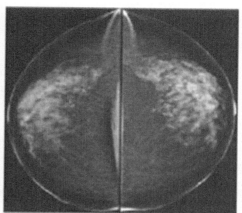

*Source:* Swissradiology

## 2.2 Computer Tomography Laser Mammography

It observes the blood circulation of tumours, and the most advantage of this Tomography laser mammography is there will be no breast compression and women feel comfortable while using this type of system. This expert system is designed especially for women who have heavy or dense breasts.

## 2.3 Digital Tomosynthesis Mammography

It involves rotating the x-ray machinery in a circle around the breast while taking several images. The method reduces the risk of imbricating structures from a particular angle will abstruse a carcinoma, likely generating abnormalities more noticeable. Presently, the most substantial obstacle to the acceptance of the tomographic technology is the amount of time that it takes to rebuild the image.

## 2.4 Digital Infrared Imaging

To do this imaging they increase circulation to the cells by transferring chemical signals to keep present blood vessels open, convert inactive vessels, and produce novel ones. The increased vascular movement repeatedly results in an rise in outward temperatures of the breast near the position of tumour, which can be seen through thermo graphic devices.

## 2.5 Optical Imaging

It is a technology used to see the haemoglobin level, identifying possible malignancies. Imaging the absorption of near-infrared light in breast tissue can quantify the haemoglobin level and amount of blood providing variance between the solid vasculature usually connected with carcinoma and healthy tissue.

## 2.6 Image Guided Biopsy

It play a vital part in assisting physicians do breast biopsies, particularly of abnormal regions that cannot be handled but can be imaged on a regular mammogram and also with ultrasound. By use of a computer and perusing devices to get information about the exact place of the image in three magnitudes. A needle is then injected into the breast and a tissue sample is acquired for a complete analysis to test the sample.

## 2.7 Magnetic Resonance Imaging

Without use of radiation it involves a strong magnet associated to a computer generates complete images of the breast. Every MRI produces number of images of the breast from all angles. A radiologist then investigates the images to detect abnormal sections that may need further examination. While doing the test the patient lie down on her stomach on the perusing board. The breast hangs into a depression on scanning board which comprises coils that identify the magnetic signal. Clinical trials are being done to decide if MRI is appreciated for screening certain women at high threat for breast carcinoma.

## 2.8 Elastography

Plotting the mechanical properties such as rigidity or pliability of breast nerve can detect abnormalities that are frequently linked with cancer tumour. This type of cancer discovery is termed as Elastography. Elastography combines mechanical pulsations with imaging modalities like magnetic resonance. So imaging the actions of the breast tissue in reaction to mechanical pulsations can determine abnormalities in the pliability of the breast tumours that may not be spotted by mammography.

## 2.9 Electrical Potential Measurement

This method associated to electrodes applied to the skin to take dimensions of electrical potential at different places on the breast. The variance in electric charge is calculated in regions of doubtful conclusions in comparison with electrodes located in a different place on the chest. The irregular development of cancer cells may result in an ionic rise with potassium pushing out of the cells and sodium pushing into cells.

## 2.10 Sonography (Ultrasound)

Sonography is an imaging system in which high-frequency sound waves are echoed from internal tissues. Their resonances gives an image called a sonogram. Ultrasound is not now used for routine breast cancer screening as it does not constantly notice certain initial signs of cancer such as micro calcifications, a calcium deposits in the breast that cannot be fingered but can be seen on a regular mammogram, and are the most common gauge of ductal carcinoma.

## 2.11 Diffraction Enhanced Imaging

In this a silicon crystal is located between the object being studied and the digital indicator where the image is recorded and the crystal diffracts a specific wavelength of x-ray giving two images. The first one is related to x-ray absorption and the second one is related to refraction. Refraction is a procedure where light, including x-rays, diverges in direction slightly due to variances in the thickness of the material it passes through. Hence the combination of these two images give more detail in the nerve and tissue.

## 2.12 Positron Emission Tomography (PET)

It is a technique by which cellular and molecular measures can be evaluated. Radioactive tracers injected into the blood to plot the underlying biochemistry. It tests create live computerized pictures of chemical changes of a tissue. An injection is given to a patient that contains sugar and radioactive material. This can be absorbed by cells with higher metabolism, such as tumours. However, this test is limited in identifying metastatic cancer that has moved from the breast to another place in the body. This scans are more precise in noticing larger and more antagonistic tumours linked with metastatic cancers than they are in finding smaller tumours.

## 2.13 Magnetic Resonance Spectroscopy (MRS)

This method can calculate the metabolism of pathological specimens and find biochemical variations, which closely connected with the existence of tumours. This method is costly and unverified, and therefore restricted to academic medical research centres.

# 3.0 THERMORHYTHMOMETRY

It depends upon similar principles as infrared thermography to support find breast cancer, the method uses a different approach. Here the probes are located on the breast that tests the skin temperature frequently to find differences which may related to neoangiogenesis and carcinoma. To find abnormal levels that could be missed with tests that only observe the breast for a particular time, possibly missing cautionary signs that are only evident by examining the circadian temperature of patients.

## 3.1 Electrical Impedance Scanning

Various tissues have various levels of electrical resistance Electrical impedance is lower in cancerous breast tissue compared to healthy breast tissue. So electrical impedance scanning devices are used along with regular mammography to support notice breast carcinoma.

This scanning device contains of a scanning probe and a computer screen that shows two-dimensional pictures of the breast. It will not emit radiation but very small amount of current, is transferred into the body. The current moves through the breast, where it is tested by the scanning probe and displays as bright white spots on a computer screen. The scanner sends the picture right to a computer, permitting the physician to move the probe around the breast to get the best interpretation of the place where it is being examined.

## 3.2  Microwave Imaging

Recording the variances in the electrical properties can be proficient by using low-energy microwaves. Because there will be heavy water content in tumours when we observe with a healthy tissue, variances in breast tissue can be analysed by changes occurred in electrical properties. But micro calcifications, indicates of early breast cancer, can be found much smaller with mammography. Breast cancers have the possibility to show more contrast at microwave frequencies than at the x-ray frequencies which are used for mammograms.

## 4.0  COVID-19 ANXIETY ON BREAST CARCINOMA SUFFERING WOMEN

The COVID-19 disease has resulted severe impacts on people worldwide at different levels and especially on the Women Health. The medical care research and development is anticipated to show a sudden deterioration of women health in lockdown period. Severe stress, fear of death worsen the Breast carcinoma patient's metabolism rate and it can be assumed from the present circumstances brought about by the COVID-19 that the expert system techniques or methods applied on a women may provide how much anxiety and depression they are facing when they exposed to the information regarding this COVID-19 pandemic. The scientists are estimated to slowly improve post-COVID-19, which will current eye-catching chances for expert systems across regions of the world in the next few years to help the doctors in treating the patient's best possible way and reducing the risk of dying. There are various techniques that support people lessen anxiety and depression.

Scientists instructs a computer or expert system to calculate electrocardiograms to predict irregular heartbeat of people. Researchers developed a neural network to study electrocardiogram to find patients at high risk of dying. Expert System can observe electrocardiogram test results, to determine patients at increased threat of irregular heartbeat. This gives more indication that we are on the margin of a change in medicine where expert systems will be functioning with doctors to advance patient care.

Anxiety and overthinking are frequently used words in present situation as many people are suffering from this kind of stress. But there is no successful application of expert system technology in developing people emotions.

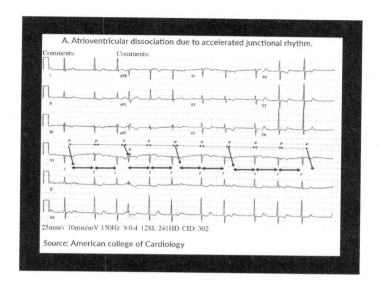

Source: American college of Cardiology

# 5.0 RECENT DEVELOPMENTS OF EXPERT SYSTEM IN MEDICAL CARE SECTOR

## 5.1 India-made MRI Machine by Arjun Arunachalam at Voxelgrids

This device can be transported to any place in India, as well as to remote areas, and possibly take medical imaging to the underserved parts. Peenya hub a healthcare modernization by a small firm promises to give high quality medical imaging, medical diagnosis and treatment accessible to places of India that are medically underserved. MRI machine created by Voxelgrids Innovations Private Limited is totally made in India and reduces some of the primary risks linked with common use of MRI in terms of size time and cost.

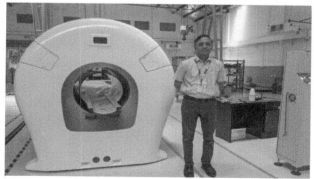

Source:https://swarajyamag.com/technology/innovative-india-made-mri-machine-can-make-medical-imaging-affordable-and-accessible

## 5.2  OncoStem Development of CanAssist Breast

CanAssist Breast is a prognostic expert system introduced by OncoStem that categorises the patients as low or high-risk based on the patient's threat of breast cancer reappearance over five years. It gives information regarding the risk of reappearance of early-stage, breast carcinoma patient's receptor-positive of hormone. This test examines acute biomarkers in the tumour to measure the danger of reappearance, and assists doctors or oncologists to identify treatment procedure.

## 5.3  LungXpert by Sasikala Devi

Sasikala Devi, senior assistant professor at SASTRA Deemed University, developed LungXpert, which helps doctors to have early detection of common heart and pulmonary diseases.

## 5.4  SigTuple Technologies

SigTuple Technologies that has leveraged expert systems including robotics and data science to advance smart screening solutions, to make healthcare inexpensive as well as precise and accessible for all.

## 5.5  Artivatic.ai by Layak Singh

Artivatic.ai won the challenge in the medical care sector with their invention DARVIN, which is devoted to healthcare. This DARVIN, platform designed for hospitals, healthcare institutions, insurance companies, patients, clinics and more.

# 6.0 CONCLUSION

Expert systems that have been trained with live cases to perform complicated tasks. A number of medical expert systems techniques are there and can act as assistants to doctors, clinicians, assisting in laboratory analysis. This clinical examination proved that the concurrent use of this expert systems techniques improved the diagnostic performance of doctors in the recognition of breast carcinoma without delaying their workflow. Expert systems are helpful for decision making issues and very essential for healthcare prognosis. The expert systems is proficient in facing, challenging decisions and issues.

Even tremendous technology introduced in market the cases and deaths rates is gradually increasing from many decades because of lack of awareness about the technology or self-testing and not taking proper precautions. There can be conducted lots of programs especially in rural areas to get awareness of deadliest diseases and early detection by this expert systems may help many women in the world and may reduce the breast cancer risk.

# REFERENCES

Diekmann F, Meyer H, Diekmann S, et al. Thick Slices from Tomosynthesis Data Sets: Phantom Study for the Evaluation of Different Algorithms. Journal of Digital Imaging. 2009;22:519–526.

Eberhard JW, Albagli D, Schmitz A. Mammography tomosynthesis system for high performance 3D imaging. In: Astley SM, B M, R C, Zwiggelaar R, editors. 8th Intl Workshop on Digital Mammography, Lecture Notes in Computer Science -- Digital Mammography. Manchester, U.K: Springer-Verlag; 2006. pp. 137–143.

Eells TD, Barrett MS, Wright JH, Thase M. Computer-assisted cognitive-behavior therapy for depression. Psychotherapy (Chic) 2014 Jun; 51(2):191–7. doi: 10.1037/a0032406.

Ferlay J, Colombet M, Soerjomataram I, et al. Global and Regional Estimates of the Incidence and Mortality for 38 Cancers: GLOBOCAN 2018. International Agency for Research on Cancer/World Health Organization; 2018.

Good WF, Abrams GS, Catullo VJ, et al. Digital Breast Tomosynthesis: A Pilot Observer Study. Am J Roentgenol. 2008;190:865–869.

Helvie MA, Roubidoux MA, Hadjiiski L, Zhang Y, Carson PL, Chan H-P. Tomosynthesis mammography versus conventional mammography: comparison of breast masses detection and characterization. Radiological Society of North America 93rd Scientific Assembly and Annual Meeting; Chicago, IL. 2007.

Huang Y, Zhao N. Generalized anxiety disorder, depressive symptoms and sleep quality during COVID-19 outbreak in China: a web-based cross-sectional survey. Psychiatry Res. 2020:112954. doi: 10.1016/j.psychres.2020.112954.

Ma, Y., Wang, Z., Lu, J.L., Wang, G., Li, P., Ma, T., Xie, Y., Zheng, Z.: Extracting Micro-calcification Clusters on Mammograms for Early Breast Cancer Detection. In: Proceedings of the 2006 IEEE International Conference on Information Acquisition, Weihai, Shandong, China, August 20–23, pp. 499–504 (2006)

Mohanty A, Kabi A, Mohanty AP. Health problems in healthcare workers: A review. J Family Med Prim Care. 2019; 8:2568.

Newman MG, Szkodny LE, Llera SJ, Przeworski A. A review of technology-assisted self-help and minimal contact therapies for anxiety and depression: is human contact necessary for therapeutic efficacy? Clin Psychol Rev. 2011 Feb; 31(1):89–103. doi: 10.1016/j.cpr.2010.09.008.

Nishiura H, Jung SM, Linton NM, Kinoshita R, Yang Y, Hayashi K et al. The Extent of Transmission of Novel Coronavirus in Wuhan, China, 2020. J Clin Med. 2020; 9(2). https://doi.org/10.3390/jcm9020330.

Rajkumar RP. Ayurveda and COVID-19: where psychoneuroimmunology and the meaning response meet. Brain Behav Immun. 2020.

Rost T, Stein J, Löbner M, Kersting A, Luck-Sikorski C, Riedel-Heller SG. User acceptance of computerized cognitive behavioral therapy for depression: systematic review. J Med Internet Res. 2017 Sep 13; 19(9):e309. doi: 10.2196/jmir.7662.

Valencia DN. Brief review on COVID-19: the 2020 pandemic caused by SARS-CoV-2. Cureus. 2020; 12:e7386

World Health Organization (WHO). Coronavirus disease (COVID-19) pandemic. WHO; 2020. Accessed November 11, 2020. who.int/emergencies/diseases/novel-coronavirus-2019

## WEBLINKS

https://www.uicc.org

https://www.ncbi.nlm.nih.gov/

https://www.wcrf.org/dietandcancer/breast-cancer

https://swarajyamag.com/technology/innovative-india-made-mri-machine-can-make-medical-imaging-affordable-and-accessible

https://yourstory.com/herstory/2020/10/raise-2020-researcher-ai-toolkit-covid-19

# CHAPTER TWELVE

# An analysis of levels of Financial Numeracy and Attitude among the Teachers in Higher Learning Institutions in Hyderabad

**Gutti R K Prasad**
*Research Scholar, Faculty of Management*
*Kalinga University, Naya Raipur, Chhattisgarh, India*
*Email: guthi1959@gmail.com, Phone: 9542978515*

*And*

**Prof. Byju John**
*PhD, Research Supervisor and Director General*
*Department of Management*
*Kalinga University, Naya Raipur, Chhattisgarh, India*
*Email: byju.john@kalingauniversity.ac.in, Phone: 9109179430*

**Abstract**—*Financial literacy is a prerequisite for the achievement of financial goals by any individual. Due to economic liberalisation, finance is not limited to national boundaries and is across the globe's length and breadth. One can invest and borrow from anywhere in the world. After the opening up of economic gates, complex financial products are made available to investors and borrowers. To invest or borrow based on those versatile financial instruments, the person needs to have a specific financial knowledge level. This paper focuses on analysing and assessing the level of financial numeracy and attitude possessed by teachers of higher learning institutions in Hyderabad since they are the role models for their student community. For this study, a structured questionnaire has been adopted containing two sections: section 1 contains Socio-Econo-Demographic variables, and section 2 includes variables relating to financial numeracy, knowledge and attitude. Descriptive analysis has been used to analyse the data and found that 21% of the teachers' working in Higher learning institutions at Hyderabad possess a higher level of financial numeracy skills. Only 23% have a higher level of knowledge in finance, and 50% have a high financial attitude in dealing with financial matters. This study can help policymakers,* *corporate entities, and academic institutions enhance literacy levels in finance to improve individuals' economic wellness.*

**Keywords**—Financial Knowledge, Financial Numeracy, Financial Attitude, Financial Behaviour and Higher learning institutions.

# 1. INTRODUCTION

## 1.1 Background

An appropriate and sufficient understanding of financial literacy can resolve future financial concerns of different individuals. Financial learning and numeracy is a part of financial knowledge, and knowledge is a part of literacy. It consists of three elements such as financial knowledge, attitude and behaviour. This literacy and its application are essential for achieving individual financial objectives. Due to liberalisation, privatisation, and globalisation worldwide, finance is not limited to certain countries and is across the globe. Financial instruments to invest or to borrow are large in number in the financial market. Choosing the right and appropriate instrument needs a basic understanding of financial concepts to enhance economic wellness and achieve financial goals. To achieve financial objectives, one needs to make financial decisions and monitor those decisions from time to time. Economic wealth can enhance the social status of the individual.

Therefore, financial literacy and the application of such literacy lead to economic progress. This financial literacy can be achieved through education and learning programs and gaining financial numerical skills to assure appropriate economic behaviour. This study focuses on assessing teachers' ability to manage their financial numeracy and evaluate the financial attitude to make the right decisions about personal finance relating to investment, borrowing, credit card, budgeting, and meeting expenditure. Those who are aware of these matters can decide when to borrow when to invest through different financial instruments. Financial knowledge shows how an individual makes financial decisions. With knowledge and numerical skills, and the right attitude help a person create a financial vision where he wants to be in the next few years in terms of financial wealth. This knowledge affects all individuals, irrespective of their wealth, upbringing, education levels, etc. Lack of financial knowledge can lead to the acceptance of borrowings at a higher interest rate; not investing in appropriate financial securities decreases the return and increases the risk.

Financial knowledge refers to a person's comprehension of and understanding the principles of finance, procedures, and application of that knowledge to solve financial difficulties. Financial attitude can be explained as a personal feeling towards financial matters. It is the individual features that take the form of tendencies towards an economic action. Financial literacy involves understanding financial concepts such as money management, financial planning, savings, investment and budgeting, etc. and applying those concepts in real life for financial advantage. Integration of concepts and application is a difficult job in the real world. As the awareness and experience grow, there will be a change in the individual's financial behaviour.

Financial literacy is a broad word, and it includes knowledge about finance, attitude and decisions (financial behaviour). Many people have explained financial literacy in different dimensions; however, the OECD's definition in 2011 is considered more appropriate. It has described as "A combination of awareness, knowledge, skill, attitude and behaviour necessary to make sound financial decisions and ultimately achieve individual financial wellbeing".

## 1.2 Need for the study

Literacy in finance is a global concern. It is critical due to complicated financial concepts, and a lack of understanding and knowledge about financial matters leads to financial inconsistency. Young workers now have more responsibility for planning and deciding their future financial needs due to India's economic reforms. Their financial behaviour is highly influenced by high job insecurity, wage differentials, easy access to consumer credit etc. A country like India, which has an extensive teaching community in various higher learning institutions, should research this subject.

## 1.3 Problem specification

The lack of financial skills and knowledge has become a global concern that is also noticeable in developing countries. Those who do not have financial literacy have not been encouraged to accept creative financial items, do sound financial planning, and implement their plans with serious commitment (Amer Jamel et al. 2015). Therefore, knowledge of finance leads to better planning for future financial needs. The teachers are the role model in our society to influence the student community, who is the creator of wealth for the future. They are in a position to control many aspects of an individual's life. Earlier studies have shown that financial knowledge positively impacts personal management in finance. Any person with good economic understanding can plan better for his/her finance; specifically, teachers are the sources of knowledge for society's growth and development. An effort is being made to study the teaching community's financial literacy and attitude levels working in higher learning institutions in Hyderabad.

## 1.4 Study's scope

The study exclusively concentrates on understanding financial numerical skills and attitude towards teachers' finance in higher learning institutions.

## 1.5 Importance of the study

The study's importance is to identify teachers' financial skills and attitude levels working in higher learning institutions to fulfil their future financial needs.

## 1.6  Study's objective

The study's objectives consist of the following:
1.   To measure the financial numeracy levels of teachers
2.   To assess the financial attitude of teachers
3.   To provide suggestions to improve the teachers' attitude in finance.

## 1.7  Study limitations

The study limitations are
1.   It is restricted to the teachers working in higher learning institutions in Hyderabad.
2.   The method of convenience  sampling method has been chosen for this study
3.   There may be a possibility that some respondents might not give the actual situation that applies to them
4.   The sample chosen may not ensure a proportionate representation of the entire population
5.   The conclusions drawn may not be generalised

# 2.  REVIEW OF LITERATURE

Financial numeracy can be defined as processing basic numerical concepts, quantitative estimations, probability and ratios (Peters et al., 2006); Cokely et al., 2012). Financial numeracy directly affects financial management outcomes related to borrowing, savings and investments.  These numeracy skills need to be implemented in real-time financial transactions without a third party's assistance (Brett Budson Mathews 2019).

Financial attitude is defined as a state of mind, opinion and judgment of a period about finances. It is the individual characteristics that take the form of tendencies towards a financial practice or action. It shows the inclination or likelihood of a person to undertake a behaviour (IGI Global)

The attitude is the response in the form of a statement of like or dislikes or useful or un-useful related to the individual financial behaviour (Potraich et al., 2016).  Financial attitude will shape the way someone spends, hoards, and spend money wastefully (Furnham, 1984)

Financial numeracy is a part of financial knowledge (Lusardi 2012), and this knowledge with financial attitude and behaviour becomes financial literacy. Therefore, knowledge, attitude and behaviour lead to literacy.

The Standard and Poor's 2014 survey showed that India's literacy level in finance is low (25 per cent), and out of 28 nations in the study undertaken by Visa in the year 2012, India is ranked 23rd position.

**Gutti R.K.P (2020),** in his study, found that the levels of literacy in finance of students of post-graduate management studies in Hyderabad are low (33%), and male students are more financially literate than female.

In their study, **Kalyani and K Reddy (2018)** identified that the employees are technologically savvy but not financially savvy.

In their study, **Saurabh Sharma (2015)** noted that the financial literacy of young employees is not inspiring. The female literacy rate is lower than male literacy, and it is linked to levels of education and income.

**Sumit Agarwal et al. (2015)** assessed literacy in finance of a small cluster of Indian inhabitants who use an online investment service. The participants were found to be financially literate in general. Male respondents have a higher chance of getting the correct responses, which rises with education and the investor's aggressiveness.

**Agarwala et al. (2013)** conducted a survey on 3,000 people in India and determined that Indians have a lower level of financial awareness than people in other countries. Workers' and pensioners' financial behaviour and attitudes, on the other hand, remain upbeat.

**Bhushan and Medury (2013)** found that gender, levels of education, levels of earnings, nature of jobs, and workplace all affect literacy in finance; according to them, the geographic area does not involve financial literacy. In urban India, the young working people's financial literacy level is comparable with similar groups in other nations.

According to **Hsu-Tong Deng et al. (2013)**, school teachers at the elementary level have a high level of medium literacy level in finance and education.

In his paper, **Ramakrishnan R. (2012)** concluded that individuals and society need financial education to advance the economy. Consumers who can make better decisions about themselves will improve overall welfare.

The study by **Abraham and Gyensare (2012)** among 250 Cape Coast University students of undergraduate and post-graduate found that India has a lower level of financial literacy than other countries. The financial behaviour and attitude of workers and retirees, on the other hand, remain upbeat.

According to **Jason West (2012)**, financially literate people's acts do not always imply that they will behave responsibly with their money.

In comparison to people of nine other nations, **the ING Group (2011)** carried a global survey and identified that in managing finance, most Indian customers have exhibited good skills and are more optimistic in meeting any future economic obstacles. They also discovered that literacy in finance is impacted by an individual's age level, income level, and level of education. Financial literacy was higher among high-income respondents than among low-income respondents.

**Lusardi, Mitchell, and Curto (2010)** investigated literacy in finance among persons and found that only one-third of young adults have a basic understanding of interest rates, inflation, and risk diversification. Financial literacy was found to be closely linked to socioeconomic status and family financial sophistication.

**Ronald and Grable (2009)**, individuals with low financial risk tolerance levels are the least financially capable and have the most inadequate subjective net worth assessment. They are still less pleased with their financial management capabilities.

According to **Wendy and Karen (2009)**, teachers understand the importance of financial education, but few trainers coaching literacy in finance are not fully equipped to teach personal finance. They also discovered that unique finance education opportunities for teachers are in high demand.

Those who got training in personal financial management do better in their financial matters **(Lewis and Linda 2009)**. People with a low literacy level in finance have fewer chances to plan for superannuation, borrow at a high cost, and partake in the economic system **(Cole Shawn et al. 2009)**. Literacy levels vary significantly between countries and are dependent on educational success and societal connections **(Jappelli 2009)**.

According to Jane Schuchardt et al. (2009), financial education results in improved financial literacy and more positive financial behaviours, motivation, and planned behaviour.

Teachers in higher education have been studied in terms of financial literacy and expertise. Financial literacy and expertise can help everyone to increase their financial resources. In this regard, an attempt is being made to assess financial literacy ( numeracy) skills and attitude among teachers in Hyderabad's higher education institutions.

## 3. THE METHODOLOGY ADOPTED FOR THE STUDY

**Research Design:** Adopted a descriptive research method by the survey through a structured questionnaire for the present study.

**Data:** Both primary and secondary sources have been used to collect data for the study.

**Questionnaire:** A structured questionnaire has been prepared on literacy elements in finance such as financial learning, financial numeracy, financial attitude, financial knowledge, and financial behaviour in addition to socio-demographic variables and has been used to collect primary data from the teachers of higher learning institutions in Hyderabad.

**Sample Description:** The sampling unit used in this study is 130 teachers of higher learning institutions in Hyderabad in the age group above 25 years.

## 4. DATA PRESENTATION AND ANALYSIS

As per **Table 1**, out of the total 130 respondents, 42 (32.3%) are female, and 88 (67.7%) are male. The age group mostly ranges between 25 years to 65, and the majority are ranging from 35 years to 45 years (42.3%). 54 ( 41.5%) teachers are brought up from semi-urban areas, 37 (28.5%) are from urban, and the remaining 39 ( 30%) are from rural areas. Out of the job experience, 6 to 10 years of experience are 32 teachers, 28 teachers have 11 to 15 years, and 21 have 16 to 20 years, and 20 teachers have 0 to 5 years experience. About master's degree qualification stream, 44.6% (58) teachers are from the engineering stream, followed by business administration 21.5% (28), 10% (13) are from science and 6.2% (8) are from commerce and the remaining from arts, architecture and others. All the teachers have regular income from salaries, and their income ranges between Rs.25,000 to Rs.1,50,000 and above. 42.3% (55) of teachers are having income ranges between Rs.50,000 to Rs.75,000, 35.4% (46) are having income between Rs.25,000 to Rs.50,000, 13.8% (18) teachers are earnings in the range of Rs.1,00,000 to Rs.1,50,000, very few (3) are there earning more than Rs.1,50,000 and also earning less than Rs.25,000.

**Table 1.** Socio-demographic profile of the respondents

| Particulars | Details (categories) | Breakup Total | % |
|---|---|---|---|
| **Gender** | Female | 42 | 32.3 |
| | Male | 88 | 67.7 |
| | Total | 130 | 100.0 |
| **Age group** | Less than 25 years | 1 | .8 |
| | Years 25 to 35 | 43 | 33.1 |
| | Years 35 to 45 | 55 | 42.3 |
| | Years 45 to 55 | 24 | 18.5 |
| | Years 55 to 65 | 7 | 5.4 |
| | Total | 130 | 100.0 |
| **Brought up** | Urban ( city) | 37 | 28.5 |
| | Semi-Urban | 54 | 41.5 |
| | Rural | 39 | 30.0 |
| | Total | 130 | 100.0 |
| **Experience** | 0 to 10 yrs. | 52 | 40 |
| | 11 to 20 yrs. | 49 | 37.7 |
| | 21 to 30 yrs. | 22 | 16.9 |
| | 31 to 40 yrs. | 7 | 5.4 |
| | Total | 130 | 100.0 |
| **Qualifications (Master's Degree)** | Commerce | 8 | 6.2 |
| | Arts | 7 | 5.4 |
| | Business Administration | 28 | 21.5 |
| | Engineering & Technology | 66 | 50.8 |
| | Science | 13 | 10.0 |
| | Architecture | 1 | .8 |
| | Others | 7 | 5.4 |
| | Total | 130 | 100.0 |

| Income levels | <Rs.25,000 | 2 | 1.5 |
|---|---|---|---|
| | Rs.25,000 - 50,000 | 46 | 35.4 |
| | Rs. 50,000 - 75000 | 55 | 42.3 |
| | Rs.75,000 - 1,00,000 | 6 | 4.6 |
| | Rs. 1,00,000 - 1,50,000 | 18 | 13.8 |
| | More than Rs.1,50,000 | 3 | 2.3 |
| | Total | 130 | 100.0 |

## 4.2. Reliability analysis of variables

The reliability test has been performed through the latest version of SPSS software, and values are indicated in **Table-2**. Cronbach Alpha value for financial knowledge 0.928, 0.854 for financial attitude, and 0.664 for financial numeracy. All the values have more than 0.60; hence, the reliability of variables is high.

**Table 2.**   Reliability of variables

| Particulars | Cronbach Alpha | No. of items |
|---|---|---|
| Financial Numeracy | 0.664 | 10 |
| Financial Knowledge (1+2) | 0.928 | 13 |
| Financial Attitude | 0.854 | 10 |

## 4.3. Construction Financial Literacy (Numeracy) score

There are ten multiple-choice questions with one correct answer to assess the level of financial numeracy levels. Each correct response has one value (1), and a wrong reply has zero value (0). The total score is 10 (10 questions multiplied by 1 for the correct response value). As per **Table 3**, those who scored between 0 to 5 have low financial literacy (financial numerical). Those who achieved a score between 5 to 7 are treated as medium level (average). Those who scored between 8 to 10 are determined as high levels of financial literacy since the mean value is 5.7 and the median value is 6.

**Table 3.**   Distribution of score for financial literacy (Numeracy)

| Serial Number | The score for financial literacy | Level of financial literacy (Numeracy) |
|---|---|---|
| 1 | 0 to 4 | Low level |
| 2 | 5 to 7 | Medium level (average) |
| 3 | 8 to 10 | High level |

## 4.4. Levels of Financial Literacy (numeracy) of teachers

Based on **Table-4**, 21% (27) of teachers working in higher learning institutions at Hyderabad are equipped with a high level of financial literacy, 58% (76) is having a medium level of financial literacy, and 21% (27) is having a low level of financial literacy. Therefore, teachers in these institutions are highly moderately financially literate.

**Table 4.** Levels of Financial Literacy (Numeracy)

|  |  | Frequency | Per cent | Valid Percent | Cumulative Percent |
|---|---|---|---|---|---|
| Valid | High level | 27 | 20.8 | 20.8 | 20.8 |
|  | Medium level | 76 | 58.5 | 58.5 | 79.2 |
|  | Low level | 27 | 20.8 | 20.8 | 100.0 |
|  | Total | 130 | 100.0 | 100.0 |  |

## 4.5. Analysis of levels of financial knowledge

On analysing **Table-5**, one can understand that only 23% (30) of teachers have high-level financial knowledge, and 50.8% and 26.2% have medium and low financial understanding, respectively. Therefore, the study clearly showed that most teachers (51%) in higher learning institutions are moderately financially knowledgeable; this indicates that teachers have an average financial knowledge level. The reasons may be that they have working experience; they directly involved in managing their money matters; they have different financial accounts. They deal with banks and other financial institutions on routine matters for their money matters, whether to deposit or withdraw and invest elsewhere to earn a higher return.

**Table 5.** Analysis of levels of financial knowledge

|  |  | Frequency | Per cent | Valid Percent | Cumulative Percent |
|---|---|---|---|---|---|
| Valid | Low financial knowledge | 34 | 26.2 | 26.2 | 26.2 |
|  | Medium financial knowledge | 66 | 50.8 | 50.8 | 76.9 |
|  | High financial Knowledge | 30 | 23.1 | 23.1 | 100.0 |
|  | Total | 130 | 100.0 | 100.0 |  |

## 4.6 Analysis of financial attitude statements

On analysing each statement as per **Table-6**, the financial attitude of teachers about financial matters are as follows:

**Statement 1:** 27.75% of teachers indicated very real, and 34.6% stated somewhat true about the message "I am in control of my financial situation". 22.3% of respondents are not sure of control of their financial situation. The minor segment, i.e., 4.6%, indicated that they are not in control of their financial situation. The majority of teachers are in control of their financial situation.

**Statement 2:** Approximately 45% of teachers believe they will achieve their future goals with their future income, but 31.5%t are unsure. The message "capable of using future income to achieve financial goals" was disputed by 6.2%of respondents. It demonstrates that they are incapable of achieving future goals with future income, which may be because the future is uncertain and beyond their control.

**Table 6.**  Analysis of financial attitude statements relating to financial matters

| Q. NO. | Statements in relation to financial attitude | 1-Not at all true | 2-Some-what not true | 3-Not sure | 4-Some-what true | 5-Very true |
|---|---|---|---|---|---|---|
| 1 | I am in control of my financial situation | 6(4.6%) | 14(10.8%) | 29(22.3%) | 45(34.6%) | 36(27.7%) |
| 2 | I am capable of using my future income to achieve my financial goals | 8(6.2%) | 9(6.9%) | 41(31.5%) | 45(34.6%) | 27(10.8%) |
| 3 | I feel credit cards are safe and risk free | 33(24.5%) | 22(16.9%) | 37(28.5%) | 28(21.5%) | 10(7.7%) |
| 4 | I feel purchasing things are important for my happiness / comfort | 16(12.4%) | 20(15.4%) | 39(30%) | 35(26.9%) | 20(15.4%) |
| 5 | I am capable of handling my financial future | 8(6.2%) | 12(9.2%) | 26(20%) | 56(43.1% | 28(21.5%) |
| 6 | I feel cost of using  credit card is very high | 28(21.5%) | 22(16.9%) | 33(25.4%) | 24(18.5%) | 23(17.7%) |
| 7 | Regular savings is important for my future | 5(3.8%) | 7(5.4%) | 18(13.8%) | 34(26.2%) | 66(50.8%) |
| 8 | Insurance cover is important to protect  from risk | 6(4.6%) | 8(6.2%) | 23(17.7%) | 37(28.5%) | 56(43%) |
| 9 | I feel understanding credit terms are important before borrowing on loan or on credit card | 7(5.4%) | 8(6.2%) | 23(17.7%) | 36(27.7%) | 56(43%) |
| 10 | I feel money management is important issue | 5(3.8%) | 8(6.2%) | 16(12.3%) | 27(20.8%) | 74(56.9%) |

**Statement 3:** Concerning the information "I feel credit cards are safe and risk-free", only 7.7% of respondents expressed as positively accurate, and 21.5% said some that true. The reason may be that they may be using the card for their personal use and paying the card bills on time. 28.5% expressed they are not sure about the safety and riskiness of credit, and Roughly 1/4th of respondents expressed that they are not sure about the statement. The reason could be that they may not be having the card or may not be using the cards correctly.

**Statement 4:** 15.4% of teachers agree with the statement, "I feel purchasing things are important for my happiness/comfort". The reason may be that they are feeling happy with the material objects. 26.9% expressed that the statement is somewhat correct. 30% of respondents are not sure at all that purchase of things brings happiness. 12.4% of teachers do not agree with the statement totally, and the reason may be that happiness is not linked to material objects, and it is a state of mind.

**Statement 5:** The statement "I am capable of handling my financial future" has been agreed by 21.5%, and 43.1% agree somewhat. Therefore, roughly 65% of the respondent can handle their financial future without any difficulties that are a goods sign. 20% of respondents are not sure of managing their future finances, and very marginal respondents disagree with the statement; that means they need someone's help to handle their financial future.

**Statements 6:** 17.7% of respondents feel that the cost of using a credit card is very high. 25% are not sure, and roughly 22% do not agree with the statement. The reason is that the use of basic cards does not involve any cost unless the card is excessively used or cash is withdrawn or unable to meet the card bills on time.

**Statement 7:** The message "regular saving is important for my future" has been agreed upon by more than 50% respondents. That shows the importance of savings to reduce future financial troubles. 13% are not sure, and 4% of respondents have not agreed with the statement, and 13.8% of teachers are not sure. Almost 77% of teachers recognise the importance of savings for a safe financial future.

**Statement 8:** 43% of teachers have agreed about the importance of insurance cover to protect from risk, and 28.5% have somewhat agreed. That means more than 50% of respondents have agreed with the extent of insurance to reduce future risk. It shows very clearly the awareness of insurance to manage future safety. Only 17.7% are not sure, and 4.6%, i.e., a very negligible portion of respondents, disagree with the statement. It is a good sign that people are taking care of their future risk by having insurance products.

**Statement 9:** About understanding credit terms before borrowing on a loan or credit card, 43% agree with the idea, and 27.7% has somewhat agreed. That shows most teachers (71%) have felt very clearly that understanding the credit terms is essential before borrowing. It is an excellent sign to reduce future complications because once the loan agreement is signed in, later on, the borrower cannot state that they have not understood. Mainly the terms of loan and credit card are numerous; hence, special attention needs to be paid to digest the agreement's terms.

**Statement 10:** Majority (57%) of teachers have agreed that money management is an important issue. It shows the importance of money management in their daily life, and money management is financial management. 12.3% are not sure, and a very negligible portion (3.8%) has not agreed with the statement.

## 4.7. Analysis of levels of financial attitude

On analysing the financial attitude levels as per **Table-7**, 50% (65) of teachers working in higher learning institutions have a very fair (high) attitude towards financial matters. The balance has a low level of attitude towards financial issues. The high level of attitude may be due to having a high level of general education and regularly dealing with money matters in their routine life.

**Table 7.**    Analysis of levels of financial attitude

|  | Frequency | Per cent | Valid Percent | Cumulative Percent |
|---|---|---|---|---|
| High Financial attitude | 65 | 50% | 50% | 50% |
| Low Financial attitude | 65 | 50% | 50% | 100% |
| Total | 130 | 100.0 | 100.0 | |

## 5.  CONCLUSIONS AND SUGGESTIONS

### Conclusions

1.  21% of teachers are having a high level of financial literacy (numeracy) skills, and at the same time, a majority (58%) are having an average (moderate) level of financial literacy.
2.  The financial knowledge level is high for 23% of teachers preparing financial plans and budgets, managing income and expenses, bills on time, savings and investment, debt and insurance.
3.  50% (65) of teachers working in higher learning institutions have a very fair (high) attitude towards financial matters, and the balance has a low level of attitude towards financial issues.
4.  Based on financial attitude analysis, most respondents felt the importance of savings, money management, understanding credit terms before borrowing and undertake insurance to reduce risk. At the same time majority also thought that they are in control of their financial situation, manage their future financial needs, and the credit cards are not safe and risk-free. Minority percentage disagree about the importance of purchasing things for their happiness.

### Suggestions

1.  A particular orientation needs to be provided to higher learning institutions' teachers to understand various financial concepts useful in their daily lives to manage their money efficiently.
2.  Non-for-profit entity) needs to be established to propagate and impart financial literacy as a sort of orientation program to reduce the financial literacy gap and reduce financial fraud due to ignorance of financial concepts.
3.  In different languages, the basic financial concepts like savings, investment, insurance, pension need to be printed and distributed on a mass scale to realise the importance of money management.
4.  The print and electronic media need to dedicate specific columns on financial literacy concepts to improve the common public's financial literacy levels.

# REFERENCES

1. Abraham Ansong, & Michael Asiedu Gyensare (2012). Determinants of University Working-Students' Financial Literacy at the University of Cape Coast, Ghana, *International Journal of Business and Management*, vol. 7 (9), 126–135.

2. Agarwal Sumit, Gene, A., Ben, I. D, Souphala, C & Evanoff, D. D. (2015). Financial Literacy and Financial Planning: Evidence from India. *Journal of Housing Economics*, Elsevier, vol. 27(C), 4–21.

3. Agarwala, SK, Barua, S., Jacob, J. & Verma, J. R. (2013). Financial Literacy among working young in urban India, Working Paper, IIM-Ahmedabad.

4. Amer, A.A.J, Ramlan, W.K., Karim,M.R. A., Mohidin, R., and Osman, Z. (2015). The Effects of Social Influence and Financial Literacy on Savings Behavior: A Study on Students of Higher Learning Institutions in Kota Kinabalu, Sabah. *International Journal of Business and Social Science*, 6, 11(1). https:// ijbssnet.com/journals/Vol_6_No_11_1_November_2015/12.pdf.

5. Cokely, E. T., Galesic, M., Schulz, E., Ghazal, S., & Garcia-Retamero, R. (2012). Measuring risk literacy: The Berlin Numeracy Test. *Judgment and Decision Making*, vol. 7(1), 25–47.

6. Furnham, A. (1984). Many Sides Of The Coin: The Psychology Of Money Usage. Person *Individ Diff*, vol. 5(5), 501–509

7. Gutti, R. K. Prasad. (2020), An Analysis of Financial Literacy and Financial Behaviour among Management graduate students in Hyderabad. *PalArch's Journal of Archaeology of Egypt / Egyptology*, vol. 17(9), 3949–3965

8. Hsu-Tong, D, Li-Chiu Chi, Nai-Yung, T, Tseng-Chung, T., & Chun-Lin Chen. (2013). Influence of Financial Literacy of Teachers on Financial Education Teaching in Elementary Schools. *International Journal of e-Education, e-Business, e-Management and e-Learning*, vol. 3(1), 68–73

9. ING Group. (2011). ING-International Financial literacy and Consumer Resourcefulness study, ING Group, Corporate Communications. Amsterdam, Netherlands.

10. Jason West. (2012). Financial Literacy Education And Behaviour Unhinged: Combating Bias And Poor Product Design, Discussion Paper, No. 2012-01

11. Kalyani PALNS and Kavya Reddy. (2018). A study of Financial Literacy of employees at Engineering Colleges, Hyderabad. Inspira- *Journal of Modern Management & Entrepreneurship*, vol. 08(1), 40–46.

12. Lewis, M., & Linda S. K. (2009). The Impact of Financial Literacy Education on Subsequent Financial Behaviour, *Journal of Financial Counselling and Planning*, vol. 20(1), 70–83.

13. Lusardi, A., Mitchell, O.S., & Curto, V. (2010). Financial Literacy among the Young. *Journal of Consumer Affairs*, vol. 44(2), 358–380.

14. Lusardi, A (2012). Numeracy, Financial Literacy, and Financial Decision-Making, *Numeracy*. Vol. 5(1)

15. Matthews, Brett. (2019). Hidden constraints to digital financial inclusion: the oral-literate divide. Development in Practice. 29. 1-15. 10.1080/09614524.2019.1654979.

16. Potrich, A. C. G., Vieira, K. M., & Silva, W. M. D. (2016). Development Of A Financial Literacy Model For University Students. *Management Research Review*, vol. 39(3), 356–376.

17. OECD INFE (2011). Measuring financial Literacy: Core Questionnaire in Measuring Financial Literacy: Questionnaire and guidance note for conducting Internationally Compatible Survey of Financial Literacy. Paris. OECD

18. Peters E, Västfjäll D, Slovic P, Mertz CK, Mazzocco K, Dickert S. (2006). Numeracy and decision making. *Psychological Science*, vol. 17(5), 407-413. doi: 10.1111/j.1467-9280.2006.01720.x. PMID: 16683928.

19. Puneet Bushan, & Medury, Y. (2013). Financial literacy and its determinants. *International Journal of Engineering, Business and Enterprise Applications*, vol. 4(2), 155–160.

20. Ramakrishnan, R. (2012). Financial Literacy and Financial Inclusion, 29th SKOCH Summit 2012, Refuelling Growth 8th & 9th June, Mumbai, India.

21. Ronald, A. S, John, E. G. (2010). Financial Numeracy, Net Worth, and Financial Management Skills: Client Characteristics That Differ Based on Financial Risk Tolerance. *Journal of Financial Service Professionals*, 57–65.

22. Saurabh Sharma. (2015). A Study on Financial Literacy among Young Employees of Private Sector in Jaipur City. *International Journal of Marketing and Financial Management*, vol. 3(5), 11–18

23. Jane Schuchardt, Sherman, D., Hanna, Tahira K. H., Angela, C. L., Palmer, L.,& Xiao, J.J. (2009). Financial Literacy and Education Research Priorities. *Journal of Financial Counselling and Planning*, vol. 20 (1), 84–95

24. Cole Shawn, Thomas, S. & Zia Bilal (2009). Financial Literacy, Financial Decisions, and the Demand for Financial Services: Evidence from India and Indonesia. Working Paper 09-117, Harvard Business School.

25. The Standard & Poor's Ratings Services Global Financial Literacy Survey (2014) retrieved from https://gflec.org/wp-content/uploads/2015/11/3313-Finlit_Report_FINAL-5.11.16.pdf?x46739

26. Jappelli, T. (2009). Financial Literacy. Discussion Paper 09/2010-06.

27. Way, W. L. and Holden K. (2009). Teachers' Background and Capacity to Teach Personal Finance: Results of a National Study. National Endowment for Financial Education.

# CHAPTER THIRTEEN

# Impact of Covid-19 on Coaching Institutes

**Manmath Deshpande**
*Research Scholar*
*Dr. Ambedkar Institute of Management Studies and Research*
*Rashtrasant Tukdoji Maharaj Nagpur University, (India)*

**Abstract**—*There has been a boom in the segment of coaching institutes in India in the past few years, particularly since the beginning of the 21st century. The big increase in the number of coaching institutes started at least in the 1980s itself. Since almost everything in life has to be learnt through coaching, the institutes which give training are of things which encompass many spheres of human existence, such as music, public speaking, cooking, education etc. In the education sector too, the educational service organizations are of a very wide range, such as coaching for the examinations of Grade 10 and Grade 12, which are of the Boards such as CBSE, State, ICSE etc, Joint Entrance Exams of IIT (Mains and Advanced), PMT (Pre-Medical Test) or NEET, CAT (Common Admission Test), MBA CET, Campus Recruitment Training (CRT), Programming, etc.*

*A new phenomenon which has come up very recently, say post-2010, is of online coaching classes. There are institutes which sell their entire course online, such as Cracku, Edushastra, HundakaFunda, CATKing, iQuanta, 2IIM, Marrow, etc. These institutes had come much before the Covid-imposed lockdown which was imposed since March 2020.*

*The traditional, non-online coaching institutes in India saw a decline in revenue due to the lockdown. Most of them were unprepared for this sudden change where online coaching had to be taken immediately. However, with the passage of time of the lockdown, they, or most of them, became more comfortable with and adept at the use of technology to take online classes. This paper aims to identify the impact of the lockdown on the coaching institutes, the changes that were forced to occur with regards to opening up of newer markets, changing in marketing approaches, technology management, and automation in the workplace.*

**Keywords**—Lockdown, Covid 19, impact, coaching institutes, online

# 1. INTRODUCTION

Coaching has always been a part of any civilization in the history of civilization. A large number of school students in India take coaching now, and this number was ever-increasing with time, at least until the lockdown was imposed due to Covid-19. A report in *The Hindu's Business Line* on 22 December 2013 cited a report by the Asian Development Bank (ADB) published in the year 2012, which said that as many as 83 per cent students in high school in India go to private tuitions at coaching institutes. *The Indian Express* dated 26 June 2013 quoted a survey of students and guardians by the Associated Chambers of Commerce and Industry of India (ASSOCHAM) which was conducted in 10 Indian cities. This survey concluded that the educational coaching classes sector increased by 35 per cent between 2007 to 2013, and that in this period, the number of students in primary school attending tuition classes doubled, while the number of students in high school attending tuitions increased to 1.92 times.

The number of students attending coaching classes at Class 12, and graduate level was not mentioned, but this too can safely be assumed to be definitely rising, if it is not at saturation level already at Class 12 level.

# 2. LITERATURE REVIEW

Since the lockdown was announced only in March 2020, and is still in force, there do not appear to be many research papers written on the topic of its impact on coaching institutes as yet. The only literature available was the reports of newspapers and magazines on this issue, which gave statements of various stakeholders such as coaching institutes, students, teaching and non-teaching staff, parents, etc. Other research papers which covered the subject of coaching institutes (much before the lockdown) were studied.

A PTI report of 17 April 2020, around a month after the lockdown was imposed, said that many students left their coaching institutes drowning the fees already paid when the classes closed due to lockdown, and joined new online coaching institutes, paying the full fees. In that report, a student mentioned that many of the traditional coaching institutes did not have online coaching facility at that time.

An article by *The Indian Express* dated 8 June 2020 said that due to the lockdown, the admissions of major institutes coaching students for IIT JEE, of which Aakash, Resonance, Allen, FITJEE, CareerPoint, PACE, Vidyamandir were mentioned by name, declined to nearly half, or even lesser at some places, and that some institutes had difficulty in even paying rent for the places taken, at least in the cities of Kota, Delhi, Mumbai, Nagpur, Raipur and Indore. It stated that Resonance's Mumbai and Raipur centres and Allen's Indore centre got only half the admissions as compared to 2019, while it was just 30% of the 2019 figures at Resonance East Delhi centre.

The report also gave an interesting fact stating that in light of the difficult situation, these institutes reduced the initial payment for seat-booking. It gave the example of a Resonance centre in Delhi which booked seats for Rs 10,000 while this amount was Rs 60,000 in 2019. There were also complaints of late payment and reduced payments by faculties teaching at these institutes.

The article further said that these institutes were scared of the professional online classes or tutoring platforms like Byjus, Unacademy, Vedantu etc who are their rivals, reducing their admissions even more. The CEO of Vedantu stated that it had seen a 150% increase in paid subscribers for coaching for competitive exams in the three months of lockdown of March to June 2020.

*The Indian Express* dated 20 July 2020 said that the Maharashtra Class Owners Association has nearly 1 lakh classes under its ambit and quoted the association as saying that business was reduced by 70% in the four months of ban on offline coaching classes since March 2020.

*The Times of India* dated 10 February 2021 reported that this Association urged the Maharashtra Government to allow offline coaching classes, and that it said that many classes may not be able to sustain and a lot of teaching and non-teaching staff may lose jobs if the classes continue only in online mode.

## 3. TECHNOLOGY MANAGEMENT

### 3.1 Access to technology by customers

The lockdown underscored the importance of digitization all across India. Had this pandemic occurred, say in the year 2000 or 2001, it would not have been possible to hold classes online, like now. That is because, at that time very few people had access to the internet, there were almost no mobile phones in the hands of ordinary people, except the very rich, and very few people had laptops or even computers. The rural part of the country, and the lower classes even in urban areas certainly did not have access to such technology.

However, in the past few years there has been rapid growth in the access to mobile phones, internet by all sections of the society, including the underclass in urban areas, and everyone in the rural areas. According to Statista, the Internet penetration rate in India was just 4% in the year 2007, from which it grew to nearly 50% in the year 2020.

A *Hindustan Times* article of 14 August 2020 said that the number of people using the internet in India has increased massively in the past few years, according to data compiled by the World Bank. But a large percentage of the population still does not have access to the internet. This situation is so far more in rural parts of India, households with low income, which will be classified as 'poor'.

This report said that the Delhi telecom circle (which includes other parts of the National Capital Region apart from Delhi too), as of end-2019 had a total of 169 internet subscribers per 100 people, as per TRAI data. This was the highest among all the telecom circles of India, which are 22 in number. Since many people used more than one internet connection (say, one broadband connection, while another being on mobile) the number of connections per 100 people was higher than 100. But this number was as low as 32 for Bihar and Jharkhand combined. The number of internet subscribers per 100 people was less than 50 in at least six telecom circles of India at the end of 2019.

These figures also showed a massive gap in internet usage in the urban and rural areas. The national average all over India showed that there were 106 internet subscribers per 100 people in urban areas, but this number was only 30 subscribers per 100 people in rural regions.

*The Times of India* reported on 6 May 2020 that for the first time the number of internet users in rural areas crossed that of those in urban areas in India (in absolute terms), in late 2019. The report by the Internet & Mobile Association of India (IAMAI) and Nielsen said that rural India had 227 million active internet users, while this number for urban India was 205 million, as of November 2019. Those who use the internet at least once in 30 days were defined as 'Active internet users' in this report. There were another 7.1 crore (i.e. 71 million) children between the age of 5 and 11 who went online using the devices of their household.

## 3.2  Use of technology by coaching institutes

After the lockdown was imposed in India in March 2020, there were many coaching institutes which avoided taking online classes until as late as possible. However, ultimately all those who wanted to survive had to take online coaching, and they all learnt how to take online coaching soon, some of them within as few as 2 or 3 days. Online coaching emerged as a panacea. The only things needed were a computer or laptop, tablet or smartphone and a good internet connection.

For taking online classes, two of the most popular platforms were Google Meet and Zoom. There are some differences in the working of these platforms as well. For example, in Zoom, it is possible to log in with fake IDs. Even if the entry to the Zoom meeting is done with real name, it is possible to change name after that. This has resulted in some students logging in and then changing their usernames, and with fake usernames, giving a lot of abuses and disrupting the class. This has been observed many times by various faculties on Zoom and revealed to this writer in personal interactions, and it is often either very difficult or impossible to identify the person doing so. This is not possible on Google Meet. Hence, on this count Zoom needs to improve its technology.

However, there are some shortcomings which some users claimed to exist in Google Meet. There was a feedback that in Google Meet there is a good option of screen sharing, but one cannot show anything which is not on the device (say Laptop). Thus, if one in logged in from

Laptop, one can only share the screen. On Zoom, anything can be shown to students if one is logged in from mobile; one can simply shift the face of the camera and show anything written in a register etc to the students, which makes it easier. Some topics cannot be learnt by mere screen sharing, hence this facility is important to have in any technology.

In Google meet, anyone can type anything on the chat box and ask any sort of doubt, which is seen by not just the faculty, but all other students, i.e. by everyone logged in in the meeting. The benefit of this is that any doubt is seen by all other students, and any of the other students too can immediately type on the chat box and explain it to the student who asked it. However, the drawback here is that there is no facility to write in private on Google meet. If any student wants to say anything in private, only to the teacher, he or she cannot do so. Or in case a faculty asks any question, and does not want the answer to be revealed publicly so that other students who have not yet solved the question and not yet got the answer do not hear it, there is no way the answer can be told. It is seen by everyone on the chat box, on Google meet.

But on the contrary, on Zoom, there is the facility of sending a private message, where any message can be sent to any single individual. This makes it possible for students to send the answer only to the teacher, whereby other students do not automatically see the answer sent, on Zoom. If a class is being taken on Google meet, then the only way the answer can be seen by only the teacher is through other messages like in private on the teacher's personal WhatsApp number.

In such online classes, there are at times connectivity issues in case of both students as well as the teacher. If the teacher's connection is lost, the whole class halts immediately then and there. If a student's connection is lost even for a very short time, the student too can suffer if a very important thing was being taught at that very moment. After this, if the teacher repeats the part lost by a particular student due to connectivity being lost, just for him or her, a lot of time of the class is lost. Therefore, technology is very important. The use of technology in education is not a new phenomenon. The Covid-19 lockdown simply made it more prevalent.

## 4. OPENING UP OF NEWER MARKETS

It is said that 'With every adversity comes an opportunity.' This is perhaps also applicable here. Due to the lockdown, it was possible for erstwhile offline coaching institutes which were limited to one particular geographical area to get a nation-wide market. Let us take the example of an individual running a one-man coaching class 'Aptitude Development Centre' in Nagpur in the offline mode. In the lockdown, such an individual had to take classes online. This resulted in some students from other cities also joining his classes online. This was possible only due to the lockdown, which resulted in the classes being taken in the online mode and another reason could be that the offline classes were closed in other cities too. Had these offline classes been available in the other cities, students of those cities may have joined them in their cities, instead of joining an online class in a different city.

Another new market opened was the students who lived far from the location of the coaching institute within the same city. Due to the online coaching, it became accessible, easy and comfortable to attend the classes for such students. Students who were unable to join a particular institute due to too much distance, lack of transport (such as lack of personal vehicle) could join it in the online mode.

In some cities, even now, many girls are not allowed to travel at night, or even if permitted they are afraid of doing that. The coaching institutes have got even such a market segment as a new segment, since such girls can attend the classes from home in the online mode. Aptitude Development Centre, Nagpur had examples of such students got in online coaching, which it took on Google Meet or Zoom.

Professional online coaching institutes like say, Cracku or Marrow, which did not operate in the brick-and-mortar mode at all even in the pre-lockdown times, have got a lot of new customers, as reported by English dailies. Since there was no option but to go for online coaching, many students preferred the professional online institutes as compared to the brick and mortar ones. Several students revealed to this author that they did not want to go for online coaching of the brick and mortar ones. Several of the otherwise traditional brick and mortar institutes gave only recorded video lectures in their online coaching, which was not found worth going for, by many students.

## 5.  CHANGES IN MARKETING APPROACHES

Due to only online classes being available, several institutes had or have the chance to highlight what exactly better they are doing in online coaching which other institutes are not doing. In online coaching 'What we are doing better than our competitors' can differ completely from the offline coaching. In offline coaching, everyone is present in a classroom with a teacher teaching live and interacting with the students. But in the online mode, it is not necessarily so, and simply recorded lectures could be made available.

As we mentioned, some institutes which went online simply gave pre-recorded video lectures, with no live online coaching. Many students thought the fees to be too high just for getting such pre-recorded lectures. Some other institutes (e.g. Kiran Gadkari Sir's institute for coaching of Maths in Class 12, or HR Mentors institute in Nagpur city, in the initial phase of the lockdown) uploaded videos on YouTube, and many were disappointed with that as well. In such cases, there was no personal attention given to any student, and there was no live coaching at all.

One of the most popular ways of marketing coaching institutes is and was to take guest lectures in colleges, whereby the students would get a demonstration of the teaching of the teacher. But due to the lockdown, the colleges were all closed. Hence, here the other ways of marketing were (are) needed. However, such guest lectures can be taken even in the online mode in the colleges.

Due to the lockdown, students were (are) spending a lot of time on smartphones or on the social media. Hence, giving advertisements on Facebook or Instagram is a very effective way to advertise about coaching institutes in this time. It is useful even more in lockdown than other times.

In marketing, the coaching institutes also need to encourage students to join the classes. Due to the lockdown, the market size itself has reduced.

An article in *The Indian Express* dated 16 November 2020 titled "Lost in lockdown" was written by three authors namely Sucharita Iyer, Shireen Jejeebhoy and Nitya Daryanani. That gave insights from a study done by the Dasra Adolescents Collaborative and it was an attempt to understand how the COVID-19 pandemic affected the lives of the youth of India. The article said that for the study, an online survey was done which asked questions about this. The number of organizations responding to the survey was 111.

The article said that past instances showed that there is a far greater increase in the probability of girls and young women being asked to drop out, and actually dropping out of school during crises. This is the effect of the significant increase in care work and domestic work during times of crises, and also due to economic disparity making girls to help in adding to the income of the family. Females are often made to discontinue their education and are married off to reduce the financial burden of the family. It stated that this study of the Dasra Adolescents Collaborative revealed that 43 per cent of the organizations who participated in the survey stated that they knew of one or more girls, who revealed their fear of ceasing of school or whose guardians had either planned for or asked for the discontinuation of school.

After studying the report as well as the current trends due to the Covid 19 lockdown, the authors of the article published by *The Indian Express* gave some recommendations to the government, one of which was:

'Engage with parents, especially families of girls who are at risk of dropping out of school. Parents need to be made aware about the importance of completing studies, even in the time of economic hardships due to lockdown, especially those parents who may force their daughters to cease studies.'

The local franchise owner, i.e. centre head of TIME Nagpur said to this writer in a personal interaction on 3 March 2021 that TIME Nagpur's business went down by at least 40% if not to 40%, due to the lockdown. Among the various reasons, one major reason cited was the fact of many girls choosing not to go for Post-graduation (MBA) due to the lockdown. This resulted in reduction in size of the market itself, by such a significant level that a major player like TIME had to mention it, and it affected its business.

In case of reduction in market size, one must try to increase it. One can see this from the advertisements given by say, some toothpastes, saying that one should brush twice a day. They show a young boy going to sleep at night, saying 'Rinse the teeth with water' before sleeping, to which a dentist comes and says 'Don't just rinse, brush your teeth before going to sleep at night. Use XYZ toothpaste.' Now the motivation for the toothpaste makers to make everyone brush twice is a day is to increase their consumption of toothpaste, so that more toothpaste can be sold. This is basically, increasing the market size.

The same we can see even in terms of MBA. A hoarding of a major coaching institute showed a girl with the words written: '*MBA to karna hi padega.* Status. Salary. Prestige.' ('One will certainly have to do an MBA, for the sake of status, prestige, salary.') This was because the number of students going for MBA was reducing, due to various reasons such as the astronomical rise in the fees of B-schools. So the institutes had to try to make doing MBA popular again, and then hope to get students for MBA entrance exams' coaching. Exactly the same has to be done in times of lockdown.

Due to online classes, many institutes were able to save the cost of rent, at least for some time. Many of the conventional coaching centres had to pay the rent even for the time classes were not held, since their contracts were often year-wise, with their landlords. Some institutes had only monthly rental contracts, so they lost only some days of March 2020. However, after a particular point of time, majority of the institutes did not have to pay rent where physical classes were not held. This money could and should be utilized for marketing.

## 6. WORKPLACE AUTOMATION

Institutes which are basically of the offline mode, gave pre-recorded lectures to the students as their online classes. This was actually automation. But this wasn't received as well by the students as a live class. Some students were definitely happy even with this, but many were not. Automation is fine so long as it satisfies the customer. If not, it should be discontinued.

### 6.1 Coaching institutes studied

The institutes studied for this purpose of understanding the impact of Covid-19 were:
1. TIME Nagpur [TIME is a national institute coaching students for MBA entrance exams like CAT, MBA CET and other such exams, Number 1 in the country]. It gave pre-recorded video lectures made available by Head Office.
2. Kiran Gadkari's institute for Maths for Class 12 and JEE coaching, Nagpur. It uploaded lectures on YouTube.
3. HR Mentors [a local institute of Nagpur, in the same category as TIME] (study was done through its students). It initially uploaded lectures on YouTube, and later took classes on Zoom.
4. Athavale's Sulabh Classes (the No. 1 coaching institute for Class 10 of Maharashtra State Board in Nagpur city). It took live classes on Zoom or Google Meet.
5. Zoom Coaching Institute (of Class 10 coaching of various boards, in Nagpur city). It took live classes on Zoom or Google Meet.

6. Marrow - an exclusively online institute coaching students for NEET (study was done through its students)
7. Cracku - an exclusively online institute coaching students for CAT (study was done through its students)
8 Working of some other institutes like Aakash, Resonance, Allen, FITJEE, CareerPoint, PACE, Vidyamandir etc was seen through newspaper reports, all of whom took online coaching.

# 7. CONCLUSION AND RECOMMENDATIONS

Covid-19 had a huge impact on the coaching institutes. Adapting new technologies was very important, or rather necessary, for survival. While the traditional brick and mortar institutes had a lot of challenges, and mostly lost market share, they also got some opportunities like access to newer market segments.

Some recommendations for coaching institutes are:
1. Some ways of marketing like taking guest lectures in person in colleges were (are) lost due to colleges being closed offline. There should be an attempt to take guest lectures in the online mode, though it is not as easy as when colleges were open.
2. It is quite possible to give personal attention to every student even in online coaching. Many students want just that. So, institutes which take coaching live on Zoom or Google Meet and give personal attention should highlight those aspects of their coaching, which others can't give in YouTube videos or pre-recorded lectures.
3. Making short videos of 1 or maximum 2 minutes, and promoting them on Facebook, WhatsApp is another good way, since students spend a lot of time online in lockdown. This was a useful and good way even in the pre-lockdown times, but with physical classes closed in colleges, its importance increased a lot more.
4. The market size itself reduced, hence some strategy should be chosen by the institutes to incentivize the lost market to return to the sector itself. The segment of female students, mentioned by the head of TIME Nagpur as well as in the article 'Lost in lockdown' by *The Indian Express* dated 16 November 2020, needs to be specially targeted by the coaching institutes. They need to urge them to do MBA and go for similar things like government jobs, bank exams, etc whose coaching they provide.
5. The institutes could come up with the message 'Use time of lockdown to do this course by our class.'
6. Institutes should use the money saved on paying rent for physical classes on marketing.
7. Coaching institutes will benefit with a strong online learning management system with course material, tests, assignments being provided and having a facility to take anonymous feedback to ensure better learning. In all such online classes, there is a real problem of checking assignments, conducting subjective tests, proper invigilation. If all

these issues are solved with proper technology by the institutes, not only the students, but the institutes too will benefit massively.

Those institutes which were totally in the offline mode before the lockdown mostly saw a big decline. But it was the opposite in case of those which were exclusively in the online mode already.

What will happen to online coaching in the long term, after Covid-19 ends is a very interesting matter. It is possible that there will be much greater growth of the professional online coaching classes like Cracku, Marrow etc. A PTI report of 17 April 2020 quoted the CEO of NEETprep, an online coaching institute for NEET, Kapil Gupta as saying that many students were forced to take online coaching due to the lockdown may not ever revert to classroom coaching.

That report also gave the opinion of the CEO of Catalyst Group, which is another online learning platform, Akhand Swaroop Pandit, as saying that the charges of the online coaching institutes have increased in the lockdown, and that the lockdown would result in a long-term increase in the use of online coaching institutes.

But it is quite possible that it may turn out to be exactly the opposite. Students who attended online coaching may find that offline, in person coaching, is better; and as soon as they get the chance, they may abandon online coaching. Anything can happen.

Coaching institutes need to be on their toes and be ready for anything.

## REFERENCES

1. Borwankar, Vinamrata. (2021, February 10). Maharashtra: Private coaching class owners submit SOP to minister, seek nod for reopening. *The Times of India*. Retrieved from https://timesofindia. indiatimes.com/city/mumbai/pvt-coaching-class-owners-submit-sop-to-min-seek-nod-for-reopening/articleshow/80778053.cms

2. Chopra, Ritika. (2020, June 8). Coaching industry tries to reinvent itself in Covid times. *The Indian Express*. Retrieved from https://indianexpress.com/article/india/a-long-recess-6446348/

3. Dutta, Aesha. (2013, December 22). The Coaching class Industry. *The Hindu Business Line*. Retrieved from http://www.thehindubusinessline.com/industry-and-economy/the-coaching-class-industry/article5490245.ece

4. Express News Service. (2013, June 26). Private tuitions now a multi-billion rupee industry: Survey. *The New Indian Express*. Retrieved from http://www.newindianexpress.com/cities/bengaluru/Private-tuitions-now-a-multi-billion-rupee-industry-Survey/2013/06/26/article1653569.ece

5. Goradia, Abha. (2020, July 20). Coaching classes seek Maharashtra govt nod to reopen: '70% business hit in lockdown'. *The Indian Express*. Retrieved from https://indianexpress.com/article/india/coaching-classes-seek-maharashtra-govt-nod-to-reopen-70-business-hit-in-lockdown-6515252/

6. Iyer, Sucharita, Jejeebhoy, Shireen and Daryanani, Nitya. (2020, November 16). Lost in lockdown. *The Indian Express*. Retrieved from https://indianexpress.com/article/opinion/lost-in-lockdown-covid-19-7053688/

7.  Kawoosa, Vijdan Mohammad. (2020, August 14). Connectivity gets better but parts of India still logged out. *Hindustan Times*. Retrieved from https://www.hindustantimes.com/india-news/connectivity-gets-better-but-parts-of-india-still-logged-out/story-VSqXriMdGUudWb7eBcWzjN.html

8.  Mascarenhas, Patricia. (2014, April 1). The great Indian tuition and coaching industry. *DNA*. Retrieved from http://www.dnaindia.com/academy/report-the-great-indian-tuition-and-coaching-industry-1973985

9.  Mishra, Digbijay and Chanchani, Madhav. (2020, May 6). For the first time, India has more rural net users than urban. *The Times of India*. Retrieved from https://timesofindia.indiatimes.com/business/india-business/for-the-first-time-india-has-more-rural-net-users-than-urban/articleshow/75566025.cms

10. Press Trust of India. (2020, April 17). Online Coaching Portals Are Acting as Saviours for Students Hit by Coronavirus Lockdown. Retrieved from https://www.news18.com/news/tech/online-coaching-portals-are-acting-as-saviours-for-students-hit-by-coronavirus-lockdown-2580433.html

11. Statista. (2019). Internet penetration rate in India 2007-2021. Retrieved from https://www.statista.com/statistics/792074/india-internet-penetration-rate/